THE SAINT OF THE EUCHARIST

THE SAINT OF THE EUCHARIST
SAINT PASCHAL BAYLON

PATRON OF EUCHARISTIC ASSOCIATIONS

Adapted from the French of the Most Reverend Father Louis-Antoine De Porrentruy, Definitor-General of the Order of Friars-Minor Capuchins

By
Father Oswald Staniforth, O.S.F.C.

MEDIATRIX PRESS
2021

ISBN: 978-1-953746-93-1

Imprimatur.
FR. ANTONIUS A TASSON, O.S.F.C.,
Min. Provincialis Provinciae Anglicae.

Nihil obstat.
F. THOMAS BERGH, O.S.B.,
Censor Deputatus.

Imprimatur.
✠ GULIELMUS EPISCOPUS ARINDELENSIS,
Vicarius Generalis.
Westmonasterii,
Die 6 Julii, 1908.

Mediatrix Press 2021
All rights reserved. Originally published by Washbourne Ltd. 1908; this work is in the public domain. Typography and layout of this edition Mediatrix Press. No part of this work may be posted in physical or electronic format except for reviews in journals, scholarly articles or classroom use without the express permission of the publisher.

Cover art: Detail, *St. Paschal Baylon, Angel Bearer of the Eucharist,* by Giovanni Battista Tiepolo

"Sanctum Paschalem Baylon peculiarem coetuum eucharisticorum, item societatum omnium a Sanctissima Eucharistia, Patronem coelestem declaramus et constituimus."

We declare and constitute St. Paschal Baylon the special heavenly Protector of all Eucharistic Congresses and Societies.

Pope Leo XIII, in his Apostolic Letter, "Providentissimus Deus," dated November 28, 1897.

TABLE OF CONTENTS

Apostolic Letter "PROVIDENTISSIMUS DEUS." xiii
Letter of His Grace the Archbishop of Westminster . xvii
Preface to the Second Edition xix
Preface xxi

CHAPTER I
THE ANGEL OF THE HOUSE
Humble Origin—The Pasch of the Holy Spirit—Happy auguries—An inheritance of faith and piety—Martin Baylon and Elizabeth Jubera—Precocious piety of the child—Lively attraction for the Blessed Sacrament—Pious escapades—the little Franciscan Habit. 1

CHAPTER II
THE SHEPHERD LAD
The young shepherd—Two precious talismans—A scholar without a teacher—A portable shrine—The heavenly Shepherdess—Holy Vigils—The chaplet of cords—Fruitful apostolate—A good shepherd—Justice and truthfulness
. . . . 10

CHAPTER III
VOCATION
Vocations in general—Signs of a vocation—My "little Monk"—Penance and prayer—a bosom friend—Apparition of St. Francis and St. Clare—The miraculous spring—An extra-liturgical clothing—Valuable testimony. 21

CHAPTER IV
IN SIGHT OF THE PROMISED LAND
On the road to the Friary—A call at Sister Jane's—Cruel

disappointment—A long and trying wait—A soul in pain—Vision of the star and the chalice—A noble renunciation—Testimony of the shepherds........ 31

CHAPTER V
IN PORT
A fine saying of Brother Giles—The promised land of obedience—St. Peter of Alacantara and his work—Glories of the Province of St. John the Baptist—First impressions of the Novice—Growing fervour—Wonder and admiration of the elder Religious Profession 42

CHAPTER VI
THE HEART OF A SON
Three hearts in one—The true son of God—Blessed are they who dwell in the house of the Lord!—A new crusade—At prayer—Brothers to Matins!—The tireless server—Obedience—The love of God in His works . 50

CHAPTER VII
A MOTHER'S HEART
False ideas of the world concerning the Saints—The love of God and our neighbours are one—Paschal's favourites—A true servant of the poor—A recipe for soup—Travellers—A Spiritual alms—Poor but proud—A pillaged garden—Questors and cooks—Absolute trust in Providence.................................... 63

CHAPTER VIII
A GOOD SAMARITAN
Poor invalids—Comfort and healing—Little Bessy—A constrained miracle—A visit to Job's house—The revenge of a Saint—A message of death—A double prophecy—Interpreting the words of the Saint to the sick 78

CHAPTER IX
"BLESSED ARE THE PEACEMAKERS"
"Peace be to this house"—The wolf changed into a lamb—The guests of the Friary—The touchstone of charity—In the Refectory—"The Father is not at home".... 92

CHAPTER X
THE HEART OF A JUDGE
A just judge—Pronouncing judgment—Execution of the sentence—A knight clad in mail—Dry bread and pure water—A true son of St. Francis—Bitterness changed into sweetness................................. 104

CHAPTER XI
A CONFESSOR OF THE EUCHARIST
A perilous commission—Council of war on the French border—Across the Pyrenees—In the land of the Huguenots—The way of sorrow—At the gates of Orleans—A little present—An interrupted meal—A night of anguish—The lancer—Arrival at Paris—Return to Spain.. 113

CHAPTER XII
ON CATHOLIC SOIL
"Godliness is profitable to all things"—A fresh commission—*En route* for Xeres de la Frontera—The history of a vocation—Reminiscences of Paschal's youthful companion—A good book—The Prodigal's return—Various Adventures—Fifteen years after—Questing in the country—The Questor-in-Chief and his subalterns—the conventual beast of burden—Returning from quest.................. 129

CHAPTER XIII
THE SCHOOL OF THE HOLY SPIRIT
Acquired science and infused science—A theologian who

did not hail from Salamanca—Caught in his own trap—The Christmas sermon—Everything is not in books—The souls in Purgatory—"Poor Father Pedro Cabrillas!"—The Chapter at Valencia............ 157

CHAPTER XIV
THE SAFEGUARD OF DIVINE TREASURES
Humility and the Divine gifts—Brought up at the tails of sheep—A cantankerous Guardian—Superior in spite of himself—The Night of the Star—Solution of a painful doubt—Concert of praise—Precious testimony of saints
.... 170

CHAPTER XV
HEAVENWARD
Presages of approaching death—The good doctor and his patient—Last words of an apostle—The chemist's bill—Temptation of the devil—The two Pentecosts—Death while adoring the Host—The fiery chariot—Universal regret—Exposition in the choir 182

CHAPTER XVI
LOVE STRONGER THAN DEATH
Whit-Monday—Tumultuous entry of the crowd into the church—A lovely spectacle—The paralytic healed—little Kathleen—a miracle! He opens his eyes, and adores the Blessed Sacrament—Prophet and healer—*Whit-Tuesday*—Fears and commotion—The favoured people of Castellon de la Llana—The burial—Disappointment and anger of the populace—Fresh miracles—Tranquility restored 195

CHAPTER XVII
A GLORIOUS SEPULCHER
A regrettable oversight—The saint in his Shrine—The throng of pilgrims—At the Escurial—The Catholic

Kings—Illustrious visitors—Various reasons for the Saint's popularity—Propagation of his *cultus* in Spain and elsewhere............................. 209

CHAPTER XVIII
THE KNOCKS OF ST. PASCHAL

The vision of Jeremias—A vigilant sentinel—A rumour of war—A peace procession—The Counsellor of Superiors and subjects—The bouquet of jasmine—An attentive listener—The riches of evangelical poverty—"Blessed are they who have not seen and have believed"—Little Anthony Paschal and his reliquary—Father Danon's spiritual clock—A forgotten promise—Eucharistic knocks—A noisy entrance—the sacrilegious Mass—At the palace of the Viceroy of Valencia—The server at Mass—The holy priest—Mysterious colloquy...... 224

CHAPTER XIX
A GALAXY OF MIRACLES

Contrast between the life of the Saints after death and that of worldly folk—The witnesses—Doctors and surgeons—Brokers in miracle—Little children snatched from death—The bull-fight—Two beautiful visions—Salvador and his little brother—Procession of persons raised from the dead—The pedlars' Rozinante—Effects of a good sermon—The Beatification and Canonization—The banner of St. Paschal—Salutation of the Blessed Sacrament...................... 254

TO
THE REVEREND ASSOCIATES OF THE
PRIESTS' EUCHARISTIC LEAGUE
TO THE
MEMBERS OF THE VARIOUS OTHER
SOCIETIES ESTABLISHED IN HONOUR OF
THE BLESSED SACRAMENT
AND TO
ALL LOVING ADORERS OF OUR LORD'S
REAL PRESENCE
THESE PAGES ARE RESPECTFULLY AND
CORDIALLY DEDICATED, UNTO THE
GREATER GLORY OF THE DIVINE
PRISONER OF THE TABERNACLE

APOSTOLIC LETTER
"Providentissimus Deus."
ON EUCHARISTIC CONGRESSES AND ASSOCIATIONS.
Leo P. P. XIII.

In Perpetual Remembrance.

DIVINE PROVIDENCE, by which all things are unerringly and lovingly ordained, watches over the Church in such a manner that, when the times seem most inclining to evil, it causes the very bitterness of calamities to become the source of unhoped-for consolations. Although we have often seen this on former occasions, never before have the causes of Christianity and civilization been so favoured by Providence as at the present time; for, although the enemies of public peace, becoming every day more audacious, attempt with unceasing and terrible efforts to destroy the faith of Christ and trample society under foot, it has pleased Divine Providence to stem this evil current, by means of the good works and aspirations of a sublime piety.

This is chiefly proven by the extraordinary propagation of the devotion to the Most Holy Heart of Jesus, by the ever-growing fervour in the world-wide cult to Mary, and the increase in the honours paid to the glorious Spouse of the same Deipara, by the congresses of different kinds having the defence of faith for their object, and by many others calculated to promote religion and encourage charity which have either been improved upon or newly founded.

Although our soul is overjoyed at all this, nevertheless we believe that the greatest of the Divine favours lately shown to us is the remarkable increase in the devotion for the Holy Sacrament of the Eucharist, after several memorable congresses having this object in view had been held in these years; for nothing seems to us more commendable, as we have said on other occasions, than that not only should Catholics be encouraged to fearlessly profess their faith and to practise those virtues which are worthy of the Christian name, but that their love and devotion should be excited towards that admirable pledge of Divine Love which is a bond of universal peace and unity.

As we attach the greatest importance to so weighty a matter, and, moreover, have often bestowed commendation on the Eucharistic congresses, therefore, animated by hopes of their obtaining in future still more encouraging results, we now esteem it fit and opportune that a heavenly Patron be assigned to them from amongst those Saints who distinguished themselves more especially by their love towards the most August Sacrament of the Eucharist.

Now, in the glorious ranks of those, the ardour of whose piety towards the great Mystery of the faith was more evident and overflowing, Paschal Baylon holds a most prominent place; for, being gifted with a soul which aspired above all things to Heaven, after having passed his youth in spotless innocence, tending flocks, he embraced a severer mode of life, entering the Order of Minors, of the Strict Observance, and from the contemplation of the Holy Eucharist he derived that science and wisdom which placed him, though formerly an unpolished and illiterate man, in a position to solve the most difficult questions of the faith, and even to write learned and pious books. He likewise, having publicly and openly asserted the truth of the Eucharist among heretics, suffered many grievous persecutions, and, imitating the martyr, Tharsicius, he was also frequently threatened with death. Finally, he appears to have retained his great devotion even in death; for it is said that, when lying on his bier, twice he opened his eyes at the elevation of the two sacred Species.

It is therefore evident that the Catholic congresses, of which we speak, could not be placed under better patronage. Besides, as we opportunely placed studious youth under the protection of Thomas Aquinas, charitable societies under that of Vincent de Paul, sick persons and those who tend them under that of Camillus of Lellis and John of God, in like manner (and may this resolution prove beneficial and auspicious and favourable in effects to the Christian cause) we now, availing ourselves of our supreme authority, do, by virtue of these letters, declare and constitute St. Paschal Baylon the special heavenly Protector of Eucharistic congresses and of all societies, both present and future, taking their name from the most Holy Eucharist.

And from the example and protection of that Saint we confidently expect this result—that every day will see an increasing number of Christians turning with their whole soul and mind and love towards Jesus Christ our Saviour, the great and August Author of all salvation.

These letters will be valid in all future time, in spite of all that anyone may do or say to the contrary. Moreover, we desire that copies, even printed, of these letters, signed by a notary, and bearing the seal of a person invested with ecclesiastical dignity, be obeyed with as much faith as would be paid to the original.

Given at Rome, at St. Peter's, under the seal of the Fisherman, on the 28th day of November, 1897, the twentieth of our Pontificate.

A. CARD. MACCHI.

LETTER OF HIS GRACE THE ARCHBISHOP OF WESTMINSTER

WE very heartily welcome this new edition of the Life of St. Paschal Baylon, the Saint of the Holy Eucharist. Appearing, as it does, in the year in which for the first time the International Eucharistic Congress is to be held in an English-speaking country, it will enable English readers to become acquainted with the details of the life of the humble Spanish Franciscan Friar whom Leo XIII. was pleased to proclaim the special heavenly Protector of all Eucharistic Congresses and Societies.

The example and intercession of St. Paschal will aid powerfully the growth of solid devotion to the Adorable Mystery of our altars, and make It, as It used to be in the days when the Catholic Faith governed every heart in the land, the abiding source of strength in God's service, and of permanent holiness of life.

✠ FRANCIS ARCHBISHOP OF WESTMINSTER
ARCHBISHOP'S HOUSE,
Westminster, S.W.,
Feast of St. John before the Latin Gate, 1908.

PREFACE TO THE SECOND EDITION

IN presenting a second edition of "The Saint of the Eucharist" to English-speaking Catholic readers, the Fathers of the Franciscan Capuchin Province of England venture to hope that the appearance of a Life of St. Paschal will be particularly appropriate at the present moment, in view of the forthcoming Eucharistic Congress, now about to be held for the first time on British soil. It is surely fitting that the name of a Saint, whose lifelong and all-absorbing devotion to the August Sacrament of the Altar merited his selection by the Vicar of Christ, as heavenly Patron of all Eucharistic Congresses and Associations, should be rescued from the obscurity with which it appears to be surrounded at the present time in the English-speaking Catholic world. The attention of our readers is particularly invited to the Preface of the first edition, published three years ago in the United States of America. They will there note that the accounts of the miraculous events which enter so largely into the story of Paschal's life are not a mere collection of legendary tales, but are based entirely on the testimony of witnesses, cited by ecclesiastical authority to give evidence in the Processes of Beatification and Canonization.

PREFACE

THE present volume is adapted from a work written in French by the Most Rev. Father Louis-Antoine de Porrentruy, Definitor-General of the Order of Friars-Minor Capuchins, and published in Paris, in the year 1899, under the title of *"Saint Pascal Baylon Patron des Œuvres Eucharistiques."* In his preface to this work, the author explains the reasons which induced him to undertake the task of writing what was practically an entirely new Life of St. Paschal Baylon, and he is led also to relate the circumstances in which the Saint was chosen by Pope Leo XIII. as Patron of Eucharistic Associations.

In the first place, Father Louis-Antoine draws the attention of his readers to the truly admirable unity of design underlying all the Pontifical acts of Leo XIII. of happy memory, and points out the means adopted by him to infuse renewed life into various organizations, already existing in the Church, in order thereby to cope more effectually with the particular needs and requirements of the present age. Thus, the Third Order of St. Francis was remodelled by the Sovereign Pontiff, so as to serve as an antidote to the luxury and effeminacy of our times. In like manner he placed the Confraternity of the Holy Family on a more secure basis, as a help towards the sanctification of domestic fife, and repeatedly urged upon the faithful the frequent public recital of the Rosary, in order to encourage everywhere devotion towards the Mother of God. And finally the Pontiff provided, as a heavenly protector over each separate good work he took in hand for the people's benefit, the Saint, who in life had made it a special object of his care and attention.

Thus, to St. Thomas Aquinas, the Angel of the Schools, he gave charge over all who are engaged in study; St. Vincent de Paul, the apostle of charity, he proclaimed the patron of all charitable organizations; and under the patronage of St. John of God and St. Camillus of Lellis he placed whatever associations are concerned with the care of the sick, infirm, and mentally afflicted.

The Very Reverend Author then continues:

"And now a Patron must be found for Eucharistic Associations, whose flourishing development is one of the most hopeful signs of the day.

"It was most fitting, of course, that the Patron should be one whose whole heart and soul, while here on earth, had ever been centred in the Most Holy Eucharist. But numberless are the Saints, now reigning in glory, who, whilst on earth, loved Jesus in the Tabernacle with passionate tenderness. To whom, then, should the palm be awarded, when all of them seem to have an equal right to it? What a radiant procession of Eucharistic adorers must not the Pontiff have seen defile before his eyes as he reflected on the subject! The names of the best known and most illustrious amongst that holy throng would naturally occur to his mind, and each one with sufficient distinctness as to influence his selection. But the Holy Spirit, it would seem, Himself indicated to the Vicar of Christ the privileged one upon whom his choice should rest. Strange to say, he was the very last of that procession, a poor humble Friar, one on whose brow did not even shine the aureola of the priesthood; and he it was whom Leo entreated to continue the Eucharistic life and love of his mortal days, by according his heavenly protection to all the Associations connected with the Blessed Sacrament.

Preface

"In Heaven, where the true proportion of things is clearly seen in the light of the Beatific Vision, and where merit is recognized according to its just deserts, there could be no surprise at the Pontiff's selection; but on earth men are prone to judge according to a less perfect standard. When, therefore, the Sovereign Pontiff made known who was the chosen of God, there arose in certain quarters of the pious and literary world a feeling of astonishment bordering almost on disappointment. The favoured one was not the one anticipated or desired, and consequently the announcement was received with anything but enthusiasm.

"Personally, I had repeated proof of this. Some days after the issue of the Pontifical Brief a cleric, with whom I had no previous acquaintance, called upon me, and plunged abruptly into the object of his visit by saying: 'I have called upon you, because I know that you are well acquainted with the history of the Franciscan Saints. Please, then, to tell me something about this Saint, whom Rome has given us as Patron of Eucharistic Associations. I am chaplain to a Religious Community, and the Sisters have been looking everywhere for a good account of his life without being able to find it. Indeed,' he went on in a significant tone of voice, 'people can hardly understand this selection, and the preference given over the great Doctors of the Eucharist and so many holy Prelates to a person so little known. And then, again, were there no more suitable names to suggest amongst the Saints belonging to the great Franciscan Family?—St. Bonaventure receiving Holy Communion through the ministry of an Angel; St. Anthony of Padua making the mule of the heretic kneel down before the Blessed Sacrament; St. Clare holding up the monstrance before the Saracens, and changing their victory into a rout? These are striking figures—but this Paschal Baylon—!'

"Without giving any direct reply to this unexpected sally, I urged my visitor to have patience, until the appearance of a Life of the Saint, after reading which he would understand the Pontiff's choice, and would be the first to applaud it. This cleric simply voiced the prevalent opinion, and repeated what was being expressed by others. Shortly after the conversation above described, another visitor called on me, and repeated the same complaint in almost identical language.

"It was, therefore, quite opportune to make known, as soon as possible, a Patron, who was received with such ill grace. I already felt sure, that it would be sufficient to make the faithful better acquainted with the story of the Saint's life, in order to cause these prejudices to vanish, and to awaken within Eucharistic souls that filial devotion it would henceforth be incumbent on them to render him. The beautiful Responsory in honour of St. Paschal gave an additional stimulus to devote myself to compiling his Life, and I undertook the task without further delay, in the full persuasion that it was a work well pleasing to God.

"I had in my hands the Life of the Saint, written by Father John Ximenes, and that of Father Christopher of Arta, and together with these two valuable biographies, I had gathered other matter, some of which was of excellent quality. Yet even this abundance of material could not console me for the absence of a principal, not to say essential, element, namely, that of the Process of Beatification. How was it possible for anyone, deprived of the accounts of contemporaries, to depict the Saint in the brilliant hues of life? The further I advanced in my labours, the more deeply did I feel this want. I made all the inquiries I could, but no one could tell me what had become of these Processes. They did not appear on the catalogues of any of the libraries, where books of this description are usually to be found, and the Promoter of the Faith could not recollect having seen them anywhere.

"All this was very discouraging. I continued my researches, however, though still without success, until, one fine day, some good angel inspired me with the idea of consulting the Alcantarines, the Brethren of St. Paschal, by a twofold title. What was my astonishment and delight, when, in an out-of-the-way corner of the Conventual Archives, I found seven huge folios, bearing on their venerable backs this inscription in Gothic majuscules; *Processus Canonisationis Beati Paschalis Baylon* ('Processes of the Canonization of Blessed Paschal Baylon').

"My regard for them increased when, inspecting the volumes more closely, I noticed that they had passed through the fire, but that the flames had rested satisfied with devouring the margin only, without injury to the text, which remained intact.

"These folios of nearly a thousand pages each, written in a vertical, cramped handwriting, contained, in Latin and Spanish, the various Processes, instituted in view of the Canonization. For one brief moment I dreaded finding here nothing but a series of lengthy and learned discussions on the merit and authenticity of the miracles presented for the examination and judgment of the Promoter of the Faith. But my apprehension changed into joy, when I discovered that, by the disposition of Divine Providence, I had before me both the different Processes, as well as a complete Life of the Saint in its minutest details, especially as regards that interesting period which preceded his entrance into Religion, upon which his early biographers have only touched lightly.

"The especial value of this fresh material arose from the fact that the great majority of the witnesses, whose depositions figure in the various Processes of Canonization, had already given their testimony some ten or fifteen years before, on the occasion of the institution of the Process of Beatification. Fearful of not stating exactly and faithfully things, of which they now only had a dim and confused recollection, these good people requested the judge to have their first depositions, made long ago, read out to them. The petition was granted, and thanks to this fact I had under my eyes the authentic documents of the two Processes, which I was not slow to avail myself of when I once more resumed my task.

"To these manifold blessings was added another, the most precious of all. The Sovereign Pontiff, having learned from one of the prelates of his court that I was about to publish a Life of St. Paschal Baylon, founded upon original and authentic documents, deigned to make known to me that he accepted the dedication of this book and blessed the work. God grant that it may not be unworthy of this patronage!

"This Life, then, of St. Paschal Baylon, which I offer to you, gentle reader, will have obtained its wished-for end if, after reading it, you will admire with me the happy inspiration which has given to Eucharistic Associations the wonderful Patron of whom they have every reason to feel proud."

That the Reverend Author's labours have been crowned with success may be gauged from the hearty reception his book met with at all hands, and from the fact that it was soon translated into several European languages. May its present appearance in the English tongue be attended by equally auspicious results.

This book will, we trust, be particularly acceptable to the reverend clergy, who, for the most part, have enrolled themselves in the Eucharistic League. It will likewise be read with great profit and interest by members of the various other Eucharistic Associations, and by all pious souls devoted to the interests of Jesus in the Blessed Sacrament.

Hence it is to these that we have dedicated the volume.

FATHER OSWALD STANIFORTH, O.S.F.C.
St. Anthony's Mission,
Mendocino, California,
Feast of St. Paschal Baylon, May 17, 1905.

THE SAINT OF THE EUCHARIST

CHAPTER I
THE ANGEL OF THE HOUSE

HE subject of this biography, though one of the most illustrious amongst the sons of Catholic Spain, that land so singularly prolific in noble and heroic souls, belonged neither to the royal house of Castile nor to the exclusive circle of Spanish grandees. Indeed, his family was not even on the same social level as the wealthy burghers who, at the time he was born, had begun to dispute the privileges, till then so jealously guarded, of the ancient aristocracy.

It was in a secluded hamlet of the kingdom of Aragon, called Torre Hermosa, under the humble roof of an honest peasant, that Paschal, on Whit-Sunday, A.D. 1540, first saw the light.

In the Spain of that period it was a time-honoured custom for parents to name their children after the Saint on whose festival their birthday happened to fall. Accordingly, the child received the name of Paschal, because in Spain the festival of Pentecost is commonly called the "Pasch of the Holy Spirit." His early biographers assure us that it was not by chance that this name was given to him. They are delighted to find in it a providential token, presaging the entire possession by the Holy Spirit of the soul of this predestined child. And, indeed, from his tenderest years until his latest breath Paschal remained ever a faithful disciple of this Divine Teacher; and when at length he gave back his soul to God, laden with the choicest fruits of the Spirit, it was on that same Pentecostal Feast, as though, by this singular coincidence, to attest the unity and harmony of his spiritual life.

Paschal's early biographers seem to regret their inability to unfold one of those pompous genealogies so dear to the heart of a Spanish author; or to trumpet forth one of those high-sounding titles which sometimes occupy an entire page, and seem like some high and mighty señor, accompanied by his suite; but they find some compensation in awarding to his ancestors what is in truth a more just title to glory, that of having done battle, during many centuries, in defence of faith and fatherland.

The Baylons and Juberas were loyal Christians and stanch patriots. They belonged to that vigorous and valiant race which, under the standard of the Catholic Kings, delivered Spain from the Moorish yoke. The blood which flowed in their veins, say the witnesses in the Process of Beatification, remained free from all alloy; it was the old Catholic and Spanish blood, instinct with honour and with faith.[1]

One incident will suffice to show us the character of Martin Baylon, Paschal's father. As soon as he became aware of the approach of death he began to prepare for his last end with unflinching fortitude. When the Holy Viaticum was carried into his humble dwelling, he raised himself from his bed with his small remaining strength, and, casting himself upon his knees, with joined hands and bowed head, profoundly adored the Divine Monarch, Who had deigned to enter under his roof to console his last moments upon earth. All present were greatly moved by his ardent faith and piety.

His wife, Elizabeth Jubera, was a spouse in every way worthy of him.

Nothing could be finer than the concert of praise, elicited from witnesses, when questioned, during the

---

[1] "Acts of Process of Segorbe."

Ch. I: The Angel of the House

Process, as to what they knew about Paschal's mother. The panegyric of this holy woman was upon every lip. She was, say they, the pearl of the women of Torre Hermosa, a model wife and mother. So modest was she and so sparing in her conversation, that they cannot remember having heard her ever utter an idle word, or use an expression likely to give pain to others. She occupied herself entirely with her household duties, and never interfered with other people, unless it were to do them some good turn.[2] Her chief virtue was charity. Like Pica, the mother of St. Francis, she had a special love for the poor, and in her eagerness to succour them, she sometimes allowed herself to be carried to pious excess.

Now, in every country of the world there are village gossips and busybodies, who take a delight in prying into their neighbours' affairs, and in meddling in what does not concern them. In this respect Torre Hermosa was no exception to the general rule. Noticing that Elizabeth gave to the poor without stint, and that she used even to distribute to them, especially to their children, a part of the bread she had baked for the use of the household, some of her neighbours deemed it their duty to call her husband's attention to her extravagance.

"Don't you see that at the rate she is going, your wife will end by ruining you, Martin?" said they. "It is high time that you should put your foot down, and stop this almsgiving, which is beyond your means."

Elizabeth's lord and master let them have their say, and when they had ended their complaint, which was doubtless well meant, although, perhaps, due in some degree to petty jealousy, he contented himself by replying good-humouredly: "Instead of condoling with me, you ought

---

[2] "Process of Torre Hermosa."

rather to congratulate me upon possessing such a wife. I have not the slightest objection to her bestowing upon the poor a portion of what I earn in the sweat of my brow. On the contrary, I am very pleased on this account: because I know that if she gives a measure of wheat for the love of God, He will repay us as much, and more."[3] This noble answer for ever closed the mouths of Elizabeth's censors, and secured for her the freedom to follow the promptings of her charitable heart in respect to the poor.

In the atmosphere of a home so thoroughly Christian, the child's earliest impressions were all of piety and holiness. Before he could yet lisp the childish terms for father and mother, he was already able to pronounce with perfect distinctness the names of Jesus and Mary, the first words his pious mother had taught his baby lips to utter. It was enchanting to see with what seriousness he made the sign of the cross and joined his tiny hands in prayer. Whenever God and Divine subjects were referred to in his presence he used to listen with evident attention, and assumed an air of infantine gravity. The signs of such precocious piety could not escape the notice of parents so deeply imbued with the fear of God. Fervently did they thank our Lord for having sent them a little angel, and, like those gathered around the infant Baptist, they asked themselves: "What an one, think ye, shall this child be? For the hand of the Lord is with him."[4]

Other and more striking signs were soon to give to these early tokens a deeper meaning.

One fine Sunday morning Elizabeth, beaming with maternal pride, carried her little treasure in her arms when she went to High Mass in the parish church. It was the first

---

[3] "Process of Torre Hermosa."

[4] Lk. 1:66.

time the eyes of the child were to rest on the Sacred Host. During the whole of the long function Paschal remained as motionless as a statue, and watched intently every action of the priest. His eyes never wandered from the altar; and when the celebrant elevated the Host, a tremor passed through his little frame as he lay in his mother's arms.

What could have happened at this blissful moment—a moment which seemed to foreshadow the whole of his after-life? It is a secret between God and the soul; but may we not surmise that some hidden virtue must have emanated from the Sacred Host and entered into the soul of the infant?

After this occurrence he developed an irresistible attraction for the house of God, where our Divine Saviour, Jesus Christ, dwells in His tabernacle. The greatest treat his mother could give him was to take him to church to assist at the sacred Liturgy.

One day Martin Baylon and his pious wife were to experience for several hours the anguish of Mary and Joseph when they had lost the Child Jesus and were searching for Him everywhere. Their little Saint had mysteriously vanished. They called him repeatedly, and diligently explored every nook and corner of the house; but it was all in vain. Then Elizabeth hastened through the streets almost distracted, inquiring of everyone she met: "Have you seen our little Paschal? He has gone, and we don't know what has become of him. O my God! suppose the gipsies should have stolen him! These *gitanos*, or gipsies, were the terror of all poor mothers, for they bore a very bad name, and frequently carried away little children. Finally, after a fruitless search of several hours, Elizabeth felt a sudden inspiration to enter the church. Was it not in the house of God that Mary had found her lost Child?

How great was her joy and how great the astonishment of all to find this child of predestination on his knees, sprawling on the altar steps, his bright blue eyes fixed on the tabernacle, and so wrapped in silent contemplation as to be unconscious of any noise in his vicinity. Being as yet too young to stand, the little fellow had crawled to the house of God on all fours. Might we not say that, after the example of Jesus, his Divine Master and Model, he wished to vindicate thereby the rights of the Heavenly Father, and to claim for himself the privilege of serving Him without reserve?

"Son, why hast Thou done so to us? Behold, thy father and I have sought Thee sorrowing."[5] So said the Blessed Virgin to her Divine Child. Elizabeth, likewise, attempted to give utterance to a mild expostulation, but it died upon her lips, and as she began now to see that this child was meant for God alone, she only pressed him with a deeper tenderness to her bosom, and consecrated him anew to the service of his Creator.

Henceforth, whenever he was able to escape the vigilance of his parents, the little truant used to creep away and betake himself to the dwelling-place of Him who attracted him by so potent a spell. At length his parents became fearful that some harm would befall their darling, and forbade him to go out alone for the future. It was his first cross, and the end of these pious escapades.

Thus, wonderfully nurtured and trained by Divine grace, the child grew in age and wisdom, beloved alike by God and men.

Even at this tender age he began to exercise a certain influence over those around him. His brother and sister, both his elders, were the first to submit themselves to his

---

[5] Lk. 2:48.

Ch. I: The Angel of the House

influence, much to the peace and concord of the household. One word from their small brother was enough to exact from them the respect and obedience due to their parents. Never did they dare to commit the slightest fault in his presence, and he was chosen as arbiter in their childish differences.

Whilst he himself found his greatest happiness in telling his beads and performing sundry devotions before the images of the Saints, still, filled with a truly supernatural discretion, he took good care that his own tastes and predilections should never become a source of annoyance to others, nor did he in any way seek to hinder their amusements. On Sundays it was usual during the intervals between church services to play a game of bowls, either at home or with the neighbours. On such occasions, whilst the players were amusing themselves to their heart's content, Paschal used to stay with his mother and keep her company. Under her direction he went through various pious exercises, which she took great delight in teaching him.

It was at this period of our Saint's life that an incident took place which at first glance may appear somewhat puerile. Perhaps it would be such in reality, did it concern an ordinary child. As, however, his biographers have recorded it with such great care, it shows that they considered it deserving of notice. To them it seemed like an early and distant intimation of Paschal's vocation to the Seraphic Order.

To understand this incident properly, it must be borne in mind that in the ages of faith it was nothing unusual to see persons of every rank and age wearing the habit of one or other of the principal Religious Orders. People used to make a vow of wearing the habit of St. Dominic, of St. Francis, of the Trinitarians, and so forth. It was for all an edifying sight, and served as the living memento of graces and favours received from God. Those who were clothed with this sacred livery found an incentive to do honour to the religious habit by their virtues, and never to profane it by leading an ungodly life. In the Acts of the Beatification and of the Canonization at least fifty witnesses are to be met with, bound by this tie to various Religious Orders.

Amongst the children of his own age there was one little boy for whom Paschal cherished a particular affection, not merely because he was his cousin and was also of a winning disposition, but more especially because, in consequence of a vow made by his parents, he was clothed in a small Franciscan frock.

"The first time he saw me in this frock," says Francis Dalgado in his deposition, "he sidled up to me, and would not go away again. In the end I had to chase him away. One day he came to see me when I was sick in bed. No sooner had he caught sight of the Franciscan frock and girdle hanging at the foot of the bed than he laid hands on them as on so much unclaimed property. It all happened in an instant. In the twinkling of an eye Paschal was transformed into a Franciscan. Never had he appeared so grand in his own eyes. He was simply radiant. Then he began pacing backwards and forwards like a monk, with his hands in his sleeves, devoutly making sundry reverences and genuflections. In short, the more he saw of the frock, the more it took his fancy; and when required to give it up again, he became mightily crestfallen, and offered a stubborn resistance. 'I want to be a Friar,' he kept saying; 'I want to be a Friar!' It required the intervention of his mother to induce him to give me back my frock, which I had no mind to surrender so easily. About ten or twelve years later he made his appearance one fine morning at our house, dressed in some sort of religious garb. My mother congratulated him. 'That's right, Paschal dear,' she said to him; 'in your childhood you often used to repeat that you would one day become a Friar. I see that you are a boy of your word, and that you will end by entering the monastery.' "[6]

After the scene described above, Elizabeth led the culprit home, weeping bitterly and quite inconsolable because he was not allowed to become a wee Friar. The biographers see in this vexation something more than the peevishness of a child deprived of its favourite toy. In this instinctive longing for the Franciscan habit they recognize the first token of the designs of Almighty God relatively to his youthful servant.

---

[6] Deposition of Francis Dalgado of Torre Hermosa.

CHAPTER II
THE SHEPHERD LAD

PASCHAL had reached his seventh year, Martin called him into his presence and told him that from that day forward it would be his allotted task to lead to pasture the small flock which formed an important item in the family belongings.

The prospect of living under the canopy of heaven, far from the haunts of men, instead of daunting the child, filled him with delight; for it harmonized with his meditative spirit, and gratified his longing for solitude. He, indeed, carried with him into the desert two precious talismans to charm away the tedium and irksomeness of loneliness. One was the constant recollection of Jesus, really present in the Sacrament of the Altar; the other a tender devotion towards Mary, the Mother of our Divine Lord. Thus, dwelling ever in the presence and in the company of Jesus and Mary, the happy moments of Paschal's shepherd life glided by with wonderful rapidity.

On account of the filial tenderness he bore towards the Mother of God, and to win her favour more effectually, Paschal, though but a poor shepherd lad, aspired to become learned. He longed to be able to recite the Little Office of the Blessed Virgin, that Breviary of Mary's Children, and thus join his voice to that chorus of praise which rises from earth to greet the Queen of Angels and of men. But how could he hope to acquire the knowledge necessary for reading the Office? Neither school nor schoolmaster was to be found on the grassy slopes of the Sierras. A spirit less resolute would have recoiled before the impossibility of the task. Not so Paschal; for his was the indomitable

Ch. II: The Shepherd Lad

energy and perseverance of the Saints. Whatever he resolved to do he would spare no pains to carry into effect.

Now, the problem to be solved was, having nothing but his own resources to rely upon, how to acquire the art of reading. To the solution of this problem Paschal applied himself with characteristic determination and ingenuity. Armed with an Office book, which he had managed to procure, he stationed himself on the high-road to waylay the passers-by. Whenever he saw anyone coming, who seemed of promising aspect, Paschal stepped up to him, and producing his book, begged him modestly and yet persuasively to explain the meaning of certain letters or words in the Office. Who could have the heart to repulse this bright little questioner, thirsting so ardently for the waters of knowledge?

By-and-by he retired to his sheep and to solitude, there to compare notes and formulate rules and principles from the various answers he had received. Gradually light came, and eventually, to his great joy, he was able to read and understand the Little Office, which at first had been as undecipherable to him as an Egyptian hieroglyphic.

The scholar's ambition grew with success. Now that he had learned how to read, why should he not also learn how to write, so as to be able to copy out for himself some of the beautiful things to be read in books concerning God and His Saints?

Without any other assistance than his own industry and perseverance, he set himself to the accomplishment of this second task.

His note-book was composed of sundry scraps of paper gathered up here, there, and everywhere, and fastened together; whilst a reed coated interiorly with resin and closed with a brass stopper served as ink-horn. The writing-fluid itself was made out of lamp-black mixed with water, or, in default of this, the juice of certain plants. The different pieces of his literary outfit, together with the Office book, were lodged in a small leather wallet hanging from his belt in the fashion of the scribes of bygone days. Paschal never parted with these homely treasures, and the note-book was made to serve for other useful purposes, as we shall see in the sequel.

At some distance from Torre Hermosa, on the summit of a hill commanding a magnificent prospect of the surrounding country, stands the Sanctuary of Our Lady of the Sierra, where a miraculous image of the Blessed Virgin has for many centuries been venerated by the faithful. This sanctuary became the focus of Paschal's devotion to the Queen of Heaven. In its shadow he pitched his tent and fed his flock, for in that hallowed spot he felt as secure from all danger as though in the shelter of a fortress bristling with cannon.

When he was compelled reluctantly to quit for a season this favoured locality, Our Lady of the Sierra had also to start on a journey. For in a moment of inspiration Paschal had carved with his knife a little image of Our Lady upon his shepherd's crook. Three small crosses, also graven by the blade of the young sculptor, surmounted the statue, recalling the Host of the tabernacle. Such was Paschal's portable shrine. Carried in his hands, it preceded him, as the column of smoke went before the people of God in their journey through the wilderness. As long as the Sierra remained in sight it was thither that Paschal turned at the time of prayer, but as soon as it was lost to view the portable shrine took its place. When the hour for conversing with God arrived, the devout shepherd lad planted his staff in the ground and recited the Office upon his knees before the image and the Cross, as though in the presence of the Blessed Sacrament and of the Immaculate

Ch. II: The Shepherd Lad

Mother. Day and night the staff was ever close to him, and out of respect for the holy symbols carved upon it he never cast it at the wayward wanderers of his flock, as shepherds are wont to do.

Some years later on, when Paschal had left home, and whilst awaiting patiently the fulfilment of God's designs in his regard, had engaged himself in the service of a master, he felt the same attraction for the neighbourhood of Our Lady of Loretto as he had in former years for the shrine on the Sierra. So often did he lead his flock there, that certain persons, fancying that he preferred his own private devotions to the calls of duty, denounced him to the master as a negligent servant.

"Why don't you take the sheep to Orta d'Alicante, or some other good pasture-land, instead of taking them continually to Loretto, where the grass is poor and the ground almost barren?" asked the master, in a severe tone of voice. "Why, sir?" replied Paschal. "Because both the shepherd and his flock are nowhere better off than in Our Lady's territory. Just come and see what good condition my sheep are in. There are no finer or fatter ones in the whole countryside. The Mother of the Good Shepherd has taken it upon herself to look after them and to protect them. Not a single one of my lambs has fallen a prey to the grizzly wolf."[1] It was perfectly true, as the master himself had to admit, and from that time he allowed his shepherd to take the sheep wherever he thought best.

The solitude of the country was not always so undisturbed as our young hermit had supposed. At certain seasons the shepherds of a particular district used to gather together and feed their flocks on common pastures. Of course, Paschal had to submit to this custom. They were

---

[1] "Acts of Process of Beatification."

occasions for trying his virtue, and also gave him opportunities of exercising a wholesome influence over his brother-shepherds. The company was none of the choicest. Amongst these shepherds, gathered together from all kinds of places, were some noted for a coarseness of speech and roughness of behaviour, in singular contrast with the gentle reserve and angelic modesty of Paschal. Curses and ambiguous expressions rose to their lips more readily than pious ejaculations or the invocations of the Litany.

Paschal had not been trained in this school, and his delicacy of conscience was not infrequently offended when brought in contact with such characters. To their credit be it said, none of them ever thought of persecuting the holy youth on account of his piety, for they were coarse and vulgar rather than actually wicked. Still, at first some of them used to banter him and treat him as an unsociable person, because he would not join in the games and dances of his comrades. But this did not last long, for Paschal's piety was so unaffected and so genuine, that the railers were themselves the first to throw down their arms and yield to his influence. All came to understand that there was something supernatural in this mere stripling, and that he should be revered as a very Angel from the skies.

The esteem and veneration in which our young Saint was held by his brother-shepherds allowed him to continue in this seemingly unpromising soil the work he had commenced in the bosom of his own family. Without making any pretence of being such, Paschal became the apostle and the model of the shepherds, as he had previously been a pattern and an apostle to his brothers and sisters.

First of all, however, it was necessary for him to gain and to preserve his independence, and this he succeeded in accomplishing, with a vigour unusual in so young a boy. In winter-time the shepherds used to gather together at sunset, and spend the long, dark evenings in games and merry-making around a blazing fire. Paschal never would take part in these noisy gatherings; but, when he had bidden good-night to his comrades, he used to retreat into his small hut, made out of the branches of trees and leaves, where, after saying his prayers, he kindled a light. These were the precious moments reserved for spiritual reading or some light manual labour.

Francis Dalgado, that same cousin whose Franciscan frock Paschal had so keenly coveted as a small child, used sometimes to pay a surprise visit to this leafy sanctum, for he, too, was now a shepherd. One evening he discovered the young solitary busily engaged in making cords provided with sundry knots. To his inquiries about their use Paschal replied: "These cords are for Rosaries. The big knots are Paters, the smaller ones Aves. As to those yonder, they help to atone for my sins." "Your sins!" exclaimed his cousin. "How can you talk about sins—you who are so good, and are always at your prayers?" "How, indeed? Why, in a thousand ways—by not at once banishing dangerous thoughts, when they present themselves to my mind; by giving too much liberty to my senses, and perhaps by stamping my foot impatiently on the earth which supports us." And with such earnestness and warmth did he speak that his cousin could find no reply, and withdrew to ponder in silence over what he had seen and heard.[2]

Paschal let slip no occasion of giving salutary advice to his companions, and God bestowed such efficacy upon the words of this young shepherd that his counsels were accepted with the deference due to the utterances of some

---

[2] "MS. Acts of Process of Canonization."

grey-bearded sage, as is attested by all who lived with him during this period of his life.

He used to distribute amongst his comrades the hempen chaplets he had made, teaching them at the same time their proper use. Thus, he became a zealous propagator of the devotion of the Rosary, which, as a simple and easy form of prayer, became very popular amongst the shepherds, so that in course of time salutations of the Blessed Virgin took the place of the coarse phrases and blasphemous expressions hitherto too often heard in the camp.

The sorrowful and the afflicted were always the objects of Paschal's solicitude; for, young as he was, he already realized that the trials and sufferings of life, when borne with resignation, are a means to expiate sin and to acquire merit; whilst, when received in an angry and rebellious spirit, they estrange from God and poison the wells of piety. Sometimes he was grieved to hear his comrades break forth into imprecations and blasphemies against God and His Saints when any misfortune or accident happened to them. Paschal was determined to remedy this evil, so that whenever in the course of his travels he found some soul soured by affliction he would not abandon that sore-tried soul until he had changed bitterness into sweetness.

"Come now, cheer up, my brother! Don't be downhearted," he used to say. "All is not lost. God is good; and then Mary, our heavenly Queen, is so powerful to help us. The damage will be repaired, and you will receive back again one of these days all that you have lost. Let us bless and thank Almighty God always. Who knows? Perhaps the very trial you are now enduring is the greatest of His favours."[3]

---

[3] "Process of Canonization."

What he was towards his comrades such was he also, in due proportion, towards the dumb animals entrusted to his care. He was, in the literal sense of the term, a good shepherd towards his flock, and always treated the sheep and lambs, not forgetting the faithful and sagacious sheepdog, with the kindness due to the creatures of a good and merciful God.

Never once was he heard to cast at them an imprecation or an angry word, and when a sheep strayed from the right path he used only to say: "Come along, now; come! St. Peter and St. John, assist us!" And then he made a pretence of brandishing his staff. That was quite enough. The sheep knew and loved their master, as their master knew and loved them, and of their own accord they fell into the ranks without more ado.[4]

It sometimes happened, in spite of all the vigilance of the shepherds and their dogs, that certain greedy sheep or silly little lambs were allured by the prospect of tender sprouts to trespass upon newly sown fields and browse upon forbidden fodder. This was the despair of our young shepherd, but it is just on this point that we see his love of justice and delicacy of conscience show to greatest advantage. As he was firmly convinced that every shepherd is responsible for all the depredations committed by his flock, he considered himself bound to make restitution, even in cases where he could not be blamed for any want of proper vigilance. One might safely say that he exaggerated his responsibility. Still, what a splendid example have we not here of the respect due to the rights of our neighbour—an example all the more telling in this present age, when spoliation, injustice, and corruption are so shamelessly rampant throughout the world!

---

[4] "MS. Acts of Canonization."

In order not to defraud his neighbour even of a single farthing, Paschal always carried with him a small notebook, in which he jotted down, there and then, the nature and extent of the damage done by his sheep. In the evening he hastened to find the owner of the field or vineyard, and pay him what the latter considered his due. Then he tore up the leaf. "We met him with his flock one day," says a witness at the Process. "He pointed out a field where his sheep had been making a raid, and asked us if we knew who was the proprietor. When we had told him, I saw him produce his little lamb-skin pocket-book, and as there was no ink in his ink-horn, he made a small puncture in the ear of a sheep and wrote down the name with a drop of the animal's blood. Thinking him over-scrupulous, we sought to settle his qualms of conscience. 'If you go on in this you will soon get rid of all your profits, and will be doing a poor business.' 'I do not covet even the least portion of my neighbour's goods,' he replied. 'Small faults pave the way to greater ones, and these lead to hell. Better settle one's score here below than have to square accounts in Eternity.' "[5]

To act thus under every circumstance is nothing less than heroic.

On one occasion his mother asked him to take some goats to his old Aunt Isabella. Now, goats inspired him with a sort of horror, and he besought his mother, with tears in his eyes, not to inflict such a penance upon him. "They are such gormandizers, and so unruly," he explained. "Nothing is harder than to keep them out of mischief. They give one the slip when least expected, and then go destroying the newly sown fields, and munching the tendrils of the vines. I entreat you, mother, do not bid

---

[5] Deposition of Gaspard Herrera ("MSS. of Process of Canonization").

me make these pilferers part of my flock, for I greatly dread inflicting some injury on my neighbour." Elizabeth did not insist, and Aunt Bella's goats were entrusted to the care of a less scrupulous herdsman.

Sometimes the shepherds would try to inveigle Paschal into taking part in a raid, or into sharing in the booty; but they always found him firm as adamant, for in his eyes the goods of others were sacred and inviolable.

"During the vintage," deposes one of the witnesses, "the *Majoral* (chief shepherd) wanted him to go into a vineyard and steal grapes. This *Majoral* was a terrible fellow, and his passionate violence used to make us tremble, whilst Paschal was at that time a mere boy. 'I am not going,' said Paschal; 'it is wrong.' At this answer the surly brute broke out in a fury, and, seizing hold of the lad, dragged him by force to the vineyard. 'Go in there, or I'll kill you!' 'You may kill me, but you cannot make me take what belongs to another,' he replied.

"On returning from the foray, the *Majoral* affected to treat the holy youth as a mean coward. He thrust some of the stolen grapes under his nose, and said tauntingly: 'You shan't have a single one of these grapes. D'you hear?' 'I don't want any,' replied Paschal. 'When I do, I will buy them.' As regards myself," added the witness in his humility, "I did not possess the same courage. Either from fear or human respect I followed the *Majoral* into the vineyard, and was not the last to taste of the forbidden fruit. Evil results ensued; my digestion was so impaired that for a time it seemed as though I were going to die. Paschal took occasion from this malady to remark to me: 'What is wrongfully acquired can never do good.' "[6]

The holy youth's sincerity and truthfulness were on a

---

[6] Deposition of Paschal Carretero.

par with his rigid sense of justice. "To gain the whole world we should never allow ourselves to utter the smallest falsehood," he often used to repeat.[7]

All that his comrades related of his uprightness and sterling honesty gained him such a reputation that everyone was eager to secure his services.

When serious damage was done by the flocks in any district, the shepherds were summoned before a tribunal of the local magnates, and gave evidence upon oath. This oath, however, was never required of Paschal, because his veracity was so widely known, and so highly esteemed, that his bare word was reckoned as good security as any number of oaths. Thus did faith—that highest safeguard and sure guarantee of truth and justice—infuse into the soul of this poor shepherd lad a refinement and a spirit of honour which might have been the envy of emperors and kings.

---

[7] Deposition of Michael Zappata.

CHAPTER III
VOCATION

IT is the prerogative of that Divine Being, to Whom our whole life belongs by the titles of creation and redemption, to assign to each one of His earthly children the particular path to be pursued, in order to arrive at our true home in Heaven. Ordinarily, it is by prayer, and also by the patient study of our own character and disposition, that we are led to the knowledge of the Divine Will in our regard. In some exceptional cases, as in that of our Saint, Almighty God makes assurance doubly sure by adding supernatural evidences and miracles to the ordinary signs of a vocation.

Long before the advent of these heavenly tokens, however, all who knew Paschal, whether they were members of the family circle or outsiders, had unanimously agreed that the tastes, habits, and inclinations of the holy youth alike predestined him for the Religious State. His eldest sister, Jane, who held him as a babe at the baptismal font, had long been wont to call him her "little monk." Amongst the shepherds he was already known by anticipation as "Brother Paschal." In fact, he was never addressed by them otherwise, and as the name accorded so well with the dearest wishes of his heart, he never raised any objection to its use.

Meanwhile, he laboured to strengthen his vocation by the faithful exercise of those virtues which find their fullest expression in the Religious State.

The Religious is pre-eminently a man of Rule, of Penance, and of Prayer. These are the three distinguishing marks of the religious life, and without them it is unthinkable.

Paschal instinctively divined all this, and hence he spared no pains to make his shepherd life approximate to that of the cloister by causing regularity, penance, and prayer to enter into it.

In order not to lose any of the graces that flow from a well-ordered life, he succeeded in constructing a kind of clock, complete in all its parts, by means of which he apportioned his time and fixed the hour of each exercise. Thus, thanks to his own ingenuity, prayers and devout practices succeeded one another with monastic regularity and exactitude.

Hand in hand with the spirit of order there went the spirit of penance. Coarse and meagre fare, forced marches of long duration at every season of the year, under the scorching rays of the torrid sun, or amid boisterous gales and glacial torrents, such and other trials no less galling were the shepherd's life and his daily bread.

How vast a field open to the spirit of penance! Surely the most greedy for sacrifices would find enough satisfaction in enduring with resignation and cheerfulness the ready-made austerities and privations of so rigorous an existence.

Yet Paschal did not find in all this sufficient material to satisfy his ardour, but, as we shall see, willingly and joyously went still further, in order, like the Apostle, to complete in his own body what is wanting to the sufferings of Christ. He seemed scarcely to touch his scanty pittance with his lips. His comrades did not fail to observe it, but none of them ever dreamed of attributing his abstinence to mere parsimony. Besides, it was well known that whatever he could spare, and much of what was really needful to him, was the portion of the poor; for he gave to them unsparingly, and always from his own stock. Never would he have wished to bestow upon them anything that could be regarded as the property of his employer, and, indeed, so great was his scrupulosity on this point that no one could have induced him to give away the bread provided daily by the master.

One of the shepherds was much astonished by Paschal's fastings, and tried to find out the reason. "I want to know why you eat so little," said he in his blunt way. "Well, then, I'll tell you," said the holy youth. He spoke with the grace and good humour whose secret is known to the Saints. "Fasting suits my constitution, and does me a lot of good. I feel much nimbler, and am better able to support the fatigues of our life."[1]

Whilst so austere with himself, he was most indulgent towards others, and gave tokens of evident pleasure when his comrades enjoyed better fare than usual, or were afforded the chance of making a substantial repast.[2]

Although those who lived in close proximity to the holy youth had eyes, there were certain other penitential secrets of which God and His Angels were alone the witnesses.

On one occasion, however, the silence was broken, and the secret of the torments he inflicted upon his flesh to bring it into subjection was allowed to escape. One of the shepherds, in a burst of confidence, had opened his heart to him. Having disclosed the temptations which left him no peace either day or night, he looked up into the eyes of his confidant and said: "And you—are you, too, like the rest of men, harassed by the enemy and subject to these miseries?" Paschal, thus directly interrogated, hung his head and blushed. For the moment, humility contended

---

[1] "Process of Canonization."

[2] Ibid.

with charity for mastery in his bosom, but charity soon won the day.

"Yes, my poor brother, I also, like yourself, feel the fire of evil passions surging in my veins. But shall I tell you what I do? Arming myself with the first bramble-branch that I can lay hands on, I scourge the rebel until the sensation of pleasure is exchanged for a groan of anguish—that's what I do."[3] And he relapsed into silence, half terrified at what he had said already.

The shepherds knew his virginal delicacy of soul, and, in order not to grieve him, they carefully refrained in his presence from every unbecoming expression.

To the penances above mentioned he joined that of going barefoot, a practice particularly painful in a mountainous country, crossed by stony paths and covered with thorns and brambles.

"Why do you always go with bare feet?" one day asked Anthony Navarro, the *Majoral,* of his young shepherd.

"Because the Kingdom of Heaven suffereth violence, and is only to be gained by suffering, trial, and self-denial." Prayer is the faithful and indispensable ally of penance; for without prayer it is impossible to persevere in a life of self-abnegation and sacrifice. As we shall return to this subject again, suffice it to say, in this place, that Paschal had realized in all its fullness the counsel: "We ought always to pray and not to faint." And from the time that Elizabeth had placed the words of prayer upon his infant lips he had never ceased to utter them.

Although Paschal entertained towards all the shepherds, his comrades in toil and in affliction, sentiments of fraternal charity and loyal affection, still, up to the present he had not contracted an intimate friendship with

---

[3] "Process of Canonization."

Ch. III: Vocation

any of their number. However, God provided a friend for him in due season. Our Saint was feeding his flock in the neighbourhood of Torre Hermosa when he met for the first time the future confidant of his most hidden thoughts. Like two sister souls, these two shepherds recognized and understood each other, even before exchanging a syllable, and felt a strong mutual attraction. Even the difference in their age was no bar to their friendship. John Apparicio was almost twenty years old, whilst Paschal had scarcely turned fourteen. But amongst the Saints, age is not reckoned merely by years, and this lad would not have been out of place in a congress of grey-beards.

Our two friends loved each other with all the strength and tenderness of youth. Everything seemed in sympathy between them; they had the same tastes, the same aspirations; and from the communion of their souls there grew and ripened the noblest fruit of a holy friendship—a strong encouragement and a joyous alacrity in well-doing.

It was a fresh pleasure to meet each morning, and, whilst they tended their flocks, the two friends discoursed of the things of God, the sorrows of this world, and the happiness of Heaven. To beguile the long hours of solitude, Paschal, who had a fine melodious voice and played skilfully on the guitar,[4] sang the popular refrains of the Blessed Virgin, accompanying himself on the instrument.

On account of his habitual discretion and reserve, Paschal did not at once confide to John Apparicio the secret of his vocation, but tested his friendship for more than a year before disclosing himself. If, however, it is good to hide the secret of the King, it is also honourable to reveal and confess the works of God,[5] as the Holy Scripture

---

[4] Rebec or Rabelico, a small stringed instrument like a guitar.

[5] Tob. 2.

reminds us.

The occasion presented itself unbidden. One evening the two friends were discussing the dangers and difficulties of their shepherd life. "Oh, what a wretched occupation is ours!" exclaimed Paschal. "Our head-men are always wrangling with the proprietors, and cannot pull with their own shepherds. How I long to quit this career, where there is nothing but disputes and lawsuits, and to become a Religious." "A Religious! Well, that is an excellent idea," commented John, with evident relish. "Now, I was just expecting that. But where will you be going? Now, suppose I were in your place and wanted to leave the world, I wouldn't go a long distance away to find a home. Close here is the Cistercian Monastery of Our Lady of Huerta. Why not apply there? You could then stay in your own part of the country, and work out your salvation quietly and easily in this abbey, which they say is the best endowed in the whole kingdom." The advice came straight from a warm and faithful heart, but the ideal presented by it was not that of Paschal's dreams. To stay in his own country—there to pass a serene and unruffled existence, with scarce a single cross or trial! Why, all this was just the contrary of what he sought. "No, no!" said he, with his usual frankness. "What you are proposing now won't do at all. I want to go a long way off, where nobody will know me. I am looking for some place where I can live in poverty and complete abandonment to Divine Providence."

John quickly perceived from this answer that between his own ideas and those of his holy young friend, upon this point, there lay a wide gulf, and he abstained from pressing the matter further. A few days later the two shepherds encountered each other at the usual trysting-place.

Paschal arrived there beaming with joy, and having no

longer anything to conceal from his friend, he at once began, with great simplicity and modesty, to relate to him the great event that had occurred since their last conversation, and how he had obtained both the certainty of his vocation and abundance of light concerning the Religious Family where he would find what he sought.

"I was by myself a few paces from the lonely hermitage of Alconcela," he said, "and was kneeling at my prayers, when all of a sudden, to my great astonishment, I beheld a Franciscan Friar, accompanied by a Sister of the same Order, appear on the scene. They both came towards me, and, having saluted me as a brother, they said to me: 'On the part of God and in His name we invite you to leave the world and enter Religion.' And then in glowing words they set before me the excellence and sublimity of that holy state so dear to God. Then they left as they had come, leaving me full of consolation and of gratitude."[6]

We are not informed who these mysterious personages were. In spite of this silence, however, several of the biographers do not hesitate to recognize in these envoys from on High St. Francis and St. Clare, since they were best suited, as it would seem, for this Heaven-sent embassy. Was not Clare the Saint of that August Sacrament to which Paschal was so singularly devoted? And was not Francis the personification of that absolute detachment which our holy youth so ardently aspired to?

Not long afterwards a miracle of the highest order gave John Apparicio a proof of the reality of this vision. Let us hear his own account of it.

"During the season of the great heats we reached a spring where the shepherds used to come to drink and to water their flocks. It was situated at Cobatilla, near

---

[6] Deposition of John Apparicio.

Cabrafuentes. We found the water so thick and muddy that it was unfit to drink. 'We had better go on and try another spring,' said I to Paschal. 'No, let us stop here,' he replied. 'I undertake to find some fresh, clear water.' Thereupon he bent his steps to a barren, stony patch, set down his staff and his wallet, and began to dig into the ground. Everything indicated failure. Suddenly, however, he straightened himself up, and, taking hold of his crook again, struck the ground confidently; then, lo and behold, there gushed forth a fine fountain of water. I ran up as fast as my legs would carry me, and after we had drunk our fill, we bathed our faces in the water, which was as limpid as a mountain torrent. Our meal passed off in silence, for I was startled by what I had seen. 'In future when you want a drink, you need only strike the ground with your staff, like I did, and the water will come,' Paschal said to me.

"I must confess that I have never tried the experiment. In fact, on a subsequent occasion when the holy youth asked me if I felt thirsty, I hastened to reply in the negative, dreading to witness a repetition of the miracle.

"Shortly afterwards my friend appeared in my presence, one fine day, completely transformed from head to foot. Under his shepherd's cloak he wore a tunic of ashen grey, reaching half-way down his legs, and held round his waist by a cord. The tunic was cut according to the pattern of the Friars of the Reform. Round his neck, like a necklace, there hung a Rosary with large beads, and a sombrero with wide brim completed this picturesque costume. Whilst I was gazing at him in astonishment, Paschal, reading my thoughts, said: 'Our Lord has deigned for a second time to send one of his Friars from Heaven to urge me to quit the world and enter Religion. As you may see, it is high time to answer this appeal, and to pledge myself to the service of Our Divine Master. Comrade, farewell! And he gave me his hand. We embraced and parted, never again to see each other here below."[7]

To every query concerning the origin of his habit, Paschal invariably gave an evasive reply, which gives colour to a theory adopted by his biographers—that the habit was brought to him by St. Francis and St. Clare.

More than half a century after the parting of the two friends, when many miracles had already shed their lustre upon the servant of God, the ecclesiastical authorities issued orders that the companions and witnesses of his life should be sought for, wherever they might be found. One day an aged man of venerable mien made his appearance at Villareal. He was bowed under the weight of eighty years. Without saying who he was, or why he came there, he begged one of the Religious to lead him to the glorious tomb of their sainted Brother. He stayed there a long time on his knees absorbed in prayer. The tears which trickled down his furrowed cheeks told their own tale. The octogenarian was no other than John Apparicio, the friend and confidant of Paschal's youth. He had come from the most remote extremity of the Province to narrate for the last time all he knew to the honour and glory of God's servant. His testimony was invaluable, since he alone, during this early period of our Saint's life, enjoyed the closest friendship with him, and knew even the hidden folds of his heart.

In order to clear up all doubt upon the point, he related on oath the story of the apparition of St. Francis and St. Clare, and told how Paschal, by striking the ground with his staff, had caused a miraculous spring to gush forth. The Religious asked why he had waited so long to make known an incident of such moment. "Ah, I didn't dare to do it,"

---

[7] Deposition of John Apparicio.

said the veteran meekly. "The thing was so extraordinary, no one would have believed me; and then, perhaps, my asseverations would only have proved detrimental of my holy friend's cause. To-day all is different, and now I am upon my oath; I am ready to tell all I know without the smallest omission."

The old fellow received a great ovation at the Convent of Villareal. They would have liked to keep him there always as a living relic of the Man of God.

During his stay, John Apparicio was summoned repeatedly to give evidence before the ecclesiastical tribunal, and many visits did he pay to Paschal's tomb. At length he regretfully departed, but not before he had obtained, amongst many other heavenly favours, the most precious grace of all, the pledge of his eternal salvation. As he had been in this land of exile the confidant and bosom friend of a Saint, it seemed incredible that he should not be the sharer of his glory in the Kingdom of the Blessed. In the long ago, when they had parted, Paschal said: "Farewell, comrade, until we meet again." And with a steadfast faith and confidence that nothing could disturb, old John Apparicio looked forward to that meeting.

CHAPTER IV
IN SIGHT OF THE PROMISED LAND

AFTER bidding adieu to his faithful friend, John Apparicio, Paschal turned his steps towards Valencia, hoping to find in that kingdom the convent of his hopes and dreams.

This journey gave him an opportunity of paying a visit to his eldest sister, Jane, who lived in the village of Peñas de San Pedro, and looked after a farm belonging to Pedro Garcia Mueno, one of the principal landlords in the neighbourhood. Their meeting after so lengthy a separation was a joyous and happy one. Jane seemed scarcely able to remove her admiring gaze from her "little monk," as she used to call the Benjamin of the family. What gave her the greatest pleasure was the knowledge that he was on the point of carrying into execution the pious design he had cherished with such persistency.

To do justice to the occasion, Jane bade the farm cooks to prepare an elaborate repast. The wayfarer perceived what they were about, and lost no time in putting a stop to these preparations. "Don't put yourselves to all this trouble and inconvenience," said he, "for all the victuals I want is a piece of bread soaked in water." So, much against the grain, Jane had to let the fire out and forego the feast.

Attributing his poor appetite to the fatigues of the journey, Jane requested Garcia Mueno's housemaid, Anne, to prepare a bedroom for him. Both the women, and Jane particularly, would have dearly loved to have a little chat with Paschal—it was so long since she had seen him, and then she had such a lot to tell him. But here, again, the good Saint put down his foot. "You can retire," he said.

"I will see about putting out the lamp." Jane and Anne were thus, perforce, compelled to beat a retreat, and as they were going away they heard Paschal draw the bolt across the door of his apartment.

As the light still remained burning an hour later, and unwonted sounds were issuing from the chamber, the curiosity of these two daughters of Eve was aroused. With stealthy tread they retraced their footsteps to the room, and applied their two pairs of eyes to a convenient chink in the door to see what was going on. What they saw froze the blood in their veins, and, unable to bear the spectacle, they soon ran away crying. There in the middle of the room stood Paschal, a rough-knotted cord in his right hand, scourging himself unmercifully. His shoulders were already black and blue—nay, they were torn and lacerated—and the sanguinary discipline was not yet over.

At daybreak on the morrow the pilgrim started on his way again, fasting as on the previous day. Despite the most urgent entreaties, he would agree to take nothing with him save a little water in his calabash. "Don't you fret; I can look after myself," said he. "Besides, if I want anything, surely no one will refuse to give it to me for the love of God."

So he departed, leaving behind a profound impression of sanctity, an impression which grew still deeper when it was discovered, from the undisturbed appearance of his bed, that the brief repose he had allowed himself from his prayers and his penances had been taken upon the bare flags of his apartment.

"On hearing the story from us," says Anne in her deposition, "our master exclaimed: 'That boy is a perfect saint!' "[1]

---

[1] Deposition of Jane and of Anne.

Ch. IV: In Sight of the Promised Land

In the shadow of the walls of the ancient city of Monteforte the Friars of the Reform had built one of their first convents under the invocation of Our Lady of Loretto. It was at the gate of this Friary that Paschal knocked, and on bended knees begged for the love of God and the salvation of his soul to be admitted amongst its inmates.

The youth of the postulant, however—he was but eighteen years of age—and perhaps his quaint costume as well, caused the Superiors to demur about accepting him. Without closing the door against him irrevocably, they only held out vague and distant hopes. It was an adjournment *sine die.* Paschal accepted this repulse as a mysterious dispensation of Divine Providence. Whilst he had received from God the assurance of his vocation, the time of his reception had not been disclosed to him. It only remained for him, then, to be resigned, and to hasten the epoch of his admission by redoubled devotion and fidelity, and such, in fact, was the course he adopted.

This delay was as painful as it was protracted, for whilst resignation hallows and mitigates suffering, it does not remove its sting. His sufferings might be not ineptly compared to those of the souls in Purgatory—those beautiful and holy souls, which, although adorned with sanctifying grace, and assured of their salvation, are yet detained in a region of exile, and forcibly withheld from the vision of God in Heaven, after which they hunger with such unspeakable longing. So, too, like a soul in pain, did this perpetual postulant for two long years linger round the House of Prayer, to him the image of Paradise, from time to time, with patience never weary, renewing his fruitless application.

So as not to withdraw his bodily presence from the spot, where his heart was securely anchored, Paschal entered the service of Martin Garcia, a wealthy landowner of Monteforte, and once more resumed his former shepherd life upon the Sierras. Long before daybreak he used to arrive in the vicinity of Our Lady of Loretto, and instal himself there, like a sentinel on guard before his Sovereign's palace.

Once he had entered into prayer, nothing could disturb his recollection. He remained equally insensible to the rough winds which buffeted his face and the drenching rains which soaked him to the skin. He seemed like some adoring Angel. To tear him from the heights of contemplation and recall him to the commonplace realities of life, his comrades were often obliged to shout at him and sometimes even to give him a violent shaking.

During the time Mass was being celebrated at the convent, his fervour, already so intense, redoubled, and he was absorbed in the contemplation of the Divine Sacrifice.

The onerous duties of his state debarred him from frequent assistance at Mass on weekdays, and this privation, perhaps more than any other trial, made him desire so ardently to enter Religion. The head-men amongst the shepherds did not fail to observe his trouble, and, like the good, compassionate men they were, did their utmost to relieve it. "Oftentimes did Paschal ask my permission to hear Mass," relates Navarro, the head shepherd, "and I always accorded it with a good grace, for I deemed it a happiness to have the power of encouraging his devotion."[2]

When deprived of this favour, the holy youth supplied for it in a different way. Thanks to the tinkling of the bells, with whose expressive language he was fully conversant, Paschal used to follow the different phases of the Holy Sacrifice with the same attention as if he had been

---

[2] Deposition of Anthony Navarro.

kneeling on the altar steps. This practice, however, instead of appeasing the ardent longings of his soul, only added to their intensity. He desired to draw near, to gaze upon and adore this venerable Mystery within the sanctuary itself.

Holy Scripture declares that God delights in doing the will of those who fear Him. What, then, will He not do for those who love Him supremely, and whose souls pant for His presence as the hart panteth for the water-brooks? If, in order to fulfil the desires of His elect, it is necessary to transcend the laws of Nature, then God will not fail to work miracles, and to work them abundantly; and thus the story of the Saints is replete with these supernatural interventions. Let the worldly-minded and the weak in faith take umbrage at the frequency of the miraculous in the dealings of the Almighty with these chosen souls; for us as believers it should rather be a perpetual occasion of reverent wonder and joy.

One day, when the ringing of the bell announced the approaching elevation, Paschal, unable any longer to bear his privation, fell into a sort of agony, and in his distraction gave vent to one of those cries of desire and love which pierce the Heavens and wound the very Heart of God. "My Master—my adorable Master—oh, that I might see Thee!" he exclaimed. Scarce had this lover's plaint escaped his lips than, raising his eyes, he perceived high up in the firmament a luminous point, which riveted his gaze. It seemed like that brilliant star which led the Magi to the crib at Bethlehem. Anon it blazed with wondrous splendour, and then, as it faded away, the sky seemed to part asunder, and Paschal, gazing through this lattice in the Heavens, saw the forms of Angels prostrated before the Sacred Host, surmounting a chalice.

In presence of the Divine Majesty, Paschal fell flat on his face. Then, regaining courage, he lifted up his head and gazed upon the heavenly vision.[3]

After a few moments it occurred to Paschal's ingenuous soul that it would be selfishness to keep Heaven's favours all for himself, so, rousing himself from his ecstasy, he hurried off to summon the other shepherds.

"Kneel down!" he said, with countenance all aglow. "Kneel down! Do you not see on high yon golden chalice, and the bright rays darting from the Host?" And he pointed towards the luminous point. "It is the most Blessed Sacrament of the Altar. The Angels are adoring It. Come, let us join our adoration to theirs."

The shepherds fell upon their knees in adoration; but it was in vain that with eager glances they scanned the vault of Heaven in order to discover the marvel, which Paschal had described with such enthusiasm. They saw nothing—absolutely nothing. Yet, although the vision remained concealed from them—and here, perhaps, is the highest testimony that could have been given to Paschal's reputation for sanctity—they believed in its reality upon the bare word of their youthful comrade, as though they had themselves seen it, and did not for a moment entertain the notion of deception or illusion. All knew he was incapable of uttering a falsehood, and the large fund of common sense which formed the backbone of his placid and stable character gave no room for hallucination.

The deposition of Anthony Navarro summarizes the opinions of the shepherds on this important point:

"To behold such marvels with our eyes, we ought to have possessed the purity of soul and the holiness of that blessed youth, and we were only poor sinners, a thousand

---

[3] "Stellam quamdam valde fulgentem videbat et in illa parte aperiebatur Coelum et in eo videbat sacrosanctum mysterium Missae cui se profunde humilians venerabatur ut verum Dominum et Deum, et anima ejus remanebat consolatissima."—Deposition of Anthony Navarro.

times unworthy of such favours. Although I did not see it, I nevertheless believe in this miracle with all the strength of my soul, and upon oath I declare that I hold for true all that Paschal told me about this vision. The perfection and sanctity of his life made it probable, and, besides, he affirmed its reality on his word as a Man of God. I should, indeed, be a poor Christian if I were to hesitate in accepting the declaration of such a holy person. Hence it is that I have often related these events to others, and to-day I confirm my words with an oath."[4]

The heavenly vision was no mere passing apparition or isolated fact in the life of our Saint, but recurred with such frequency as to become, as it were, habitual.

This is the reason why hagiographers, having to settle upon what was the most characteristic feature of our Saint, have selected this miracle as expressing more accurately than any other the dominant note of his whole life, namely: *The Adoration of the Blessed Sacrament.*

Hence they are wont to represent Paschal before a Chalice and a Host presented for his adoration by Angels.

Holy Scripture tells us that it is necessary that temptation should try the souls of men, particularly those souls whom God invites to a life of perfect holiness; for it is temptation which reveals the depths of the heart and discloses its hidden motives.

Amongst these temptations, attachment to earthly goods is rightly reckoned to be one of the strongest. Indeed, how often has it not ruthlessly rendered futile the noblest aspirations and the most sublime vocations? One who has valiantly overcome this obstacle may, without undue boasting, claim that he has given to God a supreme token of love.

---

[4] Deposition of Anthony Navarro, at that time Paschal's Majoral.

On this point Paschal had already experienced a trial. He had been entreated by his brother John, and his two sisters, Anne and Lucy, to take his share of the paternal inheritance; but he had replied: "I want absolutely nothing. Keep it all for yourselves. I shall one day be a Religious, if God so will."

True, the inheritance was not large, so that its renunciation would not necessarily have entailed any great heroism. To furnish the true measure of his spirit of renunciation it was necessary that the Servant of God should be exposed to one of those occasions which sometimes shake the constancy of even the most steadfast. Without in the least knowing or intending it, Paschal's master, the estimable Martin Garcia, was destined to play the part of tempter.

The more intimately he became acquainted with the young shepherd, the more did he discover in him rare and valuable qualities. And, quite naturally, having found a real treasure, he was loth to part with it. His wife, when informed of his ideas on the point, concurred in them with all the greater readiness, because she herself felt a motherly affection for this child of benediction. As soon as he had come to a decision in the matter, Martin summoned Paschal to his presence, and, speaking with emotion, said to him without further preliminary:

"My son, both my wife and myself are getting old, and we are childless. Why should you not become our adopted son? I invite you to leave your present occupation and come and live with us in town. You shall be our child and, later on, our heir."

The old man paused, waiting to hear from Paschal's lips the decisive "Yes" which would fulfil his wishes. But Paschal's lips remained sealed. With head bowed down pensively upon his breast, the holy youth seemed a prey to painful agitation. The answer, indeed, was ready the while, though not the one expected by the master; but the difficulty was how to give it expression without wounding the feelings of the kind-hearted old man, and shattering the dream of his declining years. After some moments Paschal at length ventured to break the silence, and to tell his benefactor what he had previously told his brothers and sisters; but was careful to accompany his refusal with lively expressions of gratitude.

"I am deeply thankful for your great kindness," he said, "but I can accept nothing from you; for I have resolved to become a Friar, and to live despoiled of all things."

There was not even a moment's hesitation in choosing between the alluring future thus unfolded before him and the blood-stained cross offered him by Christ.

Martin Garcia was too sincere a Christian not to perceive the sublimity of this refusal. Far from angrily dismissing his young herdsman, his esteem for him rose still higher, and until the day of his entry into Religion, Paschal was always treated in the house as though he had been one of the family. His renunciation of a rich inheritance made quite a stir in the country, and greatly enhanced the holy youth's reputation for exalted virtue.

The inmates of the Loretto Convent were not the last to hear about all that was being said in praise of their postulant. Little by little his frequent visits to the Friary had won the sympathy of all the Friars; for they could not fail to see and to admire his angelic piety and wonderful charity. When milk was wanted for the sick, it was to him they always applied by preference, and with great willingness used he to give promptly for the love of God all that the Friars asked of him, at the same time deducting these alms from his own wages.

The shepherds amongst whom Paschal lived, who saw

him day after day in their very midst, never could detect in him the slightest fault upon any point. It seemed as though he had been gifted with impeccability, and were confirmed in grace, so that they got into the way of treating him as a creature belonging to another world, outside the ordinary conditions of mortality. And when, in later years, they were cited before the Ecclesiastical Court, charged with the Process of Beatification, they hastened with joyous alacrity from diverse Provinces, proud of having been the companions of a Saint, and keenly alive to the honour which would be reflected upon their humble corporation by his elevation to the ranks of the Blessed. Their depositions are of touching simplicity, and testify to a veneration bordering on enthusiasm. That of Stephen Lopez, who was scarcely ever separated from Paschal during the second stage of his shepherd life, is of particular importance:

"When I used to see in that youth such a love of prayer, conjoined to such a spirit of penance," he says, "sometimes the thought used to occur to me that perhaps behind that human form there was hiding away an Angel, sent by God to teach us our duty, and the way to love Him. His zeal for the glory of God and the salvation of souls was unbounded, and always in evidence. He used to admonish with great freedom, and still greater charity, such of us as swerved from the straight path, and his counsels were marked throughout by wisdom and prudence. He seemed in our midst like some alert watchman, and an intrepid defender of the commandments of God and of the Church. He spared no pains that they should be observed to the letter. He used to remind us about Vigils, Feasts, and Holidays, and for this purpose always carried about with him a calendar, carefully marked. 'To-day is Saturday, or the Vigil of some Feast,' he used to say. 'Let us stay here, and not go any further.' We used to obey him, as though he were our chief, and only struck camp on the Monday following or the morrow of the Feast. As for himself, he used to arrange his affairs so carefully on the eve of a Holiday that he was able to abstain from all manual labour, and even the appearance of it. All was ready—the small provision of bread and oil, even down to the dry grass with which he used to kindle his fire. As Easter-time drew near, his solicitude redoubled, and he urged us in the most pathetic exhortations to fulfil our duties as Christians. On hearing him speak one day, one of his comrades said: 'Now, mind you, if that boy turns Religious, he'll make a rare preacher.' "

Another deposition—that of Anthony Navarro, the *Majoral*—will serve to complete these precious details:

"I have never in my life met so perfect a Christian as this holy man, so that I was not in the least surprised when they told me he was working miracles. I am firmly convinced he is in Heaven. He has merited it hundreds of times by his saintly life. In our last interview he said to me: 'Navarro, if I die before thee, thou canst be certain that I shall not forget thee before God. Do the same for me if thou art the first to die.' I don't doubt his fidelity to our compact. I cannot express what a consolation it is to me to have so powerful an advocate before the throne of God. Every day I say a *Pater* and an *Ave,* not, indeed, to bring him relief, but to remind him of his promise."[5]

---

[5] Deposition of Anthony Navarro.

CHAPTER V
IN PORT

THE long and weary period of suspense was fast drawing to a close. It had not been so much waste time, but, on the contrary, eminently productive of rich and rare fruits in the soul of Paschal, who had now become proficient in all the virtues most pleasing to the heart of God. Surely it cannot be questioned that, if anyone was fit and worthy to be admitted into the Religious State, it was he; rather, one feels disposed to ask what the Religious State was capable of adding to such mature perfection, and what spiritual privileges Paschal could expect to enjoy there that he did not already possess? The answer to this question is indirectly furnished by Blessed Giles, the companion of St. Francis. In one of his famous sayings, to which posterity has accorded the epithet of "Golden," he points out in his original style the inappreciable gain accruing to every soul, even to that of a Saint, through leaving the world and embracing the Religious life: "As for me, I would rather have one little ounce of virtue in Religion than two pounds of perfection in the world."

And the reason he gives for this preference is the merit of Holy Obedience, who, standing like a Queen on the threshold of the Religious life, touches all that passes before her with her sceptre, or, as we might even say, her fairy wand, and, by that touch, hallows and makes it meritorious. Then, too, it is the unique privilege of obedience to safeguard the soul that is seeking God from the danger of deception and the illusions of self-love, and to impart safety and security to all her steps.

No one understood all this better than Paschal, and hence his eagerness to bend his neck beneath the sweet yoke of obedience, in which he saw only a safer and a nobler way of serving God with perfect freedom. Let us now, in the train of our postulant, enter into this Promised Land of Obedience.

The Religious Family, which now, after so long a delay, at length gave admittance to the holy youth, is known in Franciscan annals under the title of the "Reform of the Discalced Friars of Regular Observance." It had sprung like a fountain from the glowing breast of St. Peter of Alcantara, the great mystic and most austere of Spanish penitents. In the intention of the Saint it was designed to renew the golden age of Franciscanism, and cause the seraphic spirit of the Poverello and his early companions to flourish once more in full vigour.

This is not the place to relate the sacrifices and the miracles by which this dream was translated into reality; but it is to the purpose to know the judgment of the Church upon the workman and his handiwork—a judgment which finds expression in an attractive and, as we may say, a tangible form. The Church, in her supernatural wisdom, appreciates merit at its just worth, and is wont to give a true estimate of men and things, and she does not consider herself to be paying any undue honour to St. Peter of Alcantara in placing his statue beside those of the Patriarchs and Founders of the great Religious Order in the Vatican Basilica, thereby consecrating the work of this doughty Reformer, and attributing to it the dignity and excellence of a new creation. A like homage, as far as we know, has been paid solely to one other—the Reformatrix of Carmel; so that, by a providential coincidence, it has come to pass that there now stand, under the same arch in the Basilica, the statue of St.

Theresa, and, immediately opposite, that of St. Peter of Alcantara, the trusty guide of the Seraphic Virgin across the dizzy heights of mysticism, whose every path he knew by his own experience.

Ordinarily speaking, the artificer can be known by his handiwork, and the Reform effected by St. Peter of Alcantara is no exception to this general rule. What St. Gregory said of his father Benedict may be applied to him literally and with perfect truth: "Do you want to know Benedict? Then, study his Rule. Do you want to understand the Rule? Then, read Benedict's life." In other words, the Rule so faithfully reflected the mind and spirit of its author that the holy Patriarch became incarnate in his own work, and was, so to speak, identified with it.

What gives to the glorious figure of St. Peter of Alcantara a unique expression and an originality all its own is the blending together of two opposing traits, seemingly incompatible, and incapable of being combined in the same physiognomy—joy and suffering. There are found together the radiant smile of the contemplative, who already shares in anticipation the joys of the blessed, and the sorrowful mien of the penitent, atoning for the infinite malice of sin. Christian art, taking cognizance of this twofold aspect of its subject, has portrayed St. Peter of Alcantara sometimes under one of these aspects, and sometimes under the other, and occasionally it has attempted to combine the two.

Those who regard in him only the *Penitent*, represent him carrying a heavy cross up Calvary after the example of his Divine Master; whilst those who limit their attention to the *Contemplative*, portray him seated, listening in the silence of prayer to the words, whispered into his ear by the Holy Spirit, under the form of a dove. Those, finally, who would give us both the contemplative and the penitent represent St. Peter as, in a moment of ecstasy, he seizes the cross and clasps it in a passionate embrace.

These two comprehensive features in the life of the Religious Reformer indicate to us, without the need of further inquiry, in what his Reform consisted, and which were the properties characterizing it:

Heroic penance and sublime contemplation—these are writ large on every page of the marvellous history of the first Friars of the Reform, to whom Peter of Alcantara, the new Elias, bequeathed, together with his mantle, the patrimony of his spirit and his virtues. The Master, though dead, survived in his disciples, and so closely did they follow in the footsteps of their Father, that, like him, they scarcely seemed to touch the earth with their feet as they sped along their way to Heaven. One would have taken them for beings of a different world, pure spirits, emancipated from the thraldom of the flesh, superior to the needs and weaknesses of human nature. The only food and sleep they took was what was indispensable to sustain life and preserve them from dying. Watching, fasting, and the discipline was their ordinary nourishment. And it was in these frames, so emaciated by penance, that they performed works of superhuman energy and grandeur.

Zurbaran is the artist whose skilful brush has limned the manly countenances of these heroes of penance, seamed and furrowed by voluntary suffering. They would almost appal us—these Spanish Monks—were it not that the fire of their glance is tempered by the unction of Divine grace, and that the habitual union of their soul with God shines transparent through their attenuated features, softening whatever sternness is visible there.

It was into this terrestrial Paradise, the dwelling-place of Angels in the flesh, that Paschal entered.

The Province of St. John Baptist, whose adopted son he

became, fully deserved at this epoch the encomium pronounced upon it, in the Convent of St. Gregory of Orihuelha, by the Provincial, the Venerable Father Anthony Sobrino, at the time of the canonical visitation. "Brethren, in what profound esteem ought you not to hold this Province, founded by our blessed Father and his own by predilection? You can never love it as much as it deserves. All the Provinces of the Order cast upon it glances of holy envy, seeing how the Lord hath been pleased to exalt it, and confound the most determined efforts of its foes." It was, in fact, everywhere quoted as the model Province and a nursery of Saints and Apostles.

Paschal seemed created expressly to live in such an atmosphere. From the first he found himself at home there, and with expanded lungs drank in the pure, invigorating air of the mountain peaks, the native air of saintly and heroic souls, deprived of which they are condemned to droop and languish. Everything in this land, where the Holy Spirit had led him, pleased and enchanted him; each step brought some fresh surprise.

Such an impression is by no means uncommon on the threshold of the Religious life. Change and novelty are sufficient in themselves to produce and explain it. What is more unusual is perseverance, for in many cases it is but a sudden blaze which quickly spends itself and smoulders out. It was not going to be like this, however, with the new Brother. The fire of fervent enthusiasm which kindled his breast on the day of his clothing never grew cold from the effects of habit and familiarity; but, on the contrary, found in them fresh fuel to feed its flames from day to day. What had appeared estimable and lovely in the beginning only grew more venerable and more beautiful with the lapse of time, after it had been put to the test of many years' experience; and thus Paschal's life became a perpetual feast.

He could not find words to express his gratitude towards God for the blessing of his vocation. The joy, whose unfailing source lay deep hidden in the folds of his heart, was reflected in his visage; it was a modest and a recollected joy, betraying itself in a smile, which even the sharpest pang could never wrest from his lips.

Was the satisfaction felt by Paschal reciprocated by the Friars of Loretto? Were they as contented with the aspirant as he was with his new surroundings? In order to be admitted to profession, we must remember it was not enough that the novice should feel happy and wish to remain, but it was also necessary—and this was a formidable condition—that he should satisfy the strict judges who were to decide upon his fitness.

No doubt a certain reputation for sanctity had preceded Paschal into the cloister. There had been divers rumours about his visions and his miracles. But all is not gold that glitters. These premature canonizations not infrequently resemble the mirages of the desert—those enchanted landscapes which continually recede towards the horizon before the eyes of the approaching traveller, until at length they utterly vanish, leaving behind no trace, save the remembrance of a dream of beauty.

Community life is the test, in presence of which counterfeit holiness has oftentimes resolved itself into thin air. It is a ray of light which, when shed upon the Saint's halo, shows whether it be of gold or only of some worthless imitation. Paschal passed triumphantly through this ordeal in a manner to satisfy the most exacting.

When they had studied their novice continually and without intermission, under every possible light, the Religious of Loretto perceived with joy that in him there was the material that Saints are made of, and from that time forward they became more fearful of losing him than he was of being rejected by them as unworthy. Venerable men, grown old and grey under the yoke of Religion, could not conceal their mingled astonishment and admiration at the spectacle of this youthful athlete, who, although he had only just entered the lists, already excelled the most famous champions. They confessed themselves outdone and vanquished by this stripling, and acknowledged that they had everything to learn from him, and that he was a master and an example to them.

"A great blessing has been given to our Religious Family," they used to say with much consolation. "This Brother will be the honour and glory of our Reform."[1] They spoke truly and prophesied with good reason, for from such beginnings it was safe to augur a splendid future. Paschal was not of the number of those who, having made a good start, afterwards slacken their pace and look backwards. "Upwards and onwards" is the motto of the Saints, and it was his.

In order to reach sooner the more striking events in the life of the holy Brother, his biographers pass rapidly over the year of noviceship—that all-important period wherein, as in a mould, the soul of the Religious takes form and shape. Where we seek anxiously for details we find only generalities. However, from phrases such as the following one, extracted from the Process, "Never was novice so humble, so docile, and so fervent,"[2] we can legitimately deduce the broadest conclusions as to his sanctity at this period.

Some of Paschal's biographers are of opinion that he took the Franciscan habit at Elche, where the Castilian

---

[1] Acts of Process.

[2] MSS. of the Process.

novitiate was then situated. This Friary, dedicated to St. Joseph, was held by him in almost as great affection as that of Our Lady of Loretto.

As regards his profession, we know for certain that it was made at the Loretto Convent on the Feast of the Purification in the year 1565. This never-to-be-forgotten date was duly inscribed by the newly professed in the register, in which, by order of the Provincial, the names of all the Religious of the Province were entered in order of seniority.

The heavenly delights of that day were enhanced for Paschal by the thought that the most solemn act of his life had been accomplished in a sanctuary dedicated to Mary, under her auspices, and on that sweet solemnity, when the ever-blessed Virgin offered the Infant Jesus to the Eternal Father for the Divine glory and the redemption of the world. Paschal was a child of Mary, and he, too, had consecrated himself to God for the salvation of souls. It was his Mother in Heaven, who had presented him to the Lord, even as she had once presented her Divine Child in the Temple.

CHAPTER VI
THE HEART OF A SON

"ONCE transplanted into the enclosed garden of the Lord," says the Legend of the Breviary, "the Lily of the Valley flourished exceedingly and diffused abroad the odour of sanctity."

Happily for ourselves, Paschal has himself all unconsciously outlined the complete programme of his own saintly life when, in treating of the conditions necessary for salvation, he writes thus in his clear and nervous style:

"Whoever is intent upon saving his soul must have three hearts in one:

"Towards God the heart of a son.

"Towards his neighbour the heart of a mother.

"Towards himself the heart of a judge."

Without a doubt these three hearts in one beat within Paschal's breast in perfect unison, and it is only when we have studied them separately and probed each one to its inmost depths, that we shall be able to understand what our hero really was, and appreciate his merits as they deserve; for the heart is the man himself.

In the best of all prayers our Divine Master has taught His disciples how to approach God, under the law of grace, and the name by which they are to address Him when drawing near Him: "Thus shall ye pray: Our Father Who art in Heaven." If He is our Father, then we can most truly call ourselves His children, and hence the first of our duties is to love Him with the affection a good and dutiful son bears towards his father.

Filial love is a blending of the noblest sentiments to be

found in the human breast—reverence and tenderness, simple trust, and joyful submission. When it is God Who is in question, then, taking the name of Piety, whilst retaining its intrinsic nature, filial love goes the length of adoring its Object. Never was child of God more ready than Paschal was to render to the Heavenly Father this tribute of filial affection. Without awaiting the summons of the Divine Master, he threw wide open the portals of his heart—that heart so well fitted to be the abode of the Deity—and besought Our Lord to enter in, and accept as a free and spontaneous offering all the treasures of love and tenderness it contained.

A good son never feels happier than by his father's side. To quit the paternal roof is repugnant to him, to return a joy. As he shares in all his father's ideas and prepossessions, so he inclines instinctively towards everything the latter approves; whilst he shuns whatever is disliked or censured by him. And then, again, he places his father's interests before every other concern; so that persons and things are regarded by him with a friendly or an unfriendly eye, according as they promote these interests or clash with them. Such are the chief characteristics of the good and dutiful son, his father's pride and joy. We find them all fully developed, even down to the smallest detail, in the Religious life of our Saint; so that, in tracing them, we have, as it were, sketched his portrait in advance.

A Monastery is pre-eminently the abode of our Heavenly Father. There one dwells in His company and under the same roof with Him. It was for this very reason that Paschal found there his Heaven on earth; so that, as far as his own tastes were concerned, once within the cloister, he would never again have crossed its threshold.

In the midst of this blessed abode, itself a tabernacle,

there stood the Holy of Holies, where the Eucharistic God had pitched His tent, and where He held His audiences. It was there that, day and night, the saintly Brother was to be found. The conventual chapel might be called his headquarters. He had pitched his tent there close to that of his Divine Master. If he was not to be found there, it was because Obedience had summoned him elsewhere, and the moment his liberty was restored, he sought to return there, as infallibly as the stone, when left to itself, seeks the center of gravity. Need we be surprised, since behind those veils was the Beloved, Who attracted him with irresistible force?

Ever the first in Choir at the Midnight Office, he was likewise the last to leave and return to his cell. Then, after a brief period of sleep, taken in such a position as to make it a penance rather than repose, behold him again afoot on the way to the Oratory.

It is the early morning hour when he is accustomed to gain the Indulgence, popularly styled in Spain "The Indulgence of the Crusade." Being as truly patriotic as he was Catholic, Paschal would have deemed himself wanting in his duty, both as a Christian and as a Spaniard, had he neglected, even for one day, this singular privilege accorded to his country by the Sovereign Pontiffs, in recognition of her protracted and heroic struggles in defence of the Faith. The state of contemporary affairs made the Indulgence all the more precious. The enemy was once more at the gate menacing that integrity of faith and that national unity which had been acquired at the cost of so many sacrifices. It was a question now of defending the frontiers against the invasion of Protestantism, even more formidable, perhaps, than that of Islam, and to beat back the Huguenots of France and Germany, even as the doughty knights of old had driven from the realm the hordes of African Moors. The Crusade had started afresh under another form. Paschal would have belied his pedigree, had he not been found in the forefront of that glorious phalanx of holy souls, who by prayer and penance succeeded, amidst the stress of those troublous times, in saving Catholic Spain from the contagion of heresy. So, every morning, before the Friars had risen, this new Crusader might have been seen wending his way along the silent aisles of the church, and making before each altar the visit prescribed in the Papal Bull.

And now, before proceeding further, it will not be out of place to make an observation concerning the habitual posture of our Saint in prayer. It is a matter of no little importance, since, when a soul is as candid and sincere as that of Paschal, the exterior becomes a living document faithfully representing the interior. When Paschal entered into prayer, he joined his hands, the fingers being interlaced, then he raised them to the level of his forehead, and thus, with his elbows disengaged from his sides, he remained immovable upon his knees, his eyes fixed upon the Tabernacle, or upon the image of some Saint. So perfectly did this attitude, spontaneous and unaffected as it was, correspond to the rapture of his soul that it gave one the impression of a Seraph, about to spread his wings and take flight towards Heaven. One Holy Thursday he was so absorbed in contemplation of the mystery of the Eucharist as to remain for five hours in this position, as motionless as a statue.

Sometimes, for the sake of variety, or perhaps to give some relaxation to jaded Nature, he used to stand erect, with his arms extended in the form of a cross. When he thought that he was alone and without witnesses, his profound sense of God's unspeakable Majesty and of his own nothingness caused him to prostrate himself full-length upon the ground. It seemed to him matter for wonderment that the earth did not open and swallow up so undutiful a son, unworthy to behold the face of his Father.

On certain occasions he used to be raised for several feet in the air in ecstasy, and remained, as it were, floating between Heaven and earth, as long as it pleased Our Lord to keep him entranced by the vision of His Divine beauty. Being one day surprised in a moment of ecstasy, he experienced mortal confusion. Fearing, with good reason, that the Brother who had seen him would take him for a Saint, he drew him on one side and said to him: "Take care not to draw any hasty conclusions from what you have seen. There is nothing in it worth paying any attention to, as perhaps you might be tempted to think. Now, I am going to tell you the real meaning of it. Supposing a father has a son of a wayward disposition, do you know what he often does from motives of prudence? He makes everything easy for him, treats him with kindness, caresses him, striving by this gentle treatment to win his affection and to keep him from harm. It is thus that Our Lord in His mercy deigns to act towards me." We are not informed whether the Brother allowed himself to be convinced by this plausible argument.

But let us now return to the chapel where we left the holy youth in prayer. It is time to open the church to the faithful and to give the signal for the Religious to rise. These two functions appertain to the office of the Porter, and in their discharge the holy man made his spirit of faith enter in all its fullness. The keys entrusted to him, which served to open the doors of God's house, were as precious and as sacred in his eyes as though they were those of Paradise. They never left his hands until his fingers, stiffened and frozen in the clasp of death, were no longer able to hold them.

What a joy and what an honour it was, too, to have the task of rousing the soldiers of Christ from their slumbers, in order to summon them to fresh combats! Like a bugler on the point of sounding the charge, Paschal kept his station in the dormitory, awaiting the stroke of the clock, and then, in clarion tones, he cried out: "Brethren, arise! To Prime! to Prime—to sing with the Angels the praises of Our Saviour and of His Holy Mother!" Then, knocking at the door of each cell, he said with pious deliberation: "Praised be the most Holy Name of Jesus!" When this had been accomplished, he descended again to the chapel with the same earnestness and joy, in order to serve the Masses there.

Of all the occupations of his daily life as a Religious this was the one for which he had the greatest liking. On this point his pious avidity was insatiable. The more Masses there were to be served, the more he was pleased. He was on the watch, like the huntsman lying in wait for his prey, and if, for some reason or another, the usual servers were not on the spot, he eagerly hastened to replace them. Holy as it is in itself, this humble ministry is not without its stumbling-blocks and its dangers. When it recurs day after day, and is protracted beyond a certain limit of time, it is apt to grow wearisome, even for the most fervent, so that its exercise becomes a mere matter of routine. For, indeed, how is one to maintain in the same degree, for three or four hours consecutively, the same attention and recollection found in the beginning, and awakened naturally by the living memorial of Calvary? We must ask this question of the Saints, for they alone can furnish the reply and tell us how we can be preserved from our natural apathy. After serving eight or ten Masses, Paschal was as ready as ever to serve yet more, and his recollection was even greater than at his first arrival at the altar. The trial might be renewed every day, yet it found him always prepared, and brought in its train a continual increase of fervour.

The faithful who frequented the chapel did not take long in remarking the angelic piety with which the young Brother served Mass and received Holy Communion. It was enough to bring faith to an unbeliever and to cause him to cast himself upon his knees at the feet of the hidden God, Whose Presence Paschal's attitude of profound recollection seemed to render almost visible. In spite of all his precautions against attracting public attention, the sacred fire which burnt within blazed out externally, and betrayed the secrets of his soul. His face used to become suffused with a mysterious ruddy glow, like the reflection of a heavenly light, so that his countenance wore a look of unearthly beauty. People repeated these things to one another, and as our poor humanity is ever greedy for the marvellous, the throng who came to enjoy this unwonted sight increased from day to day, without the poor Brother once suspecting that he had become a spectacle to God, to Angels, and to men. Between God and the humble there is a perpetual conflict. The more they strive to be forgotten and to wrap themselves in obscurity, the more is Our Lord pleased to place upon a candlestick the light they would fain hide under a bushel. In this unequal conflict God, Who is wonderful in His Saints, always obtains the mastery. The faithful, whose curiosity was by this time thoroughly aroused, observed more in detail what had caused them edification, and thus the veneration they already had for the holy youth increased.

Paschal, as we have already seen, had amongst other offices that of Porter. Now, whether it arose from a mere coincidence, or whether it was done on purpose, it happened that, during the time when the Masses were being celebrated, the ringing of the door-bell was almost incessant. At the first sound of the bell the angelic server, tearing himself away without the least hesitation from the Divine attractions of the Tabernacle, hastened to the door to answer the summons; then, his duty as Porter being fulfilled, he speedily returned to his post upon the altar-steps, only to be called away a few moments later by a fresh summons. This true son of obedience had been trained in an excellent school, and had learned there that the duties of our state of life must have precedence of everything else, and that even ecstasy itself must take a second place, when they are in question.

Human affection, as everyone knows, finds in absence and distance two formidable and deadly enemies. "Out of sight, out of mind," says the proverb truly. To the best of our ability we study how to falsify this saying. So as not to forget our absent friends, we keep their portrait before our eyes; we hold regular correspondence with them, and by a thousand artifices strive to retain them in our company.

Our filial love towards God is subject to the same vicissitudes, and in order to make it live and thrive it needs some stimulus. Here, too, there must be some sort of sight and speech, if there is to be a survival of love. When all sight and all communication have ceased, indifference supervenes, and entire forgetfulness is not slow in following. To preserve His children from so dire a misfortune, God has bestowed upon them prayer—a wonderful resource within the reach of all; so that by means of it even the least of us can draw near our Heavenly Father and hold familiar converse with Him. Accustomed from his very infancy to find in prayer the daily bread of Divine charity, Paschal, when he had become a Religious, devoted to this exercise all the faculties and affections of his soul. Both by word and by example he pointed out prayer as the chief exercise of the Christian and Religious Life and the great means of approaching God and of becoming like Him.

"What could be nobler, more delightful, or more profitable than conversing with God?" he used to say. "If by frequenting the company of the wise and the good one becomes insensibly wiser and more virtuous, how is it possible, I would ask you, that we shall not become more and more filled with Divine wisdom and charity, when we draw near Him, Who is the unfailing source of goodness, truth, and beauty?"

The sorrowful Passion of Our Lord Jesus Christ was the favourite theme of the holy Brother's meditations. Who will not recognize in him by this token the son and disciple of the Poverello of Assisi, whose eyes were blinded by weeping over the sufferings of the crucified God? A certain exclamation, treasured up as a precious pearl by the Friars, discovers to us in what spirit and with what feelings the servant of God approached this subject. On the occasion of some Festival the Guardian of Villareal explained to his Community that, in order to gain a certain indulgence, one should recite six *Paters*, *Aves*, and *Glorias*, at the same time making a short meditation on the Sacred Wounds. "Thus, for example," he added, "at the first *Pater* you will consider the wound made by the crown of thorns, then you go on to the second *Pater*, and from that to the third." "The second *Pater*!" exclaimed Paschal, beside himself for the moment. "Why, what you require is an impossibility. How can you suppose that, having entered into the Sacred Wound, one should leave it in order to go elsewhere?" As a matter of fact, before coming to the second *Pater*, Paschal was no longer in this world, but, hidden in this retreat as in an inviolable asylum, he remained there without the power of quitting it.

Paschal could have dispensed himself, with a perfectly safe conscience, from the Community meditation, which took place in the choir twice during the day. His office of Porter placed him at the disposal of the public, and did not allow him the same facility as that enjoyed by his Brethren for remaining several hours in the appointed place. It was to be feared, too, on account of his continual journeyings to and fro between the choir and the door, that his presence at this exercise would be a source of distraction to the Community. To avoid this inconvenience, and to give the Brother some respite, the Father Guardian, without waiting until Paschal asked for the dispensation, accorded it to him spontaneously. To his astonishment and edification, the Brother Porter thereupon threw himself upon his knees and besought him, with tears in his eyes, not to deprive him of the merit and consolation he experienced in being in choir with the Religious Brethren. In his eyes the Community at prayer was the army of the Lord, drawn up in battle array, and about to take the field. And it was at this decisive moment that it was proposed he should retire into his tent. In view of such genuine desolation, the Guardian withdrew the dispensation, and no one had any ground for complaint on this account. Paschal used to remain hidden away like the Publican of the Gospel, in a corner of the choir close to the door. Gliding like a shadow, and scarcely touching the ground with his feet, he entered and left so noiselessly and with such precaution that the Religious were unconscious alike of his entrance or his exit. From the same abiding sentiment of respect for the prayer of his Brethren, Paschal energetically repressed every outburst or sensible manifestation of the ardent devotion which filled his heart to overflowing.

It was otherwise when he was alone. Then the hidden

fire broke forth in jets of flame; and devout ejaculations and exclamations of love winged their way heavenwards like fiery darts to pierce the Heart of God. It was in a certain shrubbery which covered a portion of the garden, that the holy youth used to run and hide himself, when the vehement transports of his soul became uncontrollable. This coppice, however, did not always shield him effectually from inquisitive glances, as is obvious from the following gentle remonstrance addressed to one of these curious persons: "For pity's sake, Brother, why do you follow and persecute me so?"

The filial love of the Saints towards God extends to all the manifestations of God in things created. These masters in the science of Divine love have caused to enter into their devotion towards Jesus Christ all that is involved in the work of Redemption—that is to say, Mary, His most blessed Mother; the Angels, His messengers; the Saints, His friends and courtiers; the Pope, His Vicar upon earth; the Church, the treasury of His superabundant merits.

We have already seen that Paschal was a most devout client of Our Lady before his entry into the Order. On becoming a member of the Franciscan Family, he found a fresh stimulus to strengthen and increase his love for his spiritual Mother, in the very title of a son of St. Francis. For centuries the Friars Minor had been in the front rank of the defenders of Mary's Immaculate Conception. In order to demonstrate this privilege, they had waged severe battles and gained more than one signal victory. Anticipating the homage that would one day be paid by the entire Catholic world to the Immaculate Virgin, they annually celebrated with special solemnity the Festival of her Conception. It was the Franciscan tradition, and could be traced back to the Seraphic Patriarch himself. Paschal entered into it with his whole heart, and was rejoiced at becoming, in virtue of his profession, a champion of the Immaculate Virgin, pledged to maintain her glory. Simple and unlearned as he was, yet when the occasion presented itself, he was ready to enter the lists and break a lance in honour of his Queen.

Long before the eighth of December he used to commence his preparation for the Feast. On the day itself he went about like a man beside himself with joy. If he met any one of the younger Friars in the cloister or corridors on this occasion, he would say: "On your knees, Brother, on your knees! As you believe in God, repeat with me, 'Blessed, praised, honoured and exalted, be the Immaculate Conception of this little Child' " *(Benedicta, laudata, honorificata et superexaltata sit Immaculata Infantulae Conceptio).* He never pronounced the name of Mary without at the same time profoundly inclining his head, and whenever he came across an image of the Blessed Virgin, he kissed it with a reverent tenderness, especially when it represented her as the "*Immaculata.*"

He has left us a monument of his fervent devotion towards Mary in the following prayer, which we reproduce *in extenso:* "O Virgin, full of grandeur and magnificence, Mary most holy, source of mercy, sovereign Mother of God, Blessed Queen of the earth and of Heaven, Empress of the Angels and of men, singular Advocate of sinners, after God, thou art our most assured refuge and our aid in the midst of sorrows. O sweet name of Mary, thou art overflowing with joy, with loveliness, and with strength! Beloved Daughter of the Father, most holy Mother of the Son, August Spouse of the Holy Spirit, thy servant calls thee; come, O gentle Lady, come and aid him in the hour of deep distress, foreseeing which he every day invokes thee. Come thou and abandon not thy child in the awful moment when he shall pass from time unto eternity. Blessed Virgin, for the love of God, help us!"

After the Blessed Virgin and the Angels, what Paschal admired and loved most amongst the works of God were the Saints, those masterpieces of His grace and imitators of His Divine perfections. Those he used to invoke habitually were, in addition to the canonized and beatified members of his own Order, St. Joseph, the Foster-father of Jesus Christ, and St. John, His Precursor.

From the elect of God, Paschal's veneration descended to the Sovereign Pontiff, the Holy Catholic Church, and to all objects which her blessing and consecration removed from the ranks of things profane, and rendered holy. "When you find holy water in any place," he said once, "don't go away without taking it and blessing yourself."

Such was his mode of action always and under all circumstances. Wherever upon his way through life he could discover the traces of his Father's goodness and power, he stopped to adore the Divine perfections. And thus did the fire of Divine charity, replenished through so many channels, glow ever brighter in his filial heart.

CHAPTER VII
A MOTHER'S HEART

THE modern world, occupied exclusively about earthly and material interests, knows little and cares still less about heavenly and supernatural matters. The love of God, above all things, so characteristic of the Saints, finds scanty favour in the eyes of worldlings, who regard it as an exaggerated sort of mysticism, and even as something prejudicial to the rights of man, since, whatever is given to God, is, when viewed from their standpoint, so much purloined from the birthright of humanity. To credit their assertions, one would suppose that the Saints were a kind of parasitic growth, draining the sap from the living tree of the human species. Were such the case in reality, we might well leave untold the life-story of these eminent Servants of God, and turn our attention to others more deserving of admiration. But let us be reassured on this point. Nothing could be further from the truth than these arrogant and captious assertions of the worldly minded. To set matters in their true light all that is needed is to allow the Saints to plead their own cause at the bar of humanity. With irrefutable eloquence, and holding in their hands documents whose authenticity is indisputable, they demonstrate that whatever is given to God, instead of being lost to the world, will infallibly be repaid even in this present time with hundredfold interest. So true is it that no speculation is so sure or so lucrative as to invest in heavenly securities.

The lives of these holy persons show us that the intimate union of the soul with God, called by the name of Charity, far from loosening the links that bind the individual to the common stock of humanity, does but rivet them all the more firmly, and that amongst men none are so intensely human as the Saints of God.

If God plunges them in the crucible of Divine love, it is to purge from them the dross of egotism, so that, when they have been purified from self by this alchemy, they may emerge endowed with such an ardent and disinterested affection towards all their earthly Brethren, as to be ready to serve them with the devotedness and fidelity of the best of mothers. For they have a mother's heart for their kindred, these men who have for God the heart of a son. We might have been certain of all this beforehand, because the love of God can never subsist without the love of one's neighbour, and the latter is the sure and authentic token of the former. Still, how beautiful it is to meet with ever fresh confirmation of this truth in the lives of God's holy Servants. If proofs were needed, we should find them in abundance on every page of the life of our Saint.

After the example of his Master, Paschal loved all his Brethren without exception, and, like Him also, he had the special objects of his predilection. Who could impute it to him as a fault, since they were the favourites of the Sacred Heart of Jesus—the despised, the poor, those whom the world does not care about, and often drives away, all those who, amidst sorrows and afflictions, stand in need of help and comfort in this valley of tears? Paschal loved these disconsolate beings to the very end of his life with all the strength of that supernatural tenderness which St. Francis, in his Rule, declares should exceed that of the most affectionate of mothers. This attraction for the poor had shown itself even in his childhood. We have doubtless not forgotten the important place allotted to the destitute in the modest budget of the shepherd lad of Torre Hermosa.

Fostered by grace, this natural compassionateness had increased with age. "Pity grew with me," and it attained its fullest development in religion, where it found a larger scope and more frequent opportunities for exercise.

Paschal was appointed Porter of the convent almost on the morrow of his profession, and in this capacity he was entrusted with the care of the poor. A task more in keeping with the attractions both of nature and of grace could not have been found for him. In spite of the strict poverty of the Alcantarine Reform, or doubtless on account of it, almsgiving was largely practised by the Friars. What they took with one hand they gave away with the other, and their convents became everywhere the refuge of the poor, and a visible providence in their regard. They would not otherwise have been the genuine offspring of St. Francis.

Now that he had been appointed to the office of providing for the poor, Paschal considered himself their servant. In each one of them his lively faith recognized a master, who had a strict claim upon his time, his services, and his toil. Henceforth he no longer belonged to himself, but to his poor. They disposed of him as they liked, and often, too, took advantage of his kindness with their unreasonable whims and caprices. Instead of being irksome to him, this bondage constituted his greatest happiness, so that he seemed scarcely able to live without his crowd of poor. On one occasion he was appointed to a convent situated in a retired spot at a great distance from the highroad, where the visits of the indigent persons were few and far between. Paschal felt a kind of home-sickness, and though the last one to desire a change of residence, came to beg the Superior to restore his poor people to him.[1] The more there were of them the happier he was.

---

[1] MSS. of the Process. Deposition of William de Soria.

But it is time that we should see our good Brother actually engaged in relieving the wants of the poor. What strikes us first is the sage discretion displayed by him in the exercise of his charity. One might have fancied that, following the promptings of his heart, he would have given right and left, and somewhat at random. Nothing of the kind. On the contrary, we see him observing that good order which, according to the counsel of Holy Scripture, should be found in holy charity. "He hath set in order charity in me."[2] Scrupulously taking into consideration the various requirements arising from different circumstances and conditions, Paschal divided his numerous clients into several distinct categories. There was nothing here to wound the feelings of even the most sensitive. Everyone received his due, and in addition tokens of the most refined charity.

The first category, forming the main body of Paschal's brigade of poor, was composed of those who used to gather every day at the same hour in the convent courtyard to partake of their soup.

Before we assist at the distribution, however, there is nothing to hinder us from taking a turn around the kitchen and casting a furtive glance upon the soup, simmering in the huge cauldron, which is being prepared by the holy Brother. The ingredients are bread, vegetables from the Friary garden, and the leavings of the Community repast. The last named might awaken suspicion, for leavings of any kind are not held in high repute. But Paschal has selected them with the greatest care, rejecting remorselessly whatever is unfit to be served up. To present the poor of Jesus Christ with a nauseous mess, enough to make the stomach heave, would have seemed to him like

---

[2] Cant. ii. 4.

offering an affront to Our Lord Himself. In His honour everything had to be of irreproachable cleanliness and decency. On certain days, however, vegetables were scarce, the leavings of the Community were scanty, and to crown these misfortunes, the bread for the use of the poor was doled out in meagre rations. Under these worse than unpromising conditions, it was a case of preparing substantial and nourishing soup in sufficiently large quantities to satisfy the hunger of sixty guests or more, endowed with a splendid appetite. It was a difficult problem, and one to perplex even the most resourceful of cooks.

On such occasions Paschal did not appear to be seriously troubled. He had his own little recipes for increasing his stock of vegetables and for causing unlooked-for developments in his supply of broken victuals. These recipes were not taken from any cookery-book, but from the Book of the Gospels, where the secret of moving mountains and working miracles by means of a lively faith is contained. Seasoned by an unbounded trust in Divine providence, the transparent, watery broth thickened under one's very eyes, and was slowly metamorphosed into a soup which would have done no discredit to a chef of ability and renown.

One of the lay Brothers of Villareal relates in his deposition how he assisted unbidden at the multiplication of bread and of vegetables, which puts us in mind of the multiplication of loaves and fishes in the desert: "On that particular day the usual resources were low, and nothing was left to satisfy some ten poor people. 'Let us see what is to be done,' said Paschal, in a low tone of voice; and, wondering what he would do, I kept my eyes upon him. With his habitual calmness, Paschal went into the refectory, and, gathering up all the little morsels of bread and crumbs he could find there, threw them into the cauldron with a handful of salt. Then he poured some buckets of fresh water over them, and lit the fire. At this point I came forward, and having inspected the contents of the cauldron, I said to him: 'Brother Paschal, this soup is not likely to interfere with your clients' digestion.' 'Don't trouble yourself about that,' he replied, with a smile. 'It is God's business. He can put into it whatever is wanted, and then this soup will be better and more substantial than what will be served for ourselves by-and- by in the refectory.' He spoke with perfect truth, for when I tasted it, I perceived that Almighty God had actually taken the matter in hand, and seasoned it Himself."

Let us now assist at the distribution of the soup, for it is one of Paschal's triumphs. The throng of poor people are already gathered in the courtyard awaiting the coming of the good Brother, whom they love even better than their soup. It was a feast for them to see him again day after day, and their joy is fully reciprocated by their saintly friend. See, here he is coming with his steaming cauldron. When all are arranged in proper order, he kneels down and says grace, in which all the poor people join. After this each one approaches in turn to receive his portion. The winning smile and kindly words with which he gives it, make it doubly savoury. Paschal knows each one of his clients by name, and he is also acquainted with the state of each one's affairs, so that, even whilst he is dipping his big wooden ladle in the cauldron, he finds time to give some piece of good advice, and to get some news about the invalids and those who are absent. When the distribution is over, they all kneel down again to say grace, and the company then disperses.

Besides these daily visitants, we shall find a number of travellers at the door, who were frequent callers in the

Ch. VII: A Mother's Heart

days when hotels and inns were few and far between. Amongst them were to be found workmen and apprentices, touring Spain, professional tramps, and cripples or deformed persons who preferred a Bohemian existence to the monotony and gloom of a hospital. Such characters were to be met with on all the highways of Navarre and Aragon, and sooner or later all of them would come and knock at the door of a monastery, the assured refuge of these wanderers.

Nowhere were travellers accorded so sympathetic a reception as at Villareal. This halting-place soon became known far and wide, for those who once called there notified their acquaintances. "If your route lies by way of Valencia," they used to say, "don't fail to knock at the door of the Alcantarines at Villareal. There is a Brother there worth his weight in gold. You are sure to be received with open arms, as though you were an old friend." Thus assured, they found their way to the Friary, and after experiencing the charity of the good Brother, sent others to him, so that in this way his reputation and the number of his clients went on increasing.

It was not merely material alms which he dispensed, for he knew how, with perfect tact, to conjoin with them spiritual alms, which are far more precious. Amongst these casual guests were to be found many who had forgotten even the rudiments of religion, and could not say a single prayer. Paschal became their catechist, and they did not leave the hands of this master, whose ability equalled his patience, until, besides being greatly strengthened in their faith, they were filled with a desire to return to the practice of their duties as Christians and Catholics.

We must not forget that we are in Spain, the land of Doctors, Licentiates, and Bachelors. On this account we have to make the acquaintance of another and very interesting class of necessitous persons—namely, the poor students, who were to be counted by the hundred in the central Universities and in cities endowed with important schools. Although foundations for their maintenance were not indeed wanting, yet numberless difficulties and hardships had to be faced, and there were thousands of these students who were debarred even from this means of support. All that Paschal learned about them pierced his heart, and so he left no stone unturned to come to their assistance and keep them from want. This small band were obviously his favourites, and the flower of his army. In the view of what they might one day become, he treated them with all manner of regard. He kept the best he had for them, and served them in a separate apartment and at a time when they would be unlikely to encounter the rest of his poor, so tender was he of their legitimate pride, and so anxious to encourage their efforts, and thus gain souls for God, which might otherwise be estranged from Him by suffering. "It is a duty on our part to help these young people," he used to say. "I can see amongst them some who later on will be the honour and glory of the Church, and bestow fresh lustre upon her by their learning."

People who had fallen from a state of opulence into the depths of indigence and want appeared to him doubly miserable and especially deserving of compassion. He did not wait until they had overcome themselves sufficiently to disclose the sufferings and privations on account of which they felt a kind of shame, but he made the first advance on his own side, and by insinuating himself into their confidence he opened their hearts, closed and soured by misfortune, and obtained leave to help them. Thus, after the example of the good Samaritan, he raised up these poor people, stricken in the battle of life, and dressed their wounds.

Ch. VII: A Mother's Heart

There was an old man, nearly a hundred years old, named Monserrat Crespo. He had known better days, and at one time had occupied a high station in the world, but had been completely ruined, and was left without friends or means of support. Paschal took care of him, and for years he served this erstwhile rich man as he had never been served by his own domestics in the days of his opulence. In order that the aged man might have the pleasing illusion that he was still a person of consequence, the humble Brother never addressed him without having first respectfully saluted him, and he demeaned himself in his presence like a servant awaiting his master's orders. This went on until at length the old man entered the hospital, where he died, with his last breath blessing the kind Brother who had been more than a benefactor to him. His gratitude would have been greater had he known that for years Paschal used to deprive himself of his repast in order to give it to him.

To these clients, already sufficiently numerous, must be added those who came from the neighbourhood to ask for the leaves of the aromatic and medicinal plants cultivated by Brother Paschal for the sick poor. In spite of the enclosure, the monastic garden seems to have become a piece of common ground, where everyone thought himself at liberty to take whatever he wanted, as though he were the owner.

This devastated garden leads us naturally to the chapter of difficulties which beset the holy man in the exercise of his charity. The Friars who opposed him, and sought to moderate his ardour, were, like himself, excellent Religious and friends of the poor. Their opposition need not surprise or scandalize us, as it arose from the nature of things and the different character of their employments. Paschal had by turns to face the gardener, the cook, and the questors, and occasionally all the Brethren leagued together, to bridle what they considered his excessive prodigality.

We have their testimony in the Process of Beatification. Ashamed and sorry for having contradicted a Saint, they humbly accused themselves of having failed to understand that the ordinary measure was inapplicable to him, and that he could go beyond it without undue excess.

"With much annoyance I saw my vegetables disappear as if by magic," relates the Brother Gardener. "The holy man didn't even wait till they came to maturity to pluck them and give them away to his poor people. So then one day I spoke out and addressed to him some rather caustic remarks. His only answer was to bow his head humbly and go away. As not long afterwards he had relapsed into his habitual failing, I accosted him again, and said: 'Paschal, you are a creature without prudence or moderation. It is high time the Superiors should call you to book.' On this occasion also he did not answer, but merely looked at me and smiled. The smile seemed to me like mockery, and unable to stand it any longer, I broke out: 'Stupid! do you think you're going to take me in with your hypocritical smiles and your airs of sanctity? Stop deceiving the world, you Aragonese mule!' *(Aragones tosudo).* Like a tried soldier, the holy youth did not wince under this fire of reproaches. 'Calm yourself, Brother,' he said, in a tone of entreaty. 'Our Lord will provide for us, and the vegetables will grow up again.' These kindly words put an end to our contention."[3]

It should be observed that this garden resembled the enchanted bottle, which could be continually drawn upon without ever becoming empty. Plants plucked in the

---

[3] MSS. of the Process. Deposition of Brother Pedro d'Aranda.

evening sprang up again during the night, and in the morning the beds showed no signs of the havoc wrought on the previous day.

"I was at the door of the Convent one evening," related the Syndic Apostolic of the Friars, "when I saw a troop of children come and ask the holy Brother for some leaves of blite for the sick. 'Poor little mites,' he said. 'How much I would like to give you some, but unfortunately there is not a scrap left. However, we might just as well have a look.' And, searching carefully, he found a handful of these leaves, which he distributed to the children, who went away contented. The following morning I went again to the Convent on business, and found some people there who had come to ask the Brother for some of the same sort of leaves. 'You are wasting your time,' I said; 'there is not a single one left in the garden. Yesterday evening I saw with my own eyes the last of them taken away by some children.' Just then, who should arrive upon the scene but Paschal. The people made their request to him, and to my surprise I saw him go into the garden. My surprise became stupefaction when I saw the bed where, on the previous evening, there had not been a single blade visible, completely covered with vegetables, the green leaves growing on new stalks. 'Whatever is the meaning of this?' I exclaimed. 'Yesterday evening there was nothing here, and this bed was quite bare.' 'Let us praise the goodness of God,' said the Brother, his face radiant with joy. 'The poor sick people needed these, and to give them solace and relief He has caused them to sprout up during the night. Don't you know He can create anything in an instant?' 'Oh, that's all very fine,' I said, 'but I have a notion that you have had something to do with it. Now tell the truth. Did you not by your prayers and penances endeavour to induce Almighty God to intervene?' Paschal evaded replying to this question, and left me convinced by his silence that I had divined aright."[4]

But let us now return to the subject under consideration, and from collisions with the Gardener pass to the opposition of the Questors, who were even more inclined to set bounds to the holy man's almsgiving.

Brother Martin Navarro of Valencia alludes to the strained relations between Paschal and the Questors, and in a lifelike manner depicts one of their encounters. "I lived fourteen years with the holy man," he says. "When Questor of the Convent of St. John de la Ribera de Valencia, I one day brought, with two companions, three large wallets full of bread. It was meant chiefly for the evening collation and for the Community repast. Now, about ten o'clock next day, Paschal came to me, looking somewhat embarrassed. 'Brother Martin,' said he, 'please have the charity to go quickly to the town and quest some bread; there is not a mouthful in the refectory.' 'Now, that's rather too much of a good thing,' I said. 'So you forget that yesterday evening we brought in a supply for to-day. Ah, that is you all over! You wanted to give it all away to the poor, without troubling yourself the least bit about the difficulty we should be in. Come along now, and be quick about it, too!' And I took him to the refectory, where, of course, there was no bread to be seen. 'Now we will go to the Porter's room. I have a notion we shall discover something there.' And, sure enough, in a corner was a basket full of bread, placed there for the poor. 'Aha, I've got you this time, my holy man; you must just come now and see the Guardian. We will have a little talk in his presence.' 'I beseech you, Brother,' he said, in a tone of entreaty, 'don't do that; don't show that basket to the

---

[4] MSS. of the Process. Deposition of the Syndic.

Superior.' But I had already taken possession of the offending object. Like a culprit dragged to execution, Paschal took me by the sleeve to stay the dreaded moment. When we reached the cell, I showed the basket to the Guardian. 'Just look here, and see the nice trick this Brother was going to play on us,' I said. 'He expects to go to Heaven at our expense, carrying our merits on his shoulders. We poor Questors have to pay for his place in Paradise—for us the toil, and for him the glory of giving broadcast, according to his whims and fancies, what we have collected in the sweat of our brow. What do you think about this way of carrying on? Do you approve of it?' Meanwhile, Paschal remained with his head bowed down, awaiting the sentence of the Judge. The Guardian, who was a wise and prudent man, began by allaying my irritation, and eventually said: 'What do you want me to do? This Brother Paschal is a Saint, and with Saints one cannot always do what one likes.' Hearing this expression, although it was said with a touch of irony, Paschal made his escape carrying the basket. I followed him, and saw with my own eyes how the bread he was dividing in the refectory, multiplied in his hands. That day there was more than enough both for the Community and for the poor."[5] Thus was Almighty God pleased to intervene and to show by a miracle that the rules of natural prudence are not those to be made use of in judging the conduct of the Saints.

On different occasions, especially in times of scarcity, the Guardians united with the Questors, in imposing the most painful restrictions upon Paschal's overflowing charity. One of them forbade him to distribute anything at all before midday. This prohibition threw him into the

---

[5] MSS. of the Process. Deposition of Brother Martin Navarro.

direst perplexity. "Then, father, I must refuse a crust of bread to the poor travellers who pass by during the day and count upon these alms. Only to think of it breaks my heart!" The Guardian withdrew his prohibition, and allowed him the liberty to act as he had done before.

To one of the Questors who, anxious about the needs of the Community during a time of scarcity, had begged him to curtail his donations on that account, he made the following reply, which sounded like a paraphrase of the "*Date and dabitur vobis*" of the Gospel: "Have confidence, Brother. God will not leave us in want. Understand well that every morsel of bread given to the poor, opens for us a new channel by which all that we need will reach us in the greatest abundance."

His reply to another objection is equally deserving of being recorded, since it tells us the true motives of his charity, and the reason of that religious respect with which he treated his poor people. "Don't you see," said his critics, "that amongst these beggars there are many able-bodied young men, well able to gain their livelihood? They take advantage of your charity, and in giving to them, you run the risk of encouraging laziness and vice." "It is for the love of God, and for no other motive, that I give in charity," was his reply. "Who can tell if this young man whom I repulse may not be Jesus Christ hidden under a beggar's garb? I should not like, by refusing him, to risk hearing on the Day of Judgment those terrible words: 'I was hungry, and ye gave Me not to eat.'"

Paschal, indeed, richly merited the blessing contained in the words of Holy Scripture: "Blessed is he who understandeth concerning the needy and the poor." In his eyes, enlightened by faith, the poor man was ever the living image of Christ, in poverty and affliction; and love for God's poor one of the most solid reasons for hoping to obtain eternal happiness. When Paschal was upon his deathbed, the doctor who attended the Convent brought his youngest child, to receive his blessing, and, as the choicest that could be given, he pronounced over the little child these words: "May Father, Son, and Holy Spirit bless thee, little creature of God, and may He give thee love towards the poor."[6]

---

[6] MSS. of the Process. Deposition of Doctor Benet.

CHAPTER VIII
A GOOD SAMARITAN

ALTHOUGH the poor, who were the objects of the holy Brother's solicitude, were so numerous, they were far from exhausting the riches of his charity. The sick and the afflicted were as dear to him as the poverty-stricken. After all, is not sickness closely akin to poverty? In both cases there is want. An invalid, like a poor person, lives in a state of privation, for he is bereft of almost everything which brightens and gladdens human existence. And if physical pain and mental sufferings are present, scarcely any form of misery is greater than his. No wonder, then, that the sight of such wretchedness should stir the depths of Paschal's compassionate heart.

Besides being full of sympathy for the sick and the sorrow-stricken, Paschal possessed the priceless gift of being able to soothe and charm away pain. That he made as frequent use as possible of this power his contemporaries are unanimous in testifying. "I could never sufficiently admire that holy man's charity for the sick," observes Brother Ildefonsus Comacho, Paschal's usual companion in his visits to the sick. "So deeply did he compassionate the sufferings of the patients that he sometimes mingled his tears with theirs. His least words had a marvellous efficacy, and always brought consolation and strength.[1] Sometimes it was enough to mention some suffering to him in order to obtain instant relief. "How often did it not happen that when I had told him what

---

[1] MSS. of the Process. Deposition of Brother Ildefonsus Comacho.

Ch. VIII: A Good Samaritan

ailed me, I was already half cured," relates Catherine Parrella, of Villareal.[2]

When it is added that, besides being able to soothe pain, he also possessed a wonderful power of healing maladies, it is not hard to understand the eagerness of sick people to have him at their bedside. It was a case of who should be first to secure him. People used to lie in wait for him when he went out of the Convent to quest for bread, and the good souls were in haste to point out their dwellings, where his coming was awaited, as that of a consoler and a deliverer. Visiting the sick thus entered insensibly into his plan of life, and became one of his daily occupations.

The objects of this signal favour never lost the remembrance of it, and after the death of the Saint they came forward in great numbers to relate for the glory of God and the honour of His servant the wonderful things they had witnessed.

Their depositions form in themselves a voluminous collection, from which we select the most salient facts, in order that our readers may be able to form a picture in their mind of these charitable visits.

Upon entering the sick-room the holy Brother used to recite the following short prayer: "May Jesus, Mary, Joseph, Joachim, Anne, and Catherine cure you of every ill and deliver you from all pain."

The Friars never thought of asking the Man of God, which St. Catherine it was, who figured in this glorious company, and as he himself never referred to the subject, during his lifetime, it remained a matter of doubt. The Sacristan of Villareal, desirous of ascertaining this point, went straight to the only person who could tell what had

---

[2] MSS. of the Process. Deposition of Catherine Parrella.

been in the mind of Paschal. On his knees before the tomb of the Saint he addressed to him this humble prayer: "Do not look upon my unworthiness, I beseech you, O holy Brother, but regard only Our Lord, in Whose presence we are both standing, and for His greater glory do not refuse to make known to me which St. Catherine it was whose name and protection you invoked upon the sick and afflicted. If it was the Virgin Martyr of Alexandria, knock twice upon your coffin; if St. Catherine of Sienna, then only once. The reply was not long in coming. A single energetic rap indicated the Dominican Saint.[3]

Let us now follow our holy Brother into one of these dwellings, overshadowed by sickness. Here we are in the house of an honest farmer of Villareal, who will himself proceed to relate to us what occurred under his roof: "The Servant of God came one day to our house on quest. Scarcely had he entered, when he noticed in a corner, shivering all over, our little Bessy, who was then ten years old. 'What is the matter with the little one?' said he to my wife. 'She looks very poorly.' For reply, she uncovered Bessy's neck, and showed Brother Paschal the wound which encircled it, as with a necklace of blood. Moved to tears at the sight of such sufferings at so tender an age, Paschal drew near, and in his pity passed his hand lightly over the wounded neck. At this contact the poor little thing felt great relief, and three days later the last traces of the disease had vanished. Her wizened cheeks once more shone with the glow of health, and for the first time in many years she was able to go outside and join in the pastimes of her playmates."[4]

There was a certain excellent Christian woman living

---

[3] MSS. of the Process. Deposition of Brother Joseph Castegnada.

[4] MS. Deposition of Francis Pasqualer.

Ch. VIII: A Good Samaritan

at Villareal named Hieronima Jourdan. For a long time her jaw had been in a wretched state. Remedies were unavailing, and the poor woman endured agonies each time she ate any solid food. Now, one day, when the pain was almost intolerable, Hieronima went over to the window, seeking some distraction from her suffering. Brother Paschal happened to be passing at that very moment. "Here is a piece of good luck," said Hieronima to herself, and she beckoned to the Questor to come upstairs, as though she wished to give him an alms, though in reality it was to get relief from his good and comforting words. Whilst the Brother was guilelessly scaling the staircase, the sick woman prepared her batteries. Her ambition had suddenly risen. What she now aimed at was nothing short of a miracle. She threw herself all in tears at the holy Brother's feet, and begged him for the love of God not to refuse to trace the sign of the cross upon her afflicted jaw. At this proposition, which seemed to place him in the rank of wonder-workers, Paschal's humility took alarm, and, with many fine and convincing arguments, he strove to impress upon the good woman, that it was not to a wretched sinner like himself, recourse should be had when miracles were wanted.

Pretending to be thoroughly convinced, Hieronima watched for a favourable opportunity, and then, suddenly seizing the Brother's hand, applied it to her jaw and held it there forcibly. This was quite enough to cause the inflammation to subside and to get rid of the pain. At the end of a year's time the malady returned, but the miraculous healer was no longer upon earth. Hieronima, however, had for some time foreseen the reappearance of the disease, and, like a prudent and experienced woman, she had taken her precautions accordingly. Armed with a chaplet which had rested upon the sacred remains of the holy Brother, she rolled it over her jaw. It acted as an effective substitute for the hand of the Saint, and the malady was cured this time once and for all.[5]

Not infrequently, as in the following instance, Providence, either directly or through the medium of some charitable individual, itself conducted the healer to the bedside of the sick person before the latter had thought of summoning him.

"One day," relates Frances Sebastiana Pujol, in her lengthy deposition, "I received a visit from a poor neighbour, who was literally crushed under a load of miseries of every kind. Her husband was stone-blind, and her own eyesight was in little better condition. To crown their misfortunes, an only daughter, who should have been the prop of their old age, was herself a chronic invalid. She had already submitted to one perilous operation, and was about to undergo a second. This house of sorrow resembled that of Job, for over this illness and affliction brooded the gaunt spectre of poverty. Just as the poor creature was tearfully relating her tale of woe, Brother Paschal made his appearance. He could not have arrived at a more opportune moment. Seeing my neighbour in tears, he inquired: 'Why are you weeping, Sister? Has any misfortune befallen you?' Thereupon I set to work, to put the Brother in possession of the almost desperate condition of affairs, and omitted nothing that could serve to awaken his interest in the fate of this distressed family. He listened with evident emotion, and when I had finished unravelling this long catalogue of woes, he consoled my neighbour in these words: 'Have confidence, little Sister!' Then suddenly, as though inspired from on high, he arose and said to the blind woman: 'Let us go to your house.' And he

---

[5] MSS. of the Process. Deposition of Hieronima Jourdan.

Ch. VIII: A Good Samaritan

led her to her home. I prepared to follow them, but the holy Brother cut short my pious curiosity by saying: 'No; there is no need for you to come. You can stay at home.' I did so, much against the grain, and greatly mortified by this unlooked-for prohibition.

"When Paschal entered the room where the patient was, he noticed that her throat was covered with bandages, underneath which was a poultice. 'Take all those things off,' he said, and he was obeyed. Then he approached Paula and made a large sign of the cross over the wound in her neck, accompanying it with this invocation: '*Gratia Patris et Filii et Spiritus Sancti sit tecum*' (The grace of Father and Son and Holy Spirit be with thee). Then, as the parents wanted to replace the poultice, he said to them: 'It is not wanted. Your daughter is cured.'

"Some hours after this scene, at which I should have so much liked to have been present, I noticed an unusual commotion in the street. The whole neighbourhood seemed astir, and there was a movement in the direction of the poor cottage of the Manzolas. 'What's the matter?' I inquired of the first person I met. 'What? Do you mean to say that you have not heard the news? Paula Manzola has been miraculously cured by Brother Paschal.' Next day the surgeon, not knowing what had happened, arrived with his case of instruments to perform the operation. Great was his astonishment when Paula came into his presence, and showed him that nothing remained of the wound but a scar. 'Oh, I see,' he exclaimed in a tone of conviction. 'A more able practitioner than myself has been here, and has had a hand in this affair.' He went away, giving thanks to God and congratulating his clients on having secured the attendance of such a wonderful operator. A ray of hope and joy had descended upon this mournful house, where for a long time nothing had been heard but groaning and sobbing."[6]

Paschal often returned to the house of the Manzolas. What attracted him so much to their home was, says a witness, their poverty and infirmity, the two best titles to the benevolence and intimacy of a Saint.

Another of these providential visits, made under peculiarly touching circumstances, places the charity of the Saint in a new light, whilst at the same time it shows by what means he succeeded in recruiting benefactors. Whilst he was Porter at Villareal, there lived in that city, so favourably disposed towards the sons of St. Francis, a certain young woman, who made no secret of her antipathy for them.

"I could not otherwise think about them," she says in her deposition, "than as though they had been just a lot of Turks. I had my own ideas on the subject of questing, and I didn't see why anyone should live on the bounty of God, and be always knocking at people's doors. The Alcantarines were all unwelcome to me; but the one who had the privilege of aggravating me most was that Paschal, with his everlasting smile. One might have nothing at all for him; one might even give him a mortifying refusal; yet he still continued to smile, and would come back to-morrow, as though he had met with the most cordial welcome."

Now, one fine day, Elizabeth Pallares, this enemy of Friars, was chattering on a neighbour's doorstep, when her little boy, left alone in the house, and finding the time pass slowly, bethought him of making his first bid for freedom. He was barely two years old, and not quite steady on his legs. Misfortune overtook the venturesome traveller at the very outset of his journey. Scarce had he reached the

---

[6] MSS. of the Process. Deposition of Frances Sebastiana Pujol.

landing, than he slipped and rolled downstairs. At the foot of the staircase he bumped his head against a marble column, and his skull was fractured. The injury was mortal, and the poor little fellow could not be expected to live more than a few hours. Who can depict the anguish of the mother when, upon her return, she found her boy unconscious and about to expire? Besides the death of her son, she had other consequences to fear. Her husband was far from gentle, and on the slightest pretext he was wont to add blows to reproaches. Doubtless he would saddle her with the responsibility of the child's death, and then—look out for hard words and stripes. So it was not without reason, that Elizabeth already began to consider herself the most wretched of women.

Meanwhile Paschal, his wallet on his back, was just passing the door. A neighbour, who had caught sight of him, without further ceremony invited him to enter the house of mourning. The good Brother did not need to be asked twice. Nothing could have been more welcome to him than this invitation. Well did he know that inhospitable door, on account of the many rebuffs he had received there. Now, who does not know that to reach the heart of the Saints, in the days of their mortal pilgrimage, and to win favours from them, there is no surer means than to repulse and humiliate them? Elizabeth Pallares had made extensive usage of this means. So Paschal entered the house, resolved to revenge himself—according to the fashion of the Saints.

"Brother, see the plight of my poor little babe," said the unhappy woman to him, and she pointed to the child stretched out, apparently lifeless, on his blood-stained cot. "Oh, I beseech you, entreat God that he may not die from the effects of this fall, and that his life be spared for at least one year. Then my husband will not be able to attribute his death to this accident. After that, I resign him to the will of Heaven. All I ask is that it may not be said to me morning, noon, and night: 'It was you, you wretched creature, who slew our little one. You murdered him through your carelessness.' I could not stand it; my life would be a hell upon earth."

Upon receiving this sorrowful confidence, Paschal smiled with that smile, which in such cases was a favourable augury. "Your request is so discreet and so reasonable, poor sister," he said, "that there is every ground for believing that God will grant it. Have confidence; the child will not die from this injury, and you will escape the wrath of your husband. I am going to pray for that intention." He did, in fact, set himself to pray, and the child, who, until then, had given no sign of life, opened his eyes and looked up smilingly at his mother. Catching sight of his little cap lying on the floor, he jumped out of bed to get it. His recovery was assured.

"And now, just see how hard it is for us women, with our long tongues, to keep a secret," says Elizabeth at the end of her deposition. "I burned with eagerness to relate to my husband all that had passed with Brother Paschal after the child's fall; so, when he seemed to be in good humour, I told him how I had asked the holy man a year of life for the injured child, and that he had obtained this respite from God. It was most imprudent of me. Upon this disclosure my husband became furious, and exclaimed: 'Oh, you stupid woman! Why didn't you ask the holy Brother for twenty years of life? He would have got it just as easily.' " Other miracles were afterwards wrought in this same house through the relics of the Man of God. "And all this to soften my heart, once so hard towards the Sons of St. Francis," humbly adds Elizabeth at the end of her deposition. It is needless to add that, from that time forward, the hitherto tightly shut door opened full wide to admit the Brethren of the Reform.[7]

In giving alms to the Friary the benefactors became Paschal's creditors, and this was not the least benefit which accrued to them. Nothing affecting their temporal or their eternal welfare was a matter of indifference to him. When any danger threatened them, he hastened with the greatest solicitude to their assistance, and above all was this the case, when their salvation was in jeopardy.

One day the news reached him that Damien Porquet, one of his friends and benefactors, had been taken ill, and that there was no doubt as to the gravity of his condition. Paschal left all other business on one side, and hastened, deeply preoccupied about the lot of a soul so dear to him, to the dwelling of the sick man. When he had arrived within a few paces of his destination, what was his astonishment to hear a hubbub of voices, and peals of laughter issuing from the very house, over which the Angel of Death was hovering. The thing was so strange that he could scarcely believe his ears. He had heard aright, notwithstanding. Seated at the foot of Damien's bed were his wife and his sister-in-law, in fits of laughter, whilst the sick man himself seemed to be joining heartily in this unseasonable merriment. Their hilarity arose from a fancied improvement in the condition of the patient. Deceived by appearances, the two women gave themselves up to the fond illusion that all danger was past, and that the invalid would soon recover under their care. The doctor, it is true, was of a different opinion. But, after all, the oracles of the medical profession are not infallible. So, in spite of the doctor's verdict, they held that his recovery was certain. Everybody was rejoicing on account of his

---

[7] MSS. of the Process. Deposition of Elizabeth Pallares of Valencia.

return to life. Damien formed all sorts of plans for the future, and promised novenas in thanksgiving for his restoration to health. And it was at this very moment, when hearts were dilated with hope, that Paschal entered, bearing a message of death.

It had just been revealed to him by God that the sick man had only a few hours to live, and so it became necessary for him to shatter this beautiful dream, and to convince these poor deluded people that the condition of the patient was in reality desperate. It was an exceedingly delicate task, but the Man of God was not one to conceal the truth or to shrink from the performance of his duty. "Damien," said he, as he drew near the sick man's bed, "believe me, you are deceived, and this mirth is out of place. Make your will without delay, and prepare yourself to receive the last Sacraments." This piece of advice, so straightforward, and so precise, fell like a bolt from the blue. "So ho!" said Damien, in a tone of raillery. "Your Reverence, I see, belongs to the company of the prophets." "No, my poor friend, I'm not a prophet, but I tell you death is near." "You are a doctor, then, Reverend Sir." "No, nor even that. I am neither a prophet nor a doctor, but I tell you time presses, and that you must get ready to go." At this announcement of death, poor Damien Porquet turned himself to the wall, like King Ezechias, and began to cry.

The two women, who with great difficulty had restrained themselves up to this point, now broke out, and rained upon this disturber of the feast a perfect deluge of reproaches and abuse. "Silly, ignorant fellow, that you are! Don't you see that by talking like that to the poor dear man you are killing him? Get out of this, and never show your nose inside here again, you horrid *Mohillon*."[8]

---

[8] *Mohillon*; a term of contempt for an ignorant, uncultured Friar.

Ch. VIII: A Good Samaritan

"At this moment I arrived," relates Doctor Benet, "and was a witness of this painful and humiliating scene. How much I suffered to see the holy man treated in such a way! The sister-in-law, particularly, transported by passion, said the most cruel and injurious things to him. Paschal uttered never a word, and when at length this Fury had exhausted herself, he was content with this gentle and humble defence: 'Sister, forgive me. You need not really be put out, on account of what I said, but rather help our friend to appear in a good state in the presence of Almighty God. How does it seem to yourself? Is not the soul's safety of a great deal more consequence than that of the body? If a Christian, in good health, ought not to take offence when he is reminded that he should be on his guard against the surprises of death, how much more ought one who is grievously ill be ready to accept this salutary advice without astonishment or ill-humour? *'Laudetur Jesus Christus'* (Praised be Jesus Christ). *'Mane cum Deo'* (Abide with God). And when he had thus spoken, he retired, leaving everyone greatly edified by his patience and humility."[9]

His warning took effect. Recovering from his first surprise, Damien began to say to himself that, after all, the Brother might be right, and that it would be unwise to slight the advice of such a holy man. The women, too, had been thinking, and they went to the Guardian to acquaint him with what had occurred. "What do you think about it yourself?" they asked him. "We consider this Brother to be a holy man," he replied. "You will do well to take into account what he said to you. In any case, you will run no risk in urging the sick man to fulfil his duties." The advice was followed, and Damien, now no longer under the spell

---

[9] MSS. of the Process. Deposition of Doctor Benet.

of his delusion, did all that was required of him. After setting in order his affairs, both spiritual and temporal, he gave up his soul to God, that very evening, at nine o'clock. His relatives could never sufficiently thank Our Lord for having sent them an Angel to prepare a soul for its flight to a blissful eternity.[10]

It is likewise to Doctor Benet that we are indebted for the account of another visit in which, under not less difficult circumstances, Paschal performed the charitable act of warning a poor soul of her approaching departure. "When I called one day at the house of Anna Vendrell, one of my patients, I found the people there very much agitated by something which had just happened. They told me how Brother Paschal had been summoned by the sick woman, and had been conjured by her to ask of God her restoration to health. 'Sister, this request is good only in so far as it may be in conformity to the will of God. Say, therefore, with me: "O Lord, if it be Thy good pleasure that I should quit this life, then Thy will be done."'

"Anna, however, did not see it in this light. She wanted to live, and not to die. Not, indeed, that the poor woman's joys were so numerous here below; but then she was the mother of several little children, and it seemed so hard to leave them orphans, alone in the world. So she went on insisting, and with tears besought the Brother to obtain her cure, for the sake of the little ones, who still had need of their mother. Thus urged, Paschal became silent, and appeared to be seeking an answer from God. Our Lord placed it upon his lips by revealing the secrets of the future. As if transported by the fervour of his spirit, he said in a loud tone of voice: 'Sister, we must prepare ourselves, because both of us—you and I—are soon going to make a

---

[10] Deposition of Relatives.

very long journey!' It was the journey to Eternity. Anna departed in a few days, and the holy Brother did not tarry much longer."[11]

The companions of the Saint in his visits to the sick, were not slow in perceiving that it was possible to draw favourable or unfavourable auguries, regarding the case from his manner of speaking. For instance, when he said, "Be of good heart; it's nothing much; we will pray hard for you," this was a good sign, and they knew that the illness would not have a fatal ending. But when, on the contrary, he insisted strongly and repeatedly upon conformity with the Divine will, and filial resignation to the behests of Providence, it was an unfavourable omen, and they were morally certain that there was no hope of the sick man's recovery. These forecasts were justified by the event. It was thus that, after the example of his Divine Master, this faithful Servant of God went about everywhere amongst his brethren, doing good, healing the sick, and preparing souls to appear before the tribunal of God.

---

[11] MSS. of the Process. Deposition of Doctor Benet.

CHAPTER IX
"BLESSED ARE THE PEACEMAKERS"

NOT only was Paschal an Angel of consolation, he was also an Angel of peace. "Whenever you enter a house, you shall first say, 'Peace be to this house,' " says the Seraphic Patriarch in his Rule.[1] On Paschal's lips this traditional salutation was no empty formula; for wherever he uttered it peace entered in.

Just as he was summoned to heal the sick and console the afflicted, so was he called in to adjust the differences of families, torn by dissension and discord.

"The grace he had received on this point was of a miraculous character," says Father Pedro Adam; "it was as great as that which had been accorded to him for consoling his fellow-creatures. "In his faith and large-heartedness he was always able to find arguments so persuasive and so convincing, that the most obstinate were obliged to yield to them. Our entire Province of St. John Baptist is prepared to testify to this, and the voice of the people, which is the voice of God, re-echoes it."[2]

Where the most renowned preachers and clerics had failed, and had fruitlessly expended their Latinity, this humble Brother, with a single word, succeeded in allaying inveterate hatred, and in reconciling the bitterest enemies. We shall cite only one example, but it is worth many, and at the time served not a little to enhance the already well-grounded reputation enjoyed by the Servant of God upon

---

[1] Rule of St. Francis, chap. 3.

[2] MSS. of the Process. Deposition of Father Pedro Adam, Lector of Theology.

this point.

Martin Crespo, the hero of this story, will himself relate to us its stirring and dramatic incidents: "One evening, when I was still quite young, the corpse of my father, gashed by poignards and drenched in gore, was carried into the house. He had been trapped, and cruelly assassinated, by his enemies. Although the guilty parties were clearly pointed out by public rumour, still, the necessary evidence was wanting, and the hands of justice were tied. Seeing the crime unpunished, my mother, my elder brother, and myself took an oath to execute vengeance ourselves. We swore to take no rest until we had accomplished what we regarded as a sacred duty, for it seemed to us as though the victim himself were urging us on, to take a speedy revenge at any price.

"As you will perceive, it was in my young heart that the thirst of vengeance was the keenest, and where hatred had struck its deepest roots. My mother, like the good Christian that she was, soon yielded to the advice of her ghostly father and of the friends of the family, and repudiated her oath. My elder brother was harder to gain over; but in the end he, too, gave in and foreswore his vengeful projects. I remained by myself, deeply incensed at the defection of my relatives, and reproaching them with their forgiveness as mere weakness. Years rolled by without changing my dispositions. Rather it seemed as though time only served to inflame the wound, and I became even more eager for the blood of our foes. I did not conceal it, but repeated aloud to everyone who would listen to me that as soon as I had reached man's estate I would undertake to settle accounts with them. I had just attained my seventeenth year, and was endowed with extraordinary strength and an iron will. The assassins used to tremble when they saw me coming, and the countryside was on the look out for a crime; for it was well known that I was capable of carrying out fully my terrible resolve.

"On several different occasions the Religious of Loretto had attempted my conversion; the most influential persons in Monteforte had also tried, and so had, one after another, the various preachers of Missions and Retreats; but it was all to no purpose. Instead of appeasing my wrath, these repeated admonitions only exasperated me the more. One day, carried away by passion, I even used threatening language to one of these importunate preachers, and told him plainly to mind his own business, and not to interfere with mine. Persuaded finally that any further efforts would be equally unavailing, they ended by leaving me alone.

"One Good Friday evening there was a lifelike representation, according to the custom of our country, of the Descent from the Cross. The whole population was present at the ceremony, and followed the Crucifix, borne in triumph through the streets of the town. I also took part in the procession of the *Santa Sangre,* not suspecting what was in store for me. Our friends, deeming the occasion propitious, had resolved to profit by it in order to make a last assault. Two of the Religious, with the Preacher, the Knight Carranza, and others, gradually drew nearer and nearer, and at length hemmed me in on every side. When I saw through the manœuvre, it was too late, and escape was impossible, so I had perforce to remain, and endure the oration of the Preacher. After expending the resources of his eloquence to the utmost, he concluded, in a pathetic peroration, by urging me to forgiveness in memory of Our Saviour's Passion. His fine discourse left me unmoved and cold.

" 'Have done tormenting me!' I exclaimed passionately. 'I tell you it is no use. I will not forgive them, and you don't know what I am going to do.' Brother Paschal, whom

I had not hitherto noticed, stepped forward at this juncture, and, taking me by the arm, drew me to one side. 'My son,' he said in a sorrowful tone, 'have you not just now seen Our Lord's Passion represented?' Then, regarding me with a glance which penetrated the depths of my soul, he added: 'For the love of Jesus Crucified, my son, forgive them.' 'Yes, Father,' I replied, hanging my head and weeping, 'I will do so—indeed I will. I forgive them with all my heart for the love of God.' I no longer felt the same person. As though by enchantment, the bloodthirsty wolf had been transformed into a meek lamb. All looks were turned upon us, and the issue of our mysterious conference was awaited with anxiety. When Paschal announced that I had forgiven my enemies, the relief was so great that the crowd broke out into joyous acclamations, as though the country had been spared some calamity. The Preacher," adds the witness somewhat mischievously, "appeared mortified, inasmuch as the words of a poor Brother had been of greater efficacy than all his rhetoric. So thorough was my conversion, that if either then, or at some future time, the occasion of wreaking vengeance on my father's murderers had presented itself, I should not have felt even the desire to take advantage of it. The more I reflected upon it, the more did I perceive it was a real miracle; for no merely human influence would have been capable of overcoming my resentment and of making me renounce my schemes of vengeance."[3]

The office of Porter, which made the holy Brother the servant, or rather the slave, of the poor, gave exercise to his charity in other ways. The public, not satisfied with helping themselves to everything that grew in the garden of the Friary, also fancied that they had a right to the water

---

[3] MSS. of the Process. Deposition of Martin Crespo of Monteforte

of the well, inasmuch as this water was the freshest and most limpid in the country. At the time of the great heat particularly, there used to be an endless procession of women and children armed with empty jugs and pitchers; and the poor Brother, as though he had been the official *Aguador* of the district, used to take these various vessels to the well, fill them, and carry them back to their owners at the door, as gracious towards the last of these claimants, as he had been towards any one of the long series which had preceded them throughout the livelong day.

"In my long career as a Religious," said one of the Friars called as a witness, "I have known most of the Porters of our Convent. They were picked men, and were endowed with the virtues and qualifications requisite in this delicate employment. With the exception of Blessed Paschal, however, I must confess that I never knew one who did not, at one time or another, allow himself to be carried away by some movement of ill-humour, so as to repulse the importunate and indiscreet. But who could ever boast of surprising this holy Brother into a hasty word? Always of an even temper, he performed every service done for his neighbour with such a good grace as to make it doubly acceptable."[4]

Neither must we forget the guests, who used to come and stay at the Friary, and occupied separate quarters; for they too belonged to the Porter's department. Amongst these guests were comprised Religious, secular Priests, and Benefactors. Sometimes they were so numerous that it would have taken the whole time of an able-bodied Brother to look after them. He had to prepare the rooms for them and keep them tidy, to see their meals were prepared, to serve them at the table, and, what is more,

---

[4] MSS. of the Process.

keep them company. Often they would come when least expected, and at unseasonable hours. And there were some amongst them, endowed with prodigious loquacity. Without troubling themselves in the slightest degree about the poor Brother, who had been on his feet the whole day, and sorely needed rest, they spun out their ceaseless chatter to interminable lengths. Sometimes the Porter was unable to regain his cell before eleven o'clock, but this did not prevent him from being the first in Choir at the midnight office.

There were also beings of another class who claimed and received their share of the maternal tenderness of Paschal's heart—namely, the little children. After the example of his Divine Master, this faithful disciple gave them full liberty to approach him, and when certain peevish individuals would have driven them away, he replied to them in words like those of Jesus: "Suffer the little children to come to Me, and forbid them not; for of such is the Kingdom of God."[5] The association of the holy Brother with these little innocents breathes a grace and a naïve simplicity, which is one of the charms of our Saint's life. The winsome smiles and merry gambols of these babes shed a ray of sunshine on the picture of his charity, otherwise somewhat overclouded by the saddened countenances of the poverty-stricken and the suffering.

In his deposition, one of the veterans of the Province of St. John Baptist turns back in happy vein to the recollections of his distant childhood. "My people were living at that time at Monteforte," he says. "We often used to talk amongst ourselves at home about the holy Brother of Loretto. We children lent an eager ear to the marvellous stories about the virtues and miracles which were

---

[5] Mark 10:14.

attributed to him. Our imagination was fired, and we entreated to be allowed to see this good Brother of whom such wonderful things were related.

"When I was as yet not seven years of age, I said one day to three small companions of mine, 'I'm going to see Brother Paschal. Will you come, too?' The proposal was hailed with enthusiasm, and in less time than it takes to tell, we were making our way to the Friary as fast as our legs could carry us. The good Brother seemed to be expecting us. He received us with such cordiality, and gave us so many tokens of his friendship, that when we went away it was with a promise to return there as often as we possibly could, although the distance was a respectable one for such puny legs as ours."[6]

The highest reward which the masters at Villareal could hold out before their pupils to encourage them was the prospect of a walk to Loretto and a visit to Brother Paschal.

"Come and see Brother Paschal's house! Come and see Brother Paschal!" When he saw them coming, the Man of God could scarcely contain himself for joy. The infant battalion ranged itself round him; and then Paschal used to tell them stories, in which the Almighty God, Our Lady, and obedience to parents were always introduced, and told them in so charming a way that the little ones could not help but listen. The story ended, he would pass along the ranks with a caress and a small present, such as a nosegay or a piece of fruit, for each; and the joyous band took flight again homewards. With what earnestness they retailed to their parents and teachers all that the good Brother had been telling them. The little bouquets made by his hands were put carefully aside and preserved as relics.

---

[6] MSS. of the Process.

Needless to say, the little sisters of these small boys were not going to be left out in the cold, and they also came to take their holidays at Loretto. In order not to give any occasion for jealousy, the holy man received them as kindly as their brothers, and they became, together with the latter, the most enthusiastic eulogists of the saintly Brother.

One of his religious Brethren, seeing Paschal took such a delight in the society of children, asked him why he made so much of them. "Because," he replied, in "each of these boys I see the Child Jesus, and in each of these *niñas*[7] I see Our Lady as a little girl."

Now that we have seen with what unsparing self-devotion Paschal spent himself in the service of the outside world, it remains to be seen whether he cherished the inmates of his religious home with the same maternal tenderness. Herein is to be found the true touchstone of charity.

How many people there are, whose reputation for good nature and amiability would melt away like snow beneath the rays of the noontide sun, if only those of their own household were put in the witness-box. When away from home, they are all sugar and spice, wreathed in smiles, and fascinating everyone they meet; but scarcely have they set foot upon their own threshold, than, tearing off the mask, they show themselves in their true colours, cross-grained, disagreeable people, who make life a burden to the unfortunate beings compelled to live under the same roof with them. As the German proverb says, they are "Angels abroad, and devils at home."[8]

That it was impossible Paschal should belong to this

---

[7] Little girls.

[8] "Gassenengel, Hausteufel."

odious confraternity may be assumed without further question, when we consider the profound respect he entertained for the character of a Religious, and consequently for all those who were clothed with the holy garb of Religion, both Priests and Brothers. Here, as elsewhere, he went far beyond the limits of rigid duty, and during the whole course of his religious life, and even to his dying day, it was for his Brethren in the Order that he reserved the best and choicest share of his charity. Such is unanimously attested in the Process, by all who had the happiness to live with him.

Love expresses itself in things, that in themselves are small. For to look after details, and not to neglect even the least of them, requires an attention and a devotedness which can be inspired only by the liveliest affection. The best means, then, of observing Paschal's charity towards his Brethren is to follow him in the details of one of his employments, and for this purpose we will select the most modest of all—namely, that of Refectorian. What we shall discover on this point will serve as a clue to the rest, and will dispense us from pursuing our inquiries any further. Even from a simple glance round the refectory, of which the holy man is in charge, we are enabled to derive a presumption in favour of his charity. This refectory, though of a truly seraphic poverty, is a gem of neatness and cleanliness. There is not a stain or a speck of dust to be seen there. The tables shine, not indeed with grease, but with a gloss produced by frequent washing and brisk rubbing. Proper ventilation drives away the nauseous odour, which so frequently hangs around the walls of a dining-room. There are due precautions for preserving an agreeable freshness in summer-time, and to let in the rays of the sun in winter. These are all so many mute, but expressive tokens of that perfect charity, which leaves nothing undone, and never thinks it has done enough, when there is question of procuring some solace for our neighbour. "I lived fourteen years with Brother Paschal," says Father Martin Navarro, "and I can affirm from personal knowledge that all the offices entrusted to him were fulfilled in a way which left nothing to be desired, and with perfect regularity. From morning till night he was to be seen sweeping, dusting, and washing things committed to his charge."

In conformity with Franciscan usage, the refectory was adorned with a beautiful statue of the Blessed Virgin. This was sufficient to transform it, in the eyes of Paschal, into a shrine of his glorious Queen. He constituted himself the sacristan of this small oratory, and took care that the altar was always provided with its bouquet of flowers, and its candles, which were lit on feast-days. But now the time has arrived for getting everything ready for the Community repast. Paschal enters carrying his baskets of loaves. Like a good son going to receive his mother's blessing before starting his day's work, he kneels down before the statue of Our Lady for the space of three *Credos*. It is the offering up of his work and the directing of his intention, which entered into all his actions and consecrated them to God.

As soon as his prayer is ended, he rises up again, and, taking his basket, proceeds to divide and distribute the bread. Whilst he is going about, he softly hums to himself some pious refrain. Such was his habit everywhere, more or less. Had he not been restrained by the fear of attracting attention and making himself singular, he would have sung in his fine voice the *gozos* or popular ditties in honour of the Blessed Sacrament, Our Lady, and the Saints. It was not haphazard or mechanically that the Refectorian put his loaves in their place on the table. He placed what was best and freshest before the sick Friars or those who were fatigued by work. But in order not to excite anyone's jealousy or put to shame those who were the objects of this small indulgence, everything was hidden away carefully under the napkins of the Religious.

Paschal sometimes had the assistance of the younger Brothers in his work, and the Guardians were only too pleased to place them under his direction. He taught them how to lay the table, and the secret of making the spirit of faith enter into every detail of their work. "At the beginning of the fruit season, when plums and cherries are still scarce, put only three in each place in honour of the Most Holy Trinity; when they are more plentiful, put five, in honour of the five wounds, or seven, in honour of the seven Gifts of the Holy Spirit." It is not stated whether he ever went as far as the twelve Apostles. Perhaps he might have dreaded wounding holy Poverty thereby. "When you are sweeping the floor or washing the tables, consider how greatly the soul needs being purified and freed from all stains and from the dust which adheres to it; so make a good act of contrition, and resolve to avoid every fault in future."

This man, who used scarcely to touch what was put before him, showed himself so much concerned about the least wants of his Brethren that he sought on every occasion to discover and provide for them. During the time of the long fasts, Paschal used secretly, and without attracting the attention of the other Religious, to go in search of those whom he knew required something extra; and at other times he used to prepare a little taste for the fatigued or weakly Friars, and, in order to leave them quite at their ease to enjoy his small solace, he would retire, and only came back again when they had finished their collation.

Ch. IX: Blessed Are the Peacemakers

In the discharge of his office as Porter, his exactitude in notifying the Religious, when they were wanted in the confessional or the parlour, was admirable. Were it necessary for that purpose to go up and down stairs five or six times successively, he hastened to do so each time with alacrity and with a smiling countenance.

Once upon a time his prompt and joyous obedience was put to a sore trial. Paschal came to let the Guardian know that several of his penitents were waiting for him at the confessional. The latter, for some reason or another, thought that it would be impossible for him to go just at that moment; so he told the Saint to give a message, which is sometimes made use of by the élite of fashion when they wish to be rid of inopportune visitors. "Tell those people the Guardian is not at home." Paschal, who didn't know a single word of this fine theory of mental reservation, remained as though rooted to the spot. "Very well, Father," he said, as though he had not quite caught what the Guardian had said. "I will go and tell the people you are very busy, and can't possibly hear their confessions." "No, no; I don't mean that at all," said the Guardian, getting impatient. "Go and tell them I'm not at home." At this order the holy man bent his head in thought. Then, in a grave and sad tone of voice, he said: "Father, that would be a lie, and consequently a sin, and sin is an offence against God."

He went away, leaving the Superior somewhat disconcerted, but at the same time edified, and quite convinced, this time, that one can't do everything one likes with the Saints, and that it is they who are always in the right.

CHAPTER X
THE HEART OF A JUDGE

IF it were not a recognized truth that, under the mysterious influence of Divine grace, things apparently the most opposed by nature are capable of being reconciled and even blended, some apology would be needed on entering upon this chapter, whose subject and whose title are in startling contrast, and even in seemingly obvious contradiction with what has preceded it. What, in fact, could have less in common than the filial affection of a son, or the tender devotedness of a mother, and the glacial impassiveness of a judge, whose breast is steeled against every emotion of pity or of tenderness? Seated in his tribunal, the judge is simply the guardian and avenger of the law. Scarcely is he even permitted to take cognizance of extenuating circumstances, in order to soften the rigours of the chastisement he inflicts upon the guilty.

Now, according to Blessed Paschal, if one aspires to be a Saint, he must be a judge and have the heart of a judge. When it is our neighbour who is in question, we enter upon the functions of justiciary with only too great facility, and from the eminence of our own self-constituted tribunal, pass judgments which are not distinguished by any excessive charity or leniency. Very different is our attitude when it is we ourselves who are concerned; then, by an opposite tendency of our nature, we are inclined to excuse the culprit and pronounce his acquittal. In spite, however, of the axiom, "No one is a judge in his own cause," it is a man's duty to learn how to act as a disinterested and impartial judge, even in his own proper concerns. This cannot be done without the all-powerful aid of grace, which sustains the will, and enables one to triumph over the desperate resistance of nature. Hence it was not by their own unaided strength, but by the help of God, that the Saints sought to realize that heart of a judge, which is a masterpiece of Divine grace.

It might be said of Paschal, that he exaggerated his obligations in this respect, and that he came near making an executioner of the judge. In order to be convinced of this, it is enough to read the sentence pronounced against himself by this inexorable judge. This sentence is to be found drawn up in due form in the little book which served him as a spiritual directory. It runs as follows: "Brother Paschal, strive to make the following principles sink deep into thy mind:

"1. Thou shalt have for thyself the same regard, which one is wont to have for a corpse in a state of decay. People turn away their eyes so as not to behold it, and close their nostrils in order to escape the fetid odour exhaled by it.

"2. Anyone who would treat thee according to thy deserts might without injustice tear out thine eyes, lop off thine ears, cut out thy tongue, and mutilate all thy members, because there is no one who has not, in league with his senses, rendered himself guilty of some sin, and thus merited eternal punishment.

"3. Thou shalt not be vexed when thou findest that others share thine own opinion upon these two points; and thou shalt accept as a favour, the sentence which condemns thee to be mortified in thy senses, and tormented in thy body, until thy last day, because by means of this temporal punishment one escapes eternal punishment.

"4. If thy courage fail thee in the painful carrying out of this sentence, and if at times penance appear intolerable and never-ending, then bethink thee of thy Master, Jesus Christ, and turn thy looks towards Him. He was Innocence and Holiness itself; yet for love of thee He consented to be treated as a criminal, and took upon Himself the death of the Cross." Such was the sentence pronounced by the holy man against himself. In order not to forget a single clause of it, and to have it constantly present before his mind, he was in the habit of carrying it about with him, and of re-reading it carefully every day.

No matter where the holy man was stationed, whether at Elche or Jumilla, Almanyura, Monteforte, or Villareal, Paschal's cell was sure to be the worst in the Convent. For several years his cell at Villareal was a kind of recess under the bell, used as a passage. It was narrow and cramped, and had neither door nor ceiling, so that it was open to the winds. It was his own choice, and at his urgent entreaty his Superiors allowed him to retain it, in spite of its drawbacks. The furniture was in perfect keeping with the apartment. It would have been vain to seek for even the semblance of a bed. He used to take his repose huddled up and nearly bent double, only half covered by a wretched sort of a blanket. "How can you sleep a wink in this cold and in such an extraordinary position?" asked a Brother who found him all shivering. "Oh, did you not know that in my younger days I used to look after sheep?" he replied, smiling. "I was accustomed from my childhood to sleep like this, and the habit has become so strong, that it would be difficult for me to rest in any other way." A few books of devotion, a wooden cross, and a picture of the Blessed Virgin, formed the sole adornments of the cell.

From bed and lodgings let us pass on to clothing, which was scarcely more luxurious; for it was that of the Brethren of the Reform, of great weight, and uncomfortable alike in summer and winter. In Paschal's case the penance attached to the wearing of such a habit was doubled by certain special circumstances. In the mind of the holy Brother, this habit ought to last at least as long as the one who received it on the day of his profession. Now, the cloth of which the habit was made, though strong and durable enough, was not indestructible, and after a certain period of time it gave way in divers places, and threatened to become a total wreck. As crumbling walls are repaired with fresh masonry, so did Paschal patch his gaping habit with stout pieces of cloth. At length these patches, overlapping one another, superseded the original material, and, by depriving the habit of its suppleness and ample proportions, made it as narrow as a sack, and as rigid as a metal sheath. It was thus weighed down, and imprisoned in this species of case, that Paschal hastened about his multiform employments. The under-tunic and the other portions of religious clothing little by little underwent many transformations, and still held together by means of successive additions.

But all this was mere child's play compared with what he wore concealed under the poor habit. When St. Francis, in a transport of seraphic ardour, despoiled himself of his garments, in the Palace of the Bishop of Assisi, and gave them to his father, there was disclosed the cruel hair-shirt, which lacerated the members of the noble young man; and so moved were the bystanders that they could not restrain their tears. How great would have been the amazement and the commiseration of everyone if our Saint, removing the veils which hid his secret, had exposed to view the panoply of armour, in which he was arrayed from head to foot. Never was Earl or Baron, in the palmy days of chivalry, so cased in iron and steel as this voluntary knight of penance. None of the pieces of feudal armour was wanting. There were the shoulder-guards, the neckpiece, the elbow-guards, the knee-caps, and the greaves, not to mention the cuirass, and a number of small chains holding together the various instruments of torture.

One of the earliest biographers of the Saint, in speaking of this armoury, makes a reflection on the subject which is not without originality. "Just as people of the world, in order to follow the prevailing fashion, are careful to vary the style, hue, and material of their costume, so also did the Man of God have his fashions, and his changes in the attire of penance. On certain days he preferred to wear a tunic lined with the bristles of a boar; on others a coat of mail with iron spikes."

For the great solemnities, all the jewels were taken out of their case, and the Saint, as though putting on his most luxurious finery, adorned himself with the most terrible gems that the ingenuity of Penance could invent—collars, bracelets, fine chains, iron rings, and the rest—in order to impress upon his body the marks of Christ's Passion; and the more he was weighted with these instruments of torture, the more radiant did he appear. At such times, when he happened to meet anyone, he used to say in a mysterious way: "Brother, let us rejoice. All that comes from God is good." Or, more often still: "My Love is crucified" *(Amor meus crucifixus est)*. Such was his motto, and eloquently does it speak to us of the true motive, on account of which Paschal sought for suffering so eagerly, and took in it such a strange delight. It was in order to resemble his Divine Master, fastened to the Cross, and to give Him a strong proof of his love, rather than from any fear of losing his soul, that he embraced penance with such ardour; and it was on this account, too, that in this harsh embrace his heart overflowed with joy.

To Paschal's other privations was added hunger. During ten years the holy man subsisted almost entirely upon bread and water,—"spare bread and short water."[1] Sunday was an exception. On that day a small portion of boiled vegetables, steeped in wormwood, relieved the monotony of the usual pittance. What was served to him in the refectory, was conveyed, by a deft manœuvre, into the table drawer, which became the larder of the poor. To evade observation, Paschal pretended to eat like the rest; but no one allowed himself to become the dupe of this pious ruse, inspired by humility and charity. He sometimes added to his diet some of the scraps and refuse from the refectory and kitchen, about to be thrown into the fire, or the remains of the soup which had been distributed to the poor on the previous day. Even this seemed to himself too much to concede to a sinner worthy of everlasting punishment. It was upon such a diet, of a kind to gradually undermine even the most robust constitution, that Paschal gave himself to a merciless round of unremitting toil, which ended only with his death. Here, indeed, was a convict sentenced to penal servitude for life.

To the employments of his office he added a host of other occupations. It was to him the Brethren had recourse to repair their sandals, to mend their clothes and patch their garments. And he also used to dig in the garden. Knowing his avidity for labour, people had no scruple of adding to his burdens, and of employing his multifarious talents to their utmost. During the midday siesta, customary in hot climates, Paschal, instead of taking this beneficial repose, went out to work in the garden. There he was to be seen in the blazing sun, with the perspiration streaming from his forehead, digging the beds or scraping the paths, at the same time softly singing his pious carols. "I never saw him sitting down or giving himself a

---

[1] Isa. 20:30.

moment's rest," testifies Doctor Benet, whose functions often took him to the Friary. None better understood, than this holy man, the passage in the Fifth Chapter of the Rule: "Let the Brethren to whom the Lord has given grace to work, work, yet in such a way as not to extinguish thereby the spirit of holy prayer." Paschal had received this grace of working in all its fullness, and he had such a profound detestation of Idleness, the mother of every vice, that he chased her away on every occasion. In payment for his work, the Man of God, like some down-trodden slave of olden times, received only blows and stripes, for disciplines to blood added their complement to this interminable series of self-inflictions. Thus did he carry out remorselessly the sentence pronounced against the culprit.

Sickness, which might be supposed to have relaxed somewhat this cast-iron regime, only made it harder. Illness itself was made a pretext for refusing the victim the little allowed him when in health. The pretexts adduced by Paschal were so plausible, that the Superiors and Doctors usually ended by giving in. He succeeded, not without difficulty, in persuading them that in his case illness did not proceed from any ordinary cause, but that it was directly willed by God, and consequently that it was necessary to allow the Divine Will free play, and not to attempt to hinder it by the employment of human means and artificial remedies. There was, after all, a great deal of truth in this assertion. "It was, indeed, a most peculiar case," wrote Doctor Benet, who attended the Saint in most of his attacks. "I really do not know how to classify an illness which, instead of enfeebling the patient, seemed to give him a new lease of life and caused him excessive joy." He could not sufficiently admire his patient's unalterable joyousness in the midst of excruciating torments. Blessed Andrew Hibernon, who lived with Paschal in several of the

Convents of the Province of St. John Baptist, exalts in his deposition the fidelity of the Man of God to the smallest points of the Rule, and declares that he never knew so true a son of St. Francis. "Although it would be impossible to discover in his life a single venial fault deliberately committed, and consequently matter of expiation, the holy Brother went so far along the road of mortification that he could be, in all truth, considered a prodigy of penance. We see by his example what the human body is capable of enduring. It was simply incredible."

Father Sanchez, the Guardian of Villareal, sums up this chapter, and connects it with what has preceded, in one word, when he shows how there were present, in one and the same life, two qualities, usually regarded as incompatible—harshness and sweetness. "I never knew anyone," he says, "at the same time so harsh and yet so sweet—so harsh towards self, so sweet towards others." This harshness was itself, too, another means of exercising fraternal charity for the Saint. It was to his neighbour that there went indirectly all that superabundant wealth of expiation, which this Saint needed not himself. The necessities of the needy were supplied from his superfluity; it became to them a means of salvation. His were the most precious alms—the alms of suffering and of blood. Conceit and pride, which Our Lord reprehended in the Pharisees, found no place in the austerities practised by our Saint. He was ready to relinquish them all at a sign from his Superiors. In a certain reply, deserving to be written in letters of gold, he has himself expressed his principles on this important point. The Guardian, perceiving that he was very weak, ordered a plate of fish to be set before him. He thankfully accepted it without troubling himself about his fast. The Brother who served him was somewhat surprised, and said to him: "If you practise fasting on bread and water, how is it you can take this fish?" To this Paschal replied: "Brother, obedience comes first; devotion must take the second place." Such is the proper order as well as the safeguard of penance.

CHAPTER XI
A CONFESSOR OF THE EUCHARIST

EVERYTHING seemed to indicate that Paschal would henceforth remain, as it were, fixed and rooted to the soil of the Province of St. John Baptist, and that the rest of the world would learn little or nothing about him, at least during his lifetime. But Almighty God, Who is as zealous for the honour of His Saints, as for His own, willed otherwise; and in order that the brilliant virtues of His devoted servant might illuminate other places and other lands, He ordained that providential circumstances should arise which necessitated Paschal's temporary absence from his Province, and led him first of all into France, and later on to the further extremity of Spain. The earlier of these two long journeys is of a more thrilling nature than the latter. The circumstances under which this journey was undertaken, and the episodes which marked its accomplishment, give to it the features of a march into an enemy's country.

The Minister-General of the Family of the Observance was at that time a Frenchman called Father Christopher of Cheffontaine, and he was then residing in Paris. Now, the Custos of the Discalced Friars Minor in Spain found himself obliged to have recourse to him, for the settlement of a matter of primary importance. But the question was, how to communicate with him? At this period the Kingdom of France was passing through the throes of the civil and religious war which had been enkindled by the Calvinists. Many of the Provinces to be traversed on the route to Paris were in the hands of the sectaries; and their soldiery, entrenched in impregnable strongholds, overawed the country and held every highway. In 1570, in spite of recent defeat and the loss of their bravest leaders, the Huguenots were preparing to resume the offensive, and dreamed only of reprisals and of vengeance. "At that time," writes a chronicler, "it would have been less perilous for a man to traverse the Libyan desert, infested by lions and tigers, than for a Catholic to venture into a country inhabited by Calvinists."

The risk was extreme in the case of a foreigner, and, above all, a Religious wearing the Franciscan habit. In the eyes of the Huguenots, a Friar Minor was the incarnation of "Popery," and a very imp of Rome. In this quality he could expect nothing but hatred and violence at the hands of the sectaries. It is to the honour of the Seraphic Order that for more than a century the Friars were the mark of the especial hate and persecution of heresy, on account of their unshakable loyalty to the Holy See. The Franciscan Martyrology of the French Provinces alone counts, at this sorrowful epoch, the names of a hundred Friars, done to death after enduring torments which might have been invented by a Nero or a Domitian. Everywhere the Calvinists delivered our convents to the flames, and gave no quarter to our Religious. The smug Protestants of today discreetly throw a veil over all these horrors, and, as though, forsooth, the blood-stained past had never existed, they continue to reproach us with St. Bartholomew and the massacre of their co-religionists. History, studied in the present age with greater thoroughness and impartiality than heretofore, gives to this celebrated tragedy its true significance, and reduces it to its just proportions. Receiving timely warning of a plot that was being hatched against them, the Catholics took Time by the forelock, and subjected the conspirators to the fate intended for themselves. And even supposing that the responsibility of this massacre rested entirely upon the Catholics, still one could not draw from this fact the conclusion so dear to Protestants—namely, that their forefathers were meek lambs, whilst ours were ravening wolves and bloodthirsty tigers. The truth is that, not for a day merely, but for a whole century, these gentle lambs went on perpetrating their St. Bartholomew, massacring priests, monks, and secular people with every refinement of cruelty.

Now to return to our narrative. The matter was of a nature to forbid its being confided to a secular, and to entrust it to a Religious seemed like sending him straight to the shambles. Sore, then, would have been the perplexity of the poor Custos, had not Divine Providence pointed out to him the only subject capable of undertaking such an enterprise with any chance of success; since to a courage, proof against every trial, he conjoined a consummate prudence and other endowments both of nature and grace invaluable in such difficult circumstances. So the Superior summoned Paschal into his presence—for it was in him, as may have been guessed, that his hopes centred—and after explaining to him the almost insuperable difficulties of the undertaking, asked him if he would agree to charge himself with it. What the reply would be could not be doubtful to anyone who knew the thoughts of this true and perfect Religious on the subject of Obedience. On this solemn occasion obedience, too, seemed to the holy man to be invested with a double charm; for, like all the Saints, he had dreamed of the martyr's crown; and on hearing this unlooked-for proposal of the Custos, something seemed to whisper in his ear that he was, perchance, destined for the honour of shedding his blood for the cause of Christ and His Church. So it was with the greatest alacrity and joy that he gave his consent. "I am ready to start at once," he said to the Superior. And he was so, in reality; for his preparations consisted in receiving his instructions and the blessing of the Custos. As for anything else, such as food, shelter, and other requirements of the journey, he was no more solicitous about them than if he had been an Angel from above, or a disembodied spirit. Providence would see to it; for it was to Providence that he confided all these insignificant details with the most complete self-surrender. We may add that the resources of Providence ran no risk of being exhausted on this occasion, so modest were the wants of its client and so easy was he to satisfy. A piece of dry bread seemed to him a luxury, and a bundle of twigs softer than a monarch's couch.

It was not without sadness that the Religious saw one who was like the visible Angel Guardian and the blessing of their Friary depart. Who could tell whether they would ever see him again, or if this were not his last adieu? As to the holy Brother himself, he left to God the concern of conducting him safely to his destination and of bringing him back again, too, if, indeed, the latter entered into His providential plans; and he set out to accomplish his long pilgrimage on foot as though it had been a mere jaunt, or an ordinary change of domicile. It was a long distance from Valencia to the frontiers of France, and even if our pilgrim had been provided with sinews of steel, and had covered ten to twelve leagues every day, several weeks would be required to accomplish it.

This tedious journey across the Kingdom of Valencia and Catalonia, one sufficient to test the endurance of the most intrepid pedestrian, formed, however, only the prelude of the expedition, and its relatively easy portion. Those whom the traveller encountered, spoke the same tongue, for he was still in Spain, amongst his own compatriots. Moreover, the livery of St. Francis was known and loved throughout these two Provinces, and their intensely Catholic population welcomed the coming of the Friars. So here Paschal found it easy enough to obtain the small pittance of food he required and a shakedown for the night.

On the further side of the Pyrenees there was an abrupt change in the situation, and the traveller quickly found himself involved in many difficulties. At his first halting-place on French soil it was seriously debated amongst the Friars Minor of the Convent where he stayed, whether it was expedient to allow him to continue his journey, or if it were not better to send him back to his Province. The Friars were convened to deliberate upon the case. As is usual on such occasions, opinions were divided. On the one hand some theologians of weight held to the principle that religious obedience has its limits, and that these cannot be exceeded without infringing the rights of the subject. On this ground they considered that it was unlawful for a Superior to enjoin an heroic act upon a subject, and that obedience, when it exposed a Friar to obvious danger of death, was excessive, and consequently they maintained Paschal was not obliged to obey. This view was supported by a consideration of a different character, and one that was only too well grounded. Everyone knows, said they, how the heretics thirst for blood, especially that of our Religious. The sudden apparition of a Spanish monk in their midst will certainly infuriate them, and will incite them to fresh acts of violence, and from all this the Catholic cause will derive no benefit, but will be more likely to receive some fresh blow. To these arguments, convincing as they might appear, the more fervent, relying on other principles, and inspired by motives superior to those of human wisdom and prudence, replied as follows: "Brethren, do not forget that in these troublous times our

Franciscan Friaries are in the Church Militant, God's Kingdom upon earth, like so many sacred citadels, wherein the soldiers of Christ are trained to the exercise of arms, so that, when occasion offers, they may do battle against heresy. Do not, then, try to hinder this valiant soul from going to the seat of war and entering the conflict. The greater the danger in what is required by obedience, the greater the merit in fulfilling it. To obey in matters that are easy is nothing out of the ordinary, and cannot be considered as an exercise of Christian fortitude, so conspicuous amongst the cardinal virtues. Beware, then, of taxing with imprudence what is undertaken for so noble an end; and what end could be nobler than the accomplishment of the Divine Will, made known and declared by the voice of Superiors? Even supposing that there is somewhat of excess in this matter, and that this good Brother falls a victim to his own simplicity and childlike docility, yet even then all will be to his benefit; for he will thus find a means of bartering his mortal life for eternal happiness. And furthermore, has not Our Lord said more than once that he who is too much attached to his life will run the risk of losing his soul, whilst he who is willing to sacrifice it generously will secure the salvation of his soul? It would, therefore, be contrary to the Gospel to hinder this faithful servant on his journey." This opinion, which appeared more perfect, and corresponded so well to Franciscan traditions, prevailed, and it was decided that the Brother should be allowed to go where his Superiors had sent him, cost what it might, and even at the risk of losing his life.

Paschal was rejoiced at this decision, which the Friars communicated to him, together with the motives by which it was inspired. It seemed like a fresh revelation of the designs of God regarding him upon the eve of combat.

"Whether you live or die, you have everything to gain and nothing to lose," they said to him. To this Paschal answered humbly: "I do not cling to life, and I only prize it in order that I may be able to offer it up in sacrifice to my Master, Jesus Christ. To forfeit my life for obedience's sake would be inestimable gain." And once more he started off on foot.

Behold him now, alone, without a guide, in the heart of a strange land, whose language and whose customs were equally unknown to him. Then, again, he could not hope to pass by unremarked. Everything seemed to point him out to public notice, from his habit, a mosaic of little patches, to the strangeness of a journey undertaken under such singular circumstances. The consequence was that, wherever he appeared, there was a sensation. People came hurrying out of their houses, exclaiming to each other: "Quick, quick; come and look at a sort of man you've never set eyes on before!" And the children used to follow after him as though he had belonged to some curious species of animal. Never did the vainest of fops, intent upon drawing upon himself the public gaze, succeed so admirably in exciting curiosity and wonderment. Every day it was renewed again in some different way.

The onward march of the holy man was not seriously impeded by all this attention. Absorbed in prayer and with downcast eyes, he did not so much as perceive the popular excitement, and continued his journey as though he had been alone.

Although he was still in a Catholic region, the impression made by the passage of this Friar of so singular an aspect was by no means universally favourable. If some, struck by the air of sanctity which emanated from the whole person of the traveller, approached respectfully as he passed by, and greeted him with some mark of reverence, as a servant of God, others—and they were the greater number—maintained a suspicious or even defiant attitude, and asked themselves if this were not some fanatic, who had escaped from his Convent, or, perhaps, even a spy disguised under the religious garb. And even apart from these suspicions, it occurred to the minds of many people that this apparition of a Friar was inopportune and hazardous, and that this Franciscan, whoever he was, would have been better advised to stay in his Monastery in Spain, than to come promenading through France during such critical times. The popular ferment foreboded what the holy man was to meet with upon his entry into the land of the Calvinists.

The Way of the Cross begins for him, and his Calvary has as many stations as there are towns and villages to traverse. Everywhere, to the astonishment produced at first by the novelty of the spectacle, there succeed threats and menaces, the mutterings of the storm, and soon the full fury of the tempest is unchained. One would have thought that the whole country was in danger, and that the enemy was already at the gates. The population rises *en masse*, prepared either for attack or defence. Cries are heard on all sides, "Down with the Papist!" "Death to the idolater!" And all this hubbub about a poor Friar, as inoffensive as a lamb!

It is under a cross-fire of insults and mockery that he tramps along the road, hustled, buffeted, and covered with dirt. In one village of Orleannois the peasants took up stones instead of dirt to fling at him. Orleans, the city of Joan of Arc, was at that time the chief bulwark of the sectaries, and a focus of the deadly hatred borne by them to the Catholic name. Paschal was soon to have cruel experience of this. Scarce had he arrived before the ramparts when he found himself surrounded by a band of infuriated ruffians, who quickly flung him to the ground. After administering a sound beating, these disciples of the pure and unadulterated Gospel set him on his feet again, and, by way of provoking an argument, put to him one of those captious questions, whose aim is to draw from the person interrogated an answer which, no matter what it may be, may be forged into a weapon to be turned against him. Such were the tactics of the Pharisees, who, under pretence of seeking instruction, put questions to the Divine Master, in order to ensnare Him in His speech.

To grasp aright the import of the question addressed to the Man of God, it must be borne in mind that of all things detested by the heretics, what they most abhorred were the *Mass* and the *Pope*—"the Abomination of Desolation," as they were pleased to style them in their scriptural cant. The Pope was for them Satan's Vicar, prefigured by the beast of the Apocalypse, and the Mass unmitigated idolatry, in which the adoration due to God alone was lavished upon a piece of bread. Of these two it was the Holy Eucharist which was pre-eminently the object of their hatred; and accordingly the history of those evil times records on every page the most horrible profanations of the Sacrament of the Altar. When, by treachery or by force of arms, the enemies of our faith had gained possession of a Catholic town, their primary objective was always the Tabernacle. Their supreme triumph consisted in breaking open its door, scattering the sacred particles on the ground, and trampling them under foot, or else throwing them to be devoured by dogs or swine; and these truly diabolical triumphs were renewed with each fresh success.

So now the sectaries address this question to their prisoner with scornful hate: "Papist, do you believe that God is in the Sacrament which you consecrate and call the Mass?" To affirm the Catholic doctrine on this point was to sign his death-warrant. The bloodthirsty wretches did not have to wait long for the reply. "Yes," exclaims Paschal, in the unfaltering accents of one of the early Martyrs, "I do believe it, and I most firmly maintain that God is as really present in the consecrated Host as He is in the glory of Heaven." At this manly and spirited reply of the Confessor of the faith, the sectaries foam with rage. They fancied that fear would extort some weak concession from this wretched monk, and that, in order to escape death, he would have recourse to equivocation or subterfuge. They had not realized what kind of a person they had to deal with in their prisoner; and their ignorance in this respect was to be the occasion of yet another surprise.

Not wishing to acknowledge defeat, the heretics returned to the charge, and challenged Paschal to a formal disputation on the subject of the Eucharist. Nothing could be easier, they thought, than to get the upper hand of this uncultured monk. The Man of God was not one to shirk the encounter, especially as it was a question of defending the Blessed Sacrament. So he accepted the challenge in all simplicity and joy. Has not Our Lord, in the Gospel, promised to be with His own, and has He not, as a matter of fact, on solemn occasions like the present, placed upon the lips of little ones words of light and power capable of piercing the subtlest meshes of error? With that deft manipulation, peculiar to heresy, the sectaries, hiding the hollowness and falsity of their arguments under an imposing pile of Biblical texts, endeavoured to prove that the bread after Consecration still remained bread, and that the Sacrifice of the Mass was useless, derogatory to the Passion of Christ, and the source and occasion of the most monstrous idolatry the world has ever seen. Paschal listened in sadness of soul to this long string of blasphemies. When at length his turn to speak came, he

Ch. XI: A Confessor of the Eucharist

replied to all these fallacies in due order, refuting each one with such powerful and lucid arguments, so well grounded on the Holy Scriptures, that the Protestant thesis went utterly to pieces.[1]

This, however, was only half the victory. The scaffolding of error being thrown down, it now remained to establish the validity of the Catholic thesis, and to prove the reality and Divine character of the Sacrifice of the Altar. This task the impassioned adorer of the Eucharist accomplished in so masterful a manner—he surrounded this dogma so dear to his heart with such a wealth of triumphant evidence—that at the conclusion his opponents, smarting under defeat, betook themselves once more to violence. Like the Pharisees, confounded by the eloquence of Stephen, they took up stones to hurl at him. The Confessor of the faith would there and then have become a Martyr had not God interposed miraculously. The shower of missiles, which would, under ordinary circumstances, have inevitably stretched him bleeding and lifeless upon the earth, passed clean over his head, or fell harmlessly on either side. Only one stone was allowed by the Divine permission to reach its mark. Flung with full force, it shattered Paschal's left shoulder, and until his dying day he suffered from this fracture.

"One day the holy man was conversing with me familiarly, after he had just cured me of illness, so as to enable me to accompany him on quest through the country," says a witness, "and he began to speak about his journey into France. He told me how he had once been in Orleans, an important city situated about thirty-four leagues from Paris. 'Now, listen,' he said. 'We must pray

---

[1] "Quod eum facile passint sophismatibus suis irretire tam solidis nervosisque per infusam sibi rerum theologicarum scientiam confudit."

for those poor people of Orleans. Just fancy; their beautiful church is turned into a stable, where they pen their cattle and their goats. It is a disgrace.[2] I received a little present from those folks,' he added, with a smile. 'Our Lord permitted that it should be so.' As he said nothing further to me on the subject, I really thought they had made him some gift, and it was only long after that I learned what had really happened, and that he had been stoned."[3]

On the other side of Orleans the Man of God ventured, inadvertently, into the lion's den. About midday, feeling faint from hunger, he could devise nothing better than to knock at the gate of a château, situated at a little distance from the road, and to beg a crust of bread for the love of God. This princely mansion was the residence of a powerful Huguenot noble, known far and wide for his hostility to Papists. He had just sat down to dinner when his retainers led in the poor Friar, whom they had captured in the avenue. "Well, Monk, where do you come from, and what is your business here?" quoth the seigneur, eyeing him contemptuously.

"I am a Spaniard, and I am on the way to Paris about the affairs of my Order," answered Paschal modestly. "A Spaniard, eh? A spy of the Spanish King, I'll be bound. Take him away. Just wait till dinner's over, and then we can settle his accounts for him."

The servants led the prisoner off, and left him in the grounds until dinner should be finished. The gate left ajar seemed to invite the holy man to take flight, but he didn't even think of doing so, and would doubtless have been found in the same spot had not a compassionate soul—and there are such everywhere—come out into the grounds and

---

[2] "Pestava, hecha cavallerya."

[3] MSS. of the Process. Deposition of an asthmatical patient cured by the Saint.

induced him to make good his escape. A poor woman, who was a fervent Catholic, had the happiness of giving him, for the love of God, that fragment of bread so harshly denied him at the château.

Only just delivered from one peril as though by a miracle, our traveller soon after fell into another not less formidable. Traversing at nightfall the main thoroughfare of a long, straggling village, peopled by Calvinists, his ears were suddenly assailed by the hue and cry of an enraged crowd. From insults they proceeded to blows, and yelling, "Death to the Papist," they prepared to carry their threat into execution. Once more, however, the Lord protected His faithful servant. Under the pretext that it was getting too late, a person present proposed that the execution should be postponed until the next day. "I will see that the monk is locked up, in the meantime," said he. Then, catching hold of Paschal, he dragged him to a pigsty, amidst the plaudits of the crowd, and, shoving him in, bolted the door securely. The poor Brother, sinking with hunger and exhaustion, thought that his last hour had come. To prepare himself the better for the supreme struggle, he knelt down, and, without taking a moment's repose, spent the entire night in prayer. But the pretended executioner, who had thrust him so rudely into this loathsome hole, was in reality his deliverer. Some time before daybreak there was a knock on the door of the pigsty. "Get up and go away at once, now that the popular excitement seems to have abated," said the unknown to his prisoner; and then, after handing him some provisions, he disappeared so as to avoid recognition.

In his charming biography of the Saint, Father John Ximenes has fortunately preserved one of the most characteristic episodes of this expedition into the country of the Huguenots. "One day, I do not remember apropos of what, I turned the conversation upon the subject of the journey into France," he relates, "and the holy man described to me how, on one occasion, when he was walking along the highway alone, there came riding towards him at full speed a trooper armed with a lance. 'Having looked at me for a few moments,' related Paschal, 'the trooper said abruptly, "Is God in Heaven, Monk?" "Why, of course God is in Heaven," I replied at once. The lancer seemed satisfied with this reply, and, clapping spurs to his steed, started off at full gallop.' 'But what did the man mean?' I asked the holy Brother, 'and what was his motive in asking such a question?' 'In my opinion, this Huguenot lancer expected that after I had declared that God was in Heaven, I would add that He was also in the most holy Sacrament of the Altar, and that in that case he would have run me through with his lance as an idolater. Unhappily, this idea occurred to me too late. When it did come into my mind the horseman had vanished. Alas! I was unworthy of the crown of martyrdom, and for the second time it eluded my grasp when I was about to seize it.' "[4]

More than once the knife was at the traveller's throat, but on each occasion, by a manifest disposition of Divine Providence, the heretics stopped short of completing their work. Thus it was that the dispatches, sewn between two pieces of the poor Franciscan habit, were delivered safe and entire into the hands of Father Christopher of Cheffontaine. The veneration with which the Religious of the Friary at Paris welcomed the heroic messenger can be more easily imagined than described. As for himself, after having paid a visit to the celebrated shrines of the metropolis and taken a few days' rest, he set out again

---

[4] "Life of Blessed Paschal," by Father Ximenes.

upon the road to Spain, with the same courage and the same willingness as before.

"When he left us to go into France," says one of the Brothers in his deposition at the Process of Beatification, "his locks were of the blackness of ebony; when he returned they were white as snow." With greater eloquence than the most realistic descriptions, this one fact tells us of the perils and incredible hardships undergone by the intrepid wayfarer in the course of his journey.

The Friars used to take a delight, from time to time, in going back upon this memorable journey and in asking Paschal to relate some of his episodes, as one would ask an old soldier to tell the anecdotes of his campaigning days. Although he had an habitual aversion for talking about what directly concerned himself, he willingly acceded, in this instance, to their request, because he thence found occasion of engaging them to pray with greater fervour for the triumph of Holy Church. But he was always careful to add by way of corrective: "Ah, if only I had been a true servant of God, I would never have left the hands of the heretics alive! But, being a wretched sinner, I was enabled to escape all dangers."

Soon after the completion of this never-to-be-forgotten journey, when he had the high honour of confessing Christ in His Vicar on earth and in the Sacrament of His love, at the risk of his life, Paschal composed with his own hand a booklet, filled with beautiful reflections upon the Real Presence and the Supremacy of the Pope. It is a complete vindication in a concise form of these two dogmas against the attacks of heresy. In declaring this humble Friar the Patron of all Eucharistic Associations, does it not seem as though our late Holy Father, Leo XIII, wished at one and the same time to recognize the incomparable devotion of St. Paschal to the Blessed Sacrament, and the heroism with which, under the very knife of the enemies of the Church, he confessed the Primacy of Peter and the prerogatives of the Holy See? It is thus that that great Pontiff was pleased to acquit himself of the debt of gratitude incurred by his predecessors towards this true son of the Holy Catholic Church.

CHAPTER XII
ON CATHOLIC SOIL

IN his First Epistle to Timothy, the Apostle exhorts his disciple to the practice of piety, by showing the precious fruits derived from its exercise, both in this world and the next. "Exercise thyself unto godliness, for godliness is profitable to all things, having promise of the life that now is and of that which is to come" (4:7-8). Happy are they who possess the fullness of this heavenly gift; they hold in their hand the golden key which unlocks every door, and become by that fact the most useful servants of God and of their neighbour. Such was the consoling experience of the successive Superiors of our Saint.

With marvellous readiness he gave himself to everything required of him, no matter what its nature might be, without ever refusing a task, and he succeeded admirably in whatever was entrusted to him. The harder the task seemed, the more did he feel disposed to accept it. The Superiors were not unaware of this, and on certain occasions they knew how to exploit this weakness of his. Paschal was, indeed, an inexhaustible treasure to them.

This is why we find him again on the march, charged with a commission, recalling in a distant way the one which took him to Paris. Once more it was a question of delivering important dispatches, although not to the General this time, but to the Custos of St. John Baptist, then resident at Xeres de la Fontera, about 100 leagues from Valencia. Paschal had acquitted himself so well of the first commission that the second came to him by a kind of prescription. The Superiors never even thought of confiding it to anyone else.

This tramp across the kingdoms of Valencia and Murcia and the provinces of Granada and Andalusia did not present any of the dangers which gave the expedition into France so dramatic an interest. Our Saint could hope for no other martyrdom save that of the fatigues, inconveniences, and privations incidental to so long a journey, undertaken in apostolic fashion. He indeed found such in abundance, and he added to their painfulness by means of voluntary penances. Accustomed as we are to traverse entire states, in a few hours, without experiencing any fatigue, we can scarcely imagine what a journey on foot in the sixteenth century across rough country, without either railways or good roads, must have been like. The picturesque scenery, and the lovely views, which are the delight of the tourist, were not, indeed, wanting; but what more frequently awaited one who, like the Apostles, journeyed *sine baculo et pera* (without staff or scrip), depending on the charity of friendly people, was a plentiful harvest of mortifications in every shape and form. In following our wayfarer, step by step, we shall see that a stock of energy—both physical and moral—was required for the accomplishment of such a journey.

As the Guardian of Valencia did not assign any companion to his courier, the latter covered the distance between Valencia and Xeres by himself, and he took advantage of this circumstance to bury in the silence of oblivion whatever crosses he may have had to endure at that time. So the record of his outward journey is a blank, and it would have been exactly the same with his return had not Almighty God provided a witness, who, struck by the many beautiful and edifying things he saw, has consigned them all to writing with the most religious fidelity. This valuable witness is a boy of fourteen years of age. He afterwards became the Provincial of the Province of St. John Baptist, and as such was our holy man's best friend, and also the earliest and most authentic of his biographers. We shall now hear from his lips the story of his vocation to the Seraphic Order, and a description of the journey in which he played so leading a part.

"Blessed Paschal had just arrived at Xeres, to the joy and consolation of his Brethren. He had been sent there by his Superiors at Valencia. At this time I used often to pay visits to the Friary, as the Fathers were very kind to me and allowed me to come into choir, and even to chant the Office with them. Now, one morning, when we were singing the hour of Tierce, which immediately preceded High Mass, I saw a Religious, who was a stranger to me, enter the choir. At sight of him I felt a thrill of indescribable emotion, and could not remove my eyes from him. He wore no mantle, and the habit he had on was of some coarse material, so tight that one might have taken him for a man tied up in a corn-sack. When he had taken holy water with great devotion, and prostrated himself face downwards upon the floor, he afterwards went and knelt beside the lectern, his hands raised to the height of his face. He remained thus six or seven minutes, as motionless as a statue. Although I was quite young then, and scarcely able to comprehend the things of God, yet I was struck and, as it were, fascinated by what I saw. One of the Brothers of the Convent approached the Friar, and, taking him by the sleeve, invited him to rise and take his place in the stalls. He remained there during the High Mass in an attitude so full of recollection and devotion that it brought tears to my eyes. During the few days he remained at Xeres there was some disputing over him. Everyone expected a call from him. However, the only people he visited were a relative of the Custos, and certain benefactors who wished to converse with him, and then it was by obedience that he went. When making these visits of charity he was so modest in his bearing, and showed such tact and such piety in saying just what was needed in each case, that he was everywhere regarded for a great servant of God.

"It was I myself who derived the greatest benefit from his reputation for holiness, as you will presently see. I was the eldest son in a poor but numerous family, and my mother's hope. She was practically a widow, inasmuch as my father had emigrated to Peru many years ago, and nothing had been heard of him since. Young as I was, I worked for my mother, and it was upon me that she always counted to eke out our scanty means. In a few hours the hopes she had founded upon her eldest boy, were dissipated. A robber had effected an entrance into our house, and had carried away her precious treasure, under her very eyes. This robber was none other than Brother Paschal. Scarce had he set foot in the house when, regarding me with the eye of an owner, claiming his own property, he said to my mother: 'This little one belongs to me. I claim him for Our Lord and for our holy Father, St. Francis.' And he spoke to mother words of such persuasiveness and energy, that the poor woman, who would not have exchanged me for a kingdom, allowed me to go. 'Since it is God's Will, take him,' she said, weeping; 'but go as quickly as you can, and on the quiet; for if our relatives find out that you are taking the boy away from Valencia, in order to set him to study, they will try hard to prevent it.' Under God, I must acknowledge, it is to Blessed Paschal that I shall be indebted for my eternal salvation. So we left hurriedly, and at night-time, in order to elude pursuit and capture by members of my family."

What the Venerable Father John Ximenes does not

venture to state himself, we shall supply by stating that Paschal, illumined by God, divined in this child an elect soul, and one of the future glories of the Reform of St. Peter of Alcantara. This omission supplied, we now return to the boy's narrative: "Before leaving our home, the holy man promised my mother to watch over me with a solicitude and tenderness at least equal to her own. O wellbeloved Servant of God, I here attest that you have splendidly fulfilled your promise! Until your latest breath, you were my Guardian Angel, and, like another Raphael, you conducted your new Tobias in safety. Thanks to you, he is enabled to advance with steady footsteps, and avoid the pitfalls of this present life. I cannot express all you have been to me, in the first place because it is here a question of personal concerns, and these should remain our own secret, and furthermore, because words would not suffice, and deeds alone would be a fitting acknowledgment of such services. His last words referred to me: 'Mind you, inform Father John Ximenes of my death,' he said to the Friars around him. 'Don't let him forget that it was I, who took him from his country, and gave him to the Franciscan family.'

"From the very first day's journey I was enabled, by studying my guide at close quarters, to form an idea of the austere life led by the Religious, amongst whom I was going to try my vocation. It was enough to frighten a child; but in the person of the holy man, mortification was accompanied by so sweet a charity, that, instead of being alarmed, I was attracted and gained over. I already felt a tender and filial affection for the good Brother, with all his little cares for me, and in a childish way sought for means to spare him fatigue. We had a mule with us to carry our provisions. When I seemed rather tired of walking, the holy man used to hoist me into the saddle, having previously spread his mantle over it by way of caparison. As for himself, despite my daily entreaties, he would never avail himself of this means of resting, and made the whole journey on foot, leading the animal, and looking after it, when we halted, like an ordinary muleteer. The provisions I spoke of were for me. He did not touch them, preferring to live from day to day by questing. To remain faithful to poverty, which he practised with the most extreme rigour, he would never accept of anything I bought at the inns. It was harvest-time, and ordinarily we used to sleep in barns left open for the harvest men. The good Brother used to make my little bed of straw, and, having covered me up in his mantle, he waited with the tenderness of a mother watching over the slumbers of her infant, until I was asleep. Then only would he leave me, and, kneeling down in the opposite corner of the barn, with his arms extended in the form of a cross, or with hands joined and raised to the level of his face, passed the night in prayer. More than once I pretended to be fast asleep and to snore, and then played the spy on him, and watched him at his prayers.

"During the daytime he walked almost the whole time by himself, so as to be undisturbed in his intercourse with God. He used to sing the canticles of the Blessed Sacrament with such sweetness and devotion that I listened with delight. From time to time, fearing that I would be overcome by ennui, he came and talked to me about God and heavenly things with fervent piety. Nevertheless, sometimes I was able to wrest from him some few words on other topics. For, to tell the truth, with the curiosity of a child, I wanted an explanation of everything I saw, and I teased the holy man with my endless questions.

"We had not always the same travelling companions, and various were the characters we met with. Amongst

Ch. XII: On Catholic Soil

others, I remember a knight we travelled with one evening, who was very devout to the Blessed Virgin. As we went along he told us an interesting story about Our Lady of the Rosary, and related how this good and powerful Mother had snatched him from certain death.

" 'Once when I was upon a journey, I was surprised by a troop of brigands. It was about one o'clock at night-time. They wounded me severely with their poignards, and flung me into a ditch for dead. Then they tried to catch the mule, which carried a large sum of money in a valise attached to the saddle. But the poor beast, as though divining their malice, put himself on the defensive, and let fly with his heels at the miscreants so vigorously that no one could venture near enough to capture him. Then he galloped off at full speed, and thus saved the money. As regards myself, no sooner had I recommended myself to Our Lady of the Rosary than I found myself once more upon my feet, and without so much as a scratch!' Paschal took occasion from this story, to entertain us about Divine matters, and he spoke with such efficacy that I felt myself urged to be converted once and for all. Though only a child, the fear of God and of His judgments sank so deep into my heart that I wondered that I was not crushed by the bolts of the Divine wrath, on account of my manifold failings and the negligent and imperfect manner in which I had hitherto served Almighty God. Upon that very instant, under the impulse of this salutary emotion, I took the resolution of beginning a new life, and for that purpose of making a general confession as soon as we arrived at Valencia. I communicated my ideas to the holy man, and he thanked Our Lord effusively for the conversion of his little protégé. What put the finishing stroke to my conversion was that the holy Brother was led to speak of mental prayer, of which I had not heard so much as the name, and to teach me the method of making it. 'The entire perfection of the religious soul is found in the practice of prayer,' he frequently repeated. 'But how can one meditate with fruit, when there is wandering of the mind, and superfluity of words? Recollection and silence are required, for it is by means of these that the soul disengages itself from things exterior, and is placed in a favourable condition for seeing and hearing God.

" 'When we arrive at Granada,' he said, 'you must buy one of the spiritual works of Master Louis of Granada, of the Order of Friars Preachers.' I followed his advice, and chose the 'Sinner's Guide.' This golden book, which has contributed to the sanctification of so many souls, conferred upon me the greatest benefits, and I derived such real profit from it that since I became a priest and a director of souls I have never ceased to recommend it to beginners in the interior life. I advise them in particular to read a dozen lines of it attentively every day, for I feel sure that they will not rest satisfied with this minimum, but will certainly go beyond it. From that time forward it became my constant travelling companion, and I was never without it. The good Brother himself had to moderate my ardour. Had he allowed me my own way, I would have been poring over the book day and night.

"In that noble city of Granada a mishap occurred to us which, fortunately, had no serious consequences. We had left the Convent early one morning, and had resumed our journey, when, in one of the principal thoroughfares of the city, a mounted *alguazil* rode straight up to us, and ordered a constable who accompanied him to arrest the Brother as a vagrant. After having upbraided him, in a harsh and humiliating style, with living at his neighbour's expense, and working upon the charity of the public like a tramp, he ended up where he should have started. 'Show me your papers, you foul sluggard,' said he to the Brother. As the honour of the religious habit was at stake, Paschal, putting his thirst for mortification in the background, took from his sleeve the letter of obedience which is the monk's passport, and presented it to the *alguazil*. The latter, when he had acquainted himself with its contents, returned it to the Brother, saying: 'All right; continue your journey.' I was greatly edified by the mildness and humility of the holy man; and also marvelled at the way in which, when it would have been so easy to justify himself from the first, he did not say a single word to escape this humiliation. On how many occasions was I not witness of his imperturbable patience!

"Our journey was a veritable mission, in which the Servant of God every day cast abroad a portion of the fire of fervour and charity which consumed him. Occasions for exercising his apostolic zeal were never wanting, because the route we followed was much frequented; and oftentimes travellers, impelled by curiosity or some other motive, would join us. Thereupon the Apostle would take occasion to speak to them of the necessity of serving God, or to engage them to accept the ills of life, for love of Him, in a spirit of resignation.

"At some distance from Huescar a young man drew near us. He was in a wretched plight. His clothing was in tatters, and he held in his hand one of the sleeves of his jacket, and was using it to stanch the tears and blood, which were flowing from his face. The poor boy was also famished with hunger. Paschal, stirred with compassion, cheered him up to the best of his ability, and made him take some food with us. Then the youth told us what had happened to him. Some shepherds in the neighbourhood had maliciously set their dogs on him, and they had bitten him severely. It was a wonder that, like his jacket, he had not been torn to pieces. In the meantime a Lay Brother of the Society of Jesus, journeying on foot, like ourselves, had joined us. He was a Religious of rare virtue and modesty, and he, too, was keenly interested in the sad experiences of the young man, who, finding himself treated with such charity, unburdened himself, and related a doleful tale to the two holy Brothers. It was the story, ever ancient and ever new, of the Prodigal Son. Tired of the calm and peace of the paternal roof, he had one day taken flight in order to view the world, which to his mind's eyes appeared arrayed in the most seductive hues. Like some others of the same sort, he had burned his wings; and liberty, instead of promised sweets, had provided him with only rags and tatters, and the husks of swine. The two Religious sought to persuade him to return at once to his father. In order to encourage him to take this step, so trying to his self-love, they gave him the assurance that he would be kindly received, and that all would succeed with him, if only he acted as a dutiful and obedient son in the future, and if, after making a good confession of the disorders of his past life, he became once more a good, practical Christian. This prediction was literally fulfilled. Twenty years later, as Provincial of the Province of St. John Baptist, I again came across the Jesuit Lay Brother at Valencia. Amongst other things he told me that our Prodigal, of former times, had been to see him at his residence, and that he was clothed as a grandee of Spain, and followed by two lacqueys in livery. He belonged to one of the highest families in the kingdom, and bore an illustrious name.

"Amongst the trials endured by the holy Brother on this journey I must not forget those I caused him myself. The prolonged walking, to which I was not accustomed, sometimes put me in a bad temper, and I became melancholy and irritable. Between Caravacca and

Ch. XII: On Catholic Soil

Calasparra the heat became intolerable, and I was parched with thirst. 'Brother, I can't go any further,' I said. 'Leave me under the shadow of that pine-tree.' This doleful complaint afflicted Paschal greatly, and he at once cast about for some means to help me. The plain was empty and bare, with not a building in sight. The scorching rays of the sun beat down everywhere. 'Courage, little one,' he said confidently; 'I will try and find you some water.' He thereupon set about exploring the country in all directions, and at last found a moist spot overgrown with reeds. He gathered some of them, and made me suck the pith; and this somewhat appeased my thirst, and enabled me to proceed as far as the canal which bathes Calasparra. There he bade me sit down, and, in order that the water might not do me any harm, he made me take some food beforehand.

"Next morning, in order to escape the heat, we left Calasparra before daybreak, and we lost ourselves. After wandering about for an hour or so, we came to a canal which blocked the way. It was broad and deep, and it would have been risky to attempt to jump over it. Our only resource was a tree-trunk, crooked and difficult to manage, which we threw across the canal by way of a bridge. Not wishing to expose me to danger, Paschal ventured first across this treacherous gangway. Whether it was that he stepped without sufficient care, or that the piece of wood slipped, the result was that he lost his balance and tumbled into the water like a dead weight, carrying the bridge along with him. It all happened in the twinkling of an eye, and in such a ludicrous fashion that, without reflecting on the danger incurred by the poor Brother, I burst into roars of laughter as I saw him floundering about like a spaniel thrown into the water for the first time. Weighed down with his tight-fitting and heavy habit, it was only with great difficulty that the holy man succeeded in reaching the bank. When he emerged from his involuntary bath, instead of being angry with me, his only reproach was to smile and to remain silent. This generous forgiveness made me understand better than the sharpest reprimand would have done the levity and unseemliness of my behaviour. As we had left the mule in the village, we both went on foot along the road between the Convent of St. Anne and Mount Jumilla. The Brother, seeing that I was tired, said: 'Come along, now—cheer up; I'm going to carry you to the Convent on my back.' But I would not agree to this, and only allowed him to carry my satchel. When we arrived in sight of the Friary we saw a Religious working in the garden. Paschal said to me: 'There is the Guardian of the Convent, and one of our best preachers. In our Reform, in order to preserve humility and poverty more securely, all without distinction, Fathers and Brothers, Superiors and subjects, have to employ themselves, at certain times, in manual labour.' I was much impressed by what I saw.

"Many years after this journey, when I had become a Priest and Lector of Theology, I was sent to Villareal to preach the Lent there. The Convent of Xativa, where the holy man was then staying, was on the way. I made a halt there, in order to see one whom I regarded as a father. The holy man could not conceal the joy he felt on account of this meeting, and treated me as his child of predilection. He was at that time much troubled by the fever which infects that unhealthy spot. Without letting him know, I begged the Provincial to allow him to accompany me in quality of Brother companion during the course of my Lenten station, and the Provincial consented to it, with a good grace. Paschal seemed pleased with this providential arrangement which took him back again to a Convent of Our Lady. Perhaps also it may have been revealed to him that it was there that he was to finish his earthly pilgrimage, and that it was from that hallowed spot that he was soon to take flight heavenwards. On account of his great weakness, he was offered a mount. He refused it, however, although he was well aware that the Rule of St. Francis allows this indulgence to the sick. So we performed our journey on foot.

"As we were on the point of commencing the steep ascent of Enoma, we came across a Religious belonging to another Order, who was about to climb the mountain like ourselves. He was burdened with a heavy wallet. The ever-charitable Paschal took hold of it and lifted it on to his shoulders. But he had reckoned without his host. I, in my turn, without asking his leave, took it away from him, and he had to content himself with carrying the weighty mantle of the Religious stranger. Even that was too much for one in his enfeebled condition.

"Upon leaving Alzira we were obliged to take a road which was very miry and much cut up. A poor mule was stuck so fast in the mud that, in spite of desperate efforts and vigorous applications of the master's whip, he could not extricate himself. The muleteer was loudly lamenting, because the night was coming on, and would soon render any further efforts unavailing. Paschal was made in such a way that he could never see anyone in distress without trying to assist him. In fact, he could not help doing so. So now he had to set to work. Not satisfied with merely giving the muleteer a word of encouragement, he tucked up his habit, and, wading knee deep into the mire, made straight for the mule, dragged him out of the bog, and led him to his master, who was scarcely able to express his gratitude. To one service he added another—that of helping to load the beast. Thus it was that each of the journeys I made in the Saint's company ended with an act of charity.

They left in my memory ineffaceable recollections."[1]

Besides these official missions, undertaken for the general good of the Order, and that of the Province of St. John Baptist in particular, obedience provided other occasions for our traveller to diffuse far and wide the good odour of Christ Jesus, and at the same time to serve the particular interests of his Convent. These occasions recurred periodically every year, and almost down to the time of our Saint's death.

At the season of the harvest, of the vintage, and of the ingathering of olives, or the time for sheep-shearing, there might be seen, emerging from their Convent, like a swarm of bees issuing from their hive, a certain number of Friars, who, in accordance with Franciscan usage, went about the country in order to obtain a stock of wheat, oil, raisins, and also wool for habits and blankets, by means of questing. As these different kinds of produce were seldom found in one and the same locality, and as they were gathered in at different seasons of the year, almost as many expeditions were required as things to be quested. One can easily understand that the Superiors did not lightly make choice of those who were commissioned to explore the country, wallet on back, for they took with them the honour and reputation of their Religious family, and such goods are not to be entrusted to the first comer. The Questor-in-Chief, to whom pertains the responsibility of conducting operations, is always a Friar of mature age and tried virtue, and furthermore endowed with qualities to make him agreeable to the people, and of a sort to edify them. Two or three lieutenants accompany him, with sacks and cans, to carry the produce of their quest.

Ever since the foundation of the Order, nearly all our

---

[1] MSS. of the Process. Deposition of Father John Ximenes.

Brothers who were conspicuous for holiness have exercised this humble charge, and have exalted it in the eyes of the world by the edifying manner in which they have fulfilled it. Paschal carried on in glorious fashion this time-honoured tradition of the Order, and in his turn took his station in the ranks of these venerable patriarchs. As soon as the people had caught a glimpse of him, they instinctively recognized in him the finished type of the Franciscan Questor. One had almost to repent of sending him to these good people, for wherever he went once, they didn't want anyone else, except Brother Paschal. When he arrived, there was high festival in the village, and even before he appeared, his expected coming was the chief topic of conversation in the evenings. No wonder, for it is not every day that one sees a Saint fit to be canonized during his lifetime.

He had hard work to conceal his prodigious austerities. It was soon seen that after the most exhausting fatigues during the daytime, the holy man passed his nights in adoration before the Blessed Sacrament, and that the whole of his fare consisted of a little bread and cheese. But what struck the simple folk most of all was the way in which this perpetual faster had a smile for everyone, and kept all his penances and his austerities to himself. And then he used to speak with such discernment about spiritual matters. Who could refuse to give his small portion of alms? The question was, rather, who should have the good fortune to be the first to give to him? They reckoned, and reckoned justly, that they were making a good bargain in purchasing at such a low price—at the cost of a few handfuls of figs or olives—the prayers of this holy man and his advocacy with God. In fact, the benefactors were often put under an obligation, and received more than they gave. "I often went with him on quest," says one of his confrères. "Little by little I perceived that the most salutary effects were produced amongst those who received his visits. They seemed different from other secular people, and one could distinguish them amongst a thousand on account of their earnest, Christian lives, their more assiduous frequentation of the Sacraments, and the practice of all good works."[2]

The companions of the saintly Brother knew how to appreciate the grace of living in the company of so holy a man, and of acting under his orders. They could not have had a more experienced chief, or one better capable of forming in them the virtues proper to their employment. "He taught me how to present myself at the door of our benefactors," says one of them. "When you have rapped discreetly, say in a low tone of voice: '*Loada sea nuestro Señor Jesu-Cristo*' (Praised be Our Lord Jesus Christ). Then: '*Paz haya en esta casa*' (Peace be to this house). 'For the love of God, give something to the Friars of the Convent of Our Lady of the Rosary.' This was the way he set about it himself. His first visit, on arriving at any place, was always to the Blessed Sacrament. After a long time spent in adoration before the tabernacle, the small caravan repaired to the Presbytery. The holy man, who had the most profound veneration for every priest, prostrated himself on both his knees before the parish priest or his curate, and after respectfully kissing his hand, asked his blessing and permission to quest in the parish. Under no consideration would he have thought of questing without this authorization."[3] In reading these details, do we not seem to have under our eyes that passage of the Testament of St. Francis: "The Lord gave me, and gives me still, such faith

---

[2] MSS. of the Process.

[3] Ibid.

in priests who live according to the rule of the Holy Roman Church on account of their Orders, that if they persecuted me I would have recourse to them again. ... And these and all others I will reverence, love, and honour as my masters, and I will consider no sin in them, because I see in them the Son of God, and they are my masters. And this I do because in this world I see nothing corporally of the most High Son of God, but His most Holy Body and His most Holy Blood, which they consecrate and receive, and which they alone administer to others."[4] Paschal took great delight in conversing with learned and zealous priests upon Divine matters.

"When we made a halt upon the road, the holy man always began by making us recite prayers to the most Blessed Sacrament, and at these times we invariably turned in the direction of some church or shrine."

For transporting what had been collected from one place to another, the questors generally made use of an ass or a mule. Paschal, however, until the total collapse of his strength, was always desirous of taking the place of the beast of burden, and of carrying the produce of the quest upon his own shoulders. One day some passers-by, seeing him coming along, almost bent double under the weight of two enormous oil-cans, asked him why he didn't employ a mule, like the others. "So," said he, smiling, "then you think I am not as good as a mule?"

On returning from these arduous quests, carrying a still larger stock of merits than of provisions, Paschal, deeming himself the most useless and unfaithful of servants, used to go and cast himself in tears at the feet of the Guardian, and, asking pardon for the faults committed during his absence, offered to perform the most severe penance to

---

[4] Testament of St. Francis.

atone for them. He remained thus prostrated until the Superior allowed him to rise. Such was the regular termination of these expeditions, which seemed as though arranged by God Himself for the purpose of discovering to the world some of the treasures hidden in this beautiful soul.

PASCHAL FOUND IN THE VILLAGE CHURCH.

PASCHAL INVOKING OUR LADY OF THE SIERRA.
From a Carving.

PASCHAL AND JOHN APPARICIO.

PASCHAL MIRACULOUSLY INVESTED WITH THE FRANCISCAN HABIT.

THE VISION OF THE HOST.

THE FRIARY OF ELCHE.

PASCHAL AND THE CHILDREN.

PASCHAL MEETS A HUGUENOT LANCER.

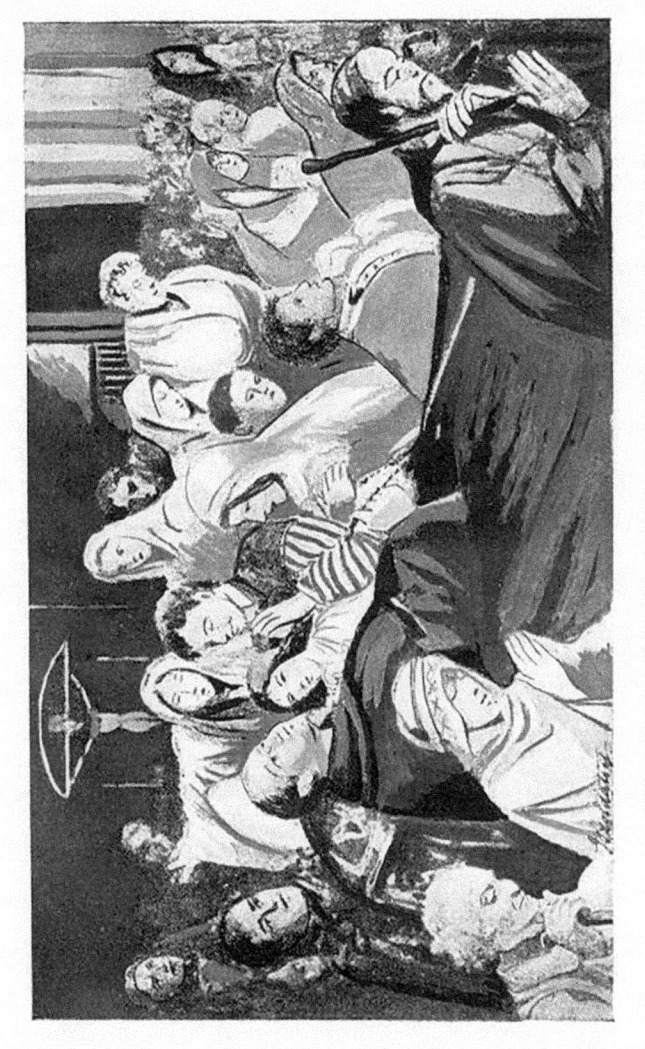

SAINT PASCHAL OPENS HIS EYES TO ADORE THE BLESSED SACRAMENT.

CANONIZATION OF SAINT PASCHAL AND FOUR OTHER SAINTS.

CHAPTER XIII
THE SCHOOL OF THE HOLY SPIRIT

IF the biography of the eminent Servants of God is invested with an exquisite charm and an absorbing interest, on account of the heroic virtues which form the warp and the woof of their lives of sanctity, the beauty and attractiveness of the story of their earthly career is greatly enhanced, when it has pleased the Father of lights to adorn their lives with miraculous gifts and favours. The marvellous, which exercises so subtle a spell over the heart and imagination of mankind, meets us on every page of our Saint's history. Almighty God showed Himself prodigal in His favours towards Blessed Paschal, and lavishly endowed him with gifts reserved for His most faithful servants. In particular, he possessed *infused science* and *the spirit of prophecy*. They were the wonder and admiration of his contemporaries, and would in themselves suffice to account for the stir made by the holy Brother.

The knowledge Paschal had acquired by study did not extend beyond the rudiments of reading and writing. And yet to this unlettered man, as to the wisest of masters, there came Bachelors, Licentiates, and Doctors. After they had asked him questions, and received his replies and his solutions, they departed in a state of amazement, declaring loudly that such light could only be derived from a supernatural source.

And, indeed, it was from God that it came directly; it was He Who, finding the soul of this simple man clear and pure as crystal, deigned to pour into it the treasures of a kind of science not contained in books, nor to be learned upon the forms of a school, and called, on that account, *infused science.* It is thus that God confounds the proud wisdom of the pretended sages of this world—"*Sapientiam Sapientium*"—and causes it to be seen how, without the aid of study and without even an effort, the human intellect can be illuminated, and carried by Him to the loftiest pinnacles of Divine knowledge.

"I am going to relate what I know from personal experience concerning the infused science of Blessed Paschal," says Father John Ximenes in his Life of the Saint. "Although the holy man did not make use of theological terms and formulas, in vogue in the schools, and replied to my questions in the vulgar idiom of Aragon, he spoke to me readily of things, which the greatest theologians only acquire by degrees, with the help of a host of metaphysical arguments. So great was the facility and so perfect the clearness of his language, that it was easy to perceive that his intellect, aided by Divine light, had penetrated to the very heart of the matter, and that he had an intuitive knowledge on the subject. I must acknowledge that on more than one occasion I tried to land him in difficulties, and to make him contradict himself. One day, in order to bewilder him, I opposed some very subtle scholastic arguments to what he had just been saying to me. He was not, however, at all confused by them, but took these arguments one by one, in the order in which they had been given, and he drew from the principles I had formulated their logical conclusions, which were opposed to sound doctrine and opened the door to error. His arguments were irrefutable. It was I who found myself in difficulties and driven to self-contradiction. This unexpected issue did not fail to abash me somewhat. It was certainly humiliating that a Lector of Philosophy and of Theology, Bachelor and Doctor of Salamanca, like myself, should be nonplussed and caught in doctrinal inaccuracy by a poor Brother, who

Ch. XIII: The School of the Holy Spirit

was a complete stranger to scientific study. I derived, however, advantage from this humiliation; for it made me see that if I was the teacher of others, I could scarcely even lay claim to the title of the disciple of this master enlightened by God."

Father Emmanuel Rodriguez, one of the ablest theologians of this epoch, abounding in learned men, wished to ascertain for himself the truth of the rumours he had heard on this subject. Once when he was on a journey he stopped at the Convent of Elche; and with the sanction of the Provincial, the Brother was summoned at his request into the Guardian's cell. It was arranged that the conversation should be led imperceptibly upon some spiritual topic, so as to give the holy man an opportunity of expressing his opinion. "Paschal came unsuspectingly to the rendezvous, and, as though incidentally, I began to discourse about certain mystical states of prayer; and asked him what his ideas were upon the subject. His answers were so exact and so much to the point, that I was encouraged to proceed further. So, entering into the region of the most incomprehensible mysteries of theology, I challenged the Brother, by my questions, to mount these heights in my company. He followed me like a man treading on well-known ground. In fact, all its features were familiar to him. To the most intricate questions he replied in his simple way, without hesitation, and with the utmost clearness. When I tried to catch him with objections, he escaped from the snare without difficulty, asserting on each point the true Catholic doctrine."

Like an examiner, who has before him some brilliant scholar, Father Emmanuel Rodriguez took a delight in protracting this trial; and thus he led the holy man from one branch of theology to another, in order to ascertain the extent of his knowledge. When the tournament was brought to an end (it had lasted several hours), Father Emmanuel, almost exhausted, whispered into the ear of the Provincial: "It is astounding. This Brother undoubtedly has infused science. If you wanted to make him a Priest one of these days, he might be sent to preach the Gospel to the people without having study; for my part, if I were a Prelate, I would have no hesitation about ordaining him, so certain am I that the Holy Spirit speaks by his lips."

What the Man of God would have been as a preacher the Religious of the Convent of Jumilla had an opportunity of judging one Christmas Day, when, in order to try his obedience, the Guardian ordered him to speak on Our Lord's Nativity to the Community assembled in choir. "I was present at this extempore sermon, and I declare that I never heard anything like it," says the Syndic of the Convent in his deposition. "Bearing in mind that he had been a shepherd in the days of his youth, the orator, with happy and touching inspiration, glided in amongst the shepherds of Bethlehem, and, as though he had been a witness of the drama of the crib, he related it all with such charm and such piety that we all melted into tears. In a series of living pictures we saw each successive scene pass before our eyes: the Angels coming down from Heaven to announce the tidings of salvation; Mary watching by the Infant Jesus, and holding Him at her breast; the shepherds approaching in their turn and taking Him into their arms, after they had adored Him as their God. He placed before us upon each of these points of the mystery certain elevating reflections, all founded on the authority of Holy Scripture and the doctrine of the Fathers. Each time he pronounced the sweet Names of Jesus and Mary he did so with such lively tenderness and so much reverence, that it was plain these names were graven on his heart. Amongst the audience were three of the best preachers of the

Province. They could scarcely believe their ears, and asked themselves whether it was all a dream or reality. We were firmly convinced that he had been inspired by God."[1]

The Servant of God had a very exalted idea of preaching, and, faithful to the exhortation of his Father, Francis, "he honoured and revered all theologians as those who minister spirit and life." When he heard the bell which announced the sermon, he was overjoyed, and thought himself bound to pray both for the preacher and for his audience. The importance attaching to the ministry of preaching led the holy man to follow, with the interest of a father, the training and the first efforts of the newly ordained Religious in sacred oratory. In particular, he sought to put them on their guard against anything calculated to transform the word of God into a merely human word. "Father," he said boldly to one of these budding orators, who was wholly intent on the effect he was going to produce, "Father, you preach yourself, instead of preaching Jesus Christ." And to another who, whilst neglecting prayer, employed all other means of attaining success: "Everything is not in books, my Brother. Believe me, the spirit of prayer and devotion will ever remain the great means of arriving at true eloquence and of making a sermon fruitful." Often, too, for the greater glory of God and the salvation of souls, he allowed himself to give counsel to the preachers of his Order, as to the choice of certain subjects. He always did so with the greatest delicacy and humility, and without in the least degree seeming to dictate to them. "Several times," relates Father Herrera, "he asked me if I would be so good as to speak on such or such a subject, already treated of with ability by certain authors, whose names he mentioned. 'Most

---

[1] MSS. of the Process. Deposition of the Syndic.

willingly,' I used to reply invariably, 'but on condition that you provide me yourself with the plan of the discourse.' He would then trace the outline with perfect facility and in such good order that I think the best of my sermons were those composed in this way."[2]

The points, on which the infused science of the Servant of God shone with most resplendent lustre, were the institution of the Blessed Sacrament and the Life of our Saviour. He spoke as though he had been present at the Last Supper, and as if he had followed the footsteps of the Divine Master, in company with the Apostles. The way, in which he used to go into details, gave reason to suppose that he saw the scenes of the Gospel enacted before his eyes. The Bible, for our Saint, was an open Book. He penetrated the meaning of the most obscure passages, and expounded the different senses with the skill of the most brilliant professor of hermeneutics. Hence it was that, before the walls of Orleans, all the Biblical apparatus of the Huguenots was shattered, by the luminous and irrefutable exegesis of this Commentator, trained in the school of the Holy Spirit.

Amongst the witnesses of these miracles of infused knowledge, we may quote Doctor Benet, who was the doctor at Villareal. "God had communicated to His Servant in prayer a wonderful knowledge of Theology and Holy Scripture," he says. "On several occasions I was privileged to attend the theological conferences of the preachers and lectors of Villareal. We all marvelled at the extraordinary facility with which this humble Friar solved difficulties and objections, quoting St. Augustine, St. Ambrose, St. Thomas Aquinas, Duns Scotus, and other Doctors with much propriety, and as though he had been doing nothing else

---

[2] MSS. of the Process. Deposition of Father Herrera.

all his life than study their works. One day I conversed with him on the subject of the glory of Paradise and the beatitude of the elect. He threw so much light upon this subject, and he spoke with such fervour, that it seemed to me as though he were already in possession of eternal bliss."

After this need we be surprised at Doctor Benet's reply to the ecclesiastical judge, when, in the course of the Process of Beatification, he was asked whether he had any relations with the Convent of the Holy Rosary? "For several years I used frequently to visit that holy house and its inmates, chiefly for three reasons. The first arose from my calling as a physician, which often brought me to the Convent; the second was the affection I have always borne the Religious of that Friary; and the third was my profound veneration for Brother Paschal, whom I regarded as a Saint, and to whom I went as often as possible to seek light, strength, and consolation, and these I ever derived from my intercourse with him."[3]

Not only did the Servant of God speak in so entrancing a fashion of things mystical and divine, but he also wrote with equal felicity upon these sublime topics. He composed, for his private use and for his own consolation, several works upon the mysteries of faith and the most abstruse questions of theology. One of these treatises came under the notice of the Ven. Don Juan de Ribera, Archbishop of Valencia and Patriarch of Antioch, one of the holiest personages of his time. When he had perused it attentively he inquired who had written such admirable matter. They introduced the holy Brother to him, and between them there sprang up a friendship, which was a source of great joy and consolation to the estimable

---

[3] MSS. of the Process, Deposition of Doctor Benet.

Prelate. The impassioned devotion of each towards the Holy Eucharist was a bond of sympathy between them. Like his saintly friend, the Ven. Ribera seemed to live only to adore and glorify the Sacrament of the Altar. Erasing from his shield the coat-of-arms of his illustrious family, he replaced it by the emblem of a monstrance issuing from a fiery furnace, surrounded with this device: "*Tibi post haec, fili, ultra quid faciam?*"(After this, my son, what more can I do for thee?) At the head of all his episcopal acts, and in the beginning of his letters, there was always inscribed the salutation of the Blessed Sacrament; and in order that its loved praises should never cease to resound in his ears, he made it a rule that all who approached him, whether friends or strangers, should say as they entered: "Praised and blessed be the most holy Sacrament of the Altar." To his two most important foundations he gave the significant titles of "Corpus Christi College" and "Convent of the Precious Blood."

When Paschal had passed to his reward, the Archbishop urgently requested some relic of him. After kissing it with the most profound respect, he placed it upon his head, and then, turning towards Father John Ximenes, who had brought it, said to him: "Father Provincial, what can we do with all our learning? The little and the simple snatch Heaven from us. We might as well throw our books into the fire!" "Not quite so fast, your Grace," replied the Provincial, with a smile. "No, no, believe me, we have no need to burn our books—the poor innocents. It is not they who are the culprits; but it is our own pride. It is that that we should take and cast away resolutely."

When the Archbishop had heard from Father Ximenes the account of the numerous miracles, wrought by his saintly friend, he heaved a sigh and said to the Provincial:

"How deeply I regret that he didn't die in my diocese. Then I would have had the happiness of busying myself about his canonization."

To this gift of science which Paschal seems to have received in its plenitude, was conjoined that of reading the secrets of hearts, together with a wonderful insight into the state of particular souls in Purgatory, and the means of assisting them. We will quote one instance. When the Servant of God was porter at Almansa, he caused a benefactress to have a certain number of Masses celebrated, for the repose of the soul of a brother she had just lost. Some time after, in a conversation with one of her nieces, she praised Paschal very highly: "Now, mind well what I'm going to tell you," she said to her. "This Brother is a great servant of God, and no one knows better than I do what a high degree of perfection he has attained. His death will be the death of a Saint, and you will see that God will glorify him without delay, with many miracles." The niece took in every word of this, and she reflected that there would be no difficulty in discovering whether her parents, lately deceased, were in Purgatory and needed her help. A few days later the aunt, who had been charged with the commission of questioning Brother Paschal on the subject, brought his reply. One of the departed souls already enjoyed the beatific vision, and for the deliverance of the other it was required by Almighty God that thirty Masses should be celebrated without delay, and certain prayers recited. When both the Masses and the prayers had been said, the aunt returned for another consultation. "You can rest satisfied now," said the holy man. "Nothing more need be done on behalf of that soul. What has already been performed is so agreeable to God, that it has been sufficient for the discharge of the remainder of the debt."

The *Gift* of *Prophecy* and frequent *Ecstasies* put the

finishing touch to Paschal's halo of sanctity. The predictions, already related in the course of the story of Paschal's life, enable us to pass rapidly over this point. It will be sufficient to give one final example, especially designed, it would seem, to show in what a degree our Saint was favoured with this wonderful gift. The faithful who frequent our Convents, come to regard themselves to a certain extent as forming part and parcel of the family, and under this aspect, they take a fraternal interest in what concerns the life and changes of the Community. It has been thus in every age. Elizabeth Xea was a typical example of one of these good souls; devoted to the Convent and interested in everything which would contribute to its welfare. Now amongst the Religious of Villareal there was a certain Father Pedro Cabrillas, whom she highly esteemed, on account of his eloquence and the abundant spiritual fruit produced by his preaching. He fell ill and the issue of his malady hung in the balance. Poor Elizabeth was greatly distressed. She made novena after novena for the speedy recovery of her favourite preacher. It seemed inconceivable that God would take so early from His vineyard, a labourer of such worth and utility. In her anguish she opened her mind to Brother Paschal. "Ah," said the holy man sorrowfully, "poor Father Pedro! his career is over, he will never preach again." "How do you know?" asked Elizabeth with warmth. We are now going to relate what he did know. Some days previously the invalid himself had entreated the holy man to pray for his restoration to health. To this the holy man replied: "I will do so willingly; but what use will it be?" This somewhat enigmatic answer left Father Pedro in a state of much perplexity. Not venturing himself to ask the meaning of it, he sent Father Didacus Castellon to the holy man. Paschal was reticent, and replied to his interlocutor: "How should

I know about such things?" The patient, becoming more and more uneasy, had recourse to strong measures, and begged the Guardian to command Brother Paschal to say definitely what God had revealed to him, concerning the issue of this malady. The Brother was trapped. Confronted with this formal precept, he bowed his head and sighed deeply. Then, his face all aglow, and, as it were, under the spur of vehement internal emotion, he turned towards the sick man and said: "Brother Preacher, the will of God is that you should soon quit this earth. It is no longer by words, but by example, that you will have to preach, during the few months you have yet to live. Patience, then. Recommend yourself to God." He pronounced these words in a grave tone of voice, and with such sadness, that no one present had a moment's doubt of what would happen. As a matter of fact, Father Pedro lived only four months longer.

On another occasion Elizabeth Xea went to consult Brother Paschal. This time her trouble was of a different kind. It was the eve of the Provincial Chapter, and she was anxious to know if there would be any changes in the staff of the Community, for such she greatly dreaded. "Who are we going to have for Provincial, Brother?" "Father John Ximenes," he said, without hesitation. At that same moment the Capitulars, assembled in the Convent of Valencia, were placing this worthy Religious at the head of the Province of St. John Baptist. "Four days before the holding of this Chapter," relates Father John Ximenes, "Father Didacus Castellon, Guardian of Villareal, the residence of the holy man, came to find me in my cell and to congratulate me on my approaching elevation to the Provincialate. I was at that time not yet thirty-two years of age and the youngest member of the Chapter. 'Now, then, none of your jokes,' said I. 'I am not joking,' he said. 'If

Brother Paschal is a prophet, and he is one in reality, you will be Provincial and I shall be a Definitor. This is how I learned it. When I was starting from Villareal, to come to the Chapter, I begged Brother Paschal not to forget his Guardian in his prayers on this important occasion. "I will do as you wish," he said, and then, making me a profound bow, he added: "Safe journey, Very Reverend Father Definitor. I announce to you that we shall have as our Provincial Father John Ximenes." ' Father Didacus Castellon, who dreaded above all things the office of Novice-Master, took care not to tell me that when the holy man had informed him that he would be Definitor, he had also said to him: 'And further, you will be Master of the Novices.' It was unprecedented in our Province, that the functions of Definitor and Master of the Novices should be conjoined in the same individual. In spite of his reticence, however, Father Didacus was invested by the Chapter with these two important offices, and everything happened as Paschal had predicted."[4]

But let us now return to the good Elizabeth Xea and her preoccupations about the Chapter, in which, to her great regret, she had not an active voice. No one is perfect here below. Devout as she was, Elizabeth had her likes, and her little dislikes as well. She began communing with herself in this fashion: "If they take away our Guardian, whose return is desired by everyone, and give us instead Father X., who never has anything to say to me—well! I'll never set foot in the Convent again, and I won't give any more alms to the Brother when he comes questing. I've had quite enough of these continual changes, which remove our Confessors and Directors, and oblige us to go to every new-comer." What was her astonishment when,

---

[4] Deposition of Father John Ximenes.

Ch. XIII: The School of the Holy Spirit 169

the following day, Brother Paschal came and without further preamble said to her: "Sister, even though it *should* happen, do not leave off doing to our Friary in the future all the good you have done in the past." So saying, he departed. Seeing herself found out, Elizabeth was abashed, and, without delay, retracted her bad resolution, promising to give her alms to the Friars of Our Lady of the Rosary, as usual, even if Father X. became Guardian.[5]

---

[5] MSS. of the Process. Deposition of Elizabeth Xea.

CHAPTER XIV
THE SAFEGUARD OF DIVINE TREASURES

WONDERFUL as are the miraculous favours which adorn the lives of the Servants of God, these do not, in themselves, constitute holiness, nor are they so much as linked with it by an indissoluble bond. Hence, from the fact that they occur in the life of any human being, it cannot be inferred with infallible certainty that that person is a Saint. Let us hasten to add, however, that there is drawn from the presence of these celestial gifts, a presumption of great weight, and a sign that is rarely misleading. For although there are not wanting some who were, for a time, endowed with the spirit of prophecy, or with infused science, and yet who figure not on the catalogue of the Saints, it still remains true, that Almighty God does not ordinarily lavish such exceptional favours on any, save the most perfect of His children. On account of their very sublimity, these choice graces require delicate manipulation, and suppose in their recipient rare and precious qualities, otherwise they are calculated to turn to his detriment. Here, as elsewhere, there is the possibility of abuse, and nowhere is abuse so disastrous. Who does not know with what deplorable facility a man is puffed up and intoxicated by the perception of his own excellence, and how difficult it is for one, endowed with these precious gifts, not to feel the temptation to make them minister to his own pride and vanity? Lest, therefore, these favours should become a snare and a stumbling-block, it is imperatively necessary

Ch. XIV: The Safeguard of Divine Treasures 171

that they be placed under some sure safeguard. Nowhere can a more faithful guardian be found for these Divine treasures than Humility. Humility alone has the power of preserving from dizziness those whom God has raised to these exalted honours. So it was into her hands that Paschal entrusted the wonderful talents with which God had enriched him. He laid no other foundation for the edifice of his spiritual perfection than that of humility; and as he aspired to raise this edifice to more than ordinary proportions, so he was careful to follow the counsel of St. Leo, and to dig these foundations as deep as possible. Although we have already brought forward numerous testimonials to Paschal's spirit of self-abasement, we shall now add certain others; since there will be no excess in speaking more at length of that virtue, which is the final test and ultimate guarantee of genuine holiness.

We have already heard from the lips of Paschal what he thought about himself; and have also seen how on many occasions he proclaimed himself the least of men, and the very scum of the earth. It now remains for us to examine the worth of these declarations. Sometimes one happens to meet people who say in tones penetrated with devotion: "I am nothing, and I am good for nothing." To these ambiguous Saints one is inclined to respond with a certain great Bishop of our own days: "Pray complete your programme of humility, and in order to assure its truthfulness, add to it, by way of appendix: 'And I believe nothing of the sort.' " And indeed these professors of make-believe humility are far from believing anything of the kind. If they are only taken at their word and treated as nonentities, they are not slow to show their resentment, and to demand what you take them for.

It was quite otherwise with our holy Brother. One of his chief anxieties was to make others share in the base opinion he had of himself, and great was his chagrin to meet so many who were incredulous on this point, and to find that instead of the contempt he sought, they bestowed upon him marks of respect and of the highest veneration. It was a far greater trial than the insults and ill-treatment which on several occasions were liberally showered on him. These latter were a treat for him. "Whatever calumnies or injuries you may have to endure, no matter how outrageous they may be, you will drink them in, like so much delicious liqueur, and accept them with a heart bounding for joy," he writes in his Rule of Life.

Let us now enumerate a few of the chief occasions wherein the blessed man had occasion to practise what he had written down. One day he inadvertently came upon some secular persons, who were in the act of committing a grave fault; and in these circumstances he deemed it his duty to give them a fraternal admonition. He did so with so much charity and discretion that it could be plainly seen that the honour of God and the welfare of his neighbour alone impelled him to speak. The guilty parties, however, did net regard it in this light. Humiliated at being caught *in flagrante delicto*, and yet more incensed at being rebuked by a mere Brother, they flew into a passion and grossly insulted him: "Just look at that hypocrite, who pretends to keep his eyes down and then steals round the corner to spy on others! Is it right that a fellow like that should be allowed to read us lessons, as though everybody didn't know that he'd been brought up at sheep's tails—the vulgar clown!" And they went on in the same strain. Brother Paschal had fallen on his knees in the meantime, and with hands joined was entreating these revilers to forgive his boldness, and the coarseness which still remained from his early occupation of tending sheep. The guilty parties had not been expecting an answer like this, and were taken aback by it. They went away, without another word, hanging their heads in shame.

Amongst the different Superiors of the holy man, there was one whose temper sometimes carried him to an excessive severity. He was possessed of a perfect horror for whatever was out of the common, and everything he noticed in Brother Paschal, the Porter, provoked and irritated him. So fault-findings rained down in plenty upon the poor Brother. The least little mistake became a pretext for breaking out into virulent reproaches. One day at Valencia, when the whole Community were present in the refectory, the accusations that were made, were so severe and so humiliating, that the Religious who were present, scarcely knew which way to look. "The patience of all was hard pushed," here remarks Father John Ximenes, "whilst that of Paschal was put to a fiery ordeal." On his knees and with bowed head Paschal listened to these mortifying remarks, with greater eagerness than if they had been his panegyric. The Guardian, emphasizing every word, added by way of peroration: "I really don't know what is going to become of you, my poor Paschal. Your self-confidence is simply boundless. And all because you fondly imagine yourself to possess a treasure. Alas! it is only too greatly to be feared that this fancied treasure is only a piece of lead or a lump of clay." Rising respectfully, Paschal then went to kiss the Superior's feet and to thank him. Just at that moment the door-bell rang, and the Porter left the refectory to answer the call. He remained absent for more than ten minutes. Brother John of Ile noticed this, and fancying that the holy man had stayed away, in order to allow his feelings to become composed, took him to one side and said in a tone of affectionate compassion: "Patience, Brother Paschal, patience!" "Why ever do you say that?" replied the holy man in astonishment. "On account of that awful scolding, which has upset all of us." "Oh, is that all? Then don't let that trouble you, Brother," returned the holy man with great joy. "Rest assured that the Holy Spirit spoke by the mouth of our Guardian today."

On another occasion he roused the ire of this same Guardian, and called forth one of his severest reprimands, on account of a very trivial fault. He had accidentally broken a bottle half full of oil, and in accordance with custom had suspended round his neck a fragment of the vessel, in order that his negligence might be known to all. Whilst decorated with this trophy, he was encountered by the Superior. "Ah, I've caught you again, have I, you careless, wasteful creature?" he exclaimed, making for Paschal as though he were going to devour him. "Get out of my sight, and don't let me see you again!" After this scene, one of the Brothers thought that it was incumbent upon him to apply a little balm to the wound, that he felt sure Paschal must be smarting under. "It's really too much of a good thing," he said to Paschal. "What proportion is there between a mere trifle like that and such a tirade?" "What is that you are saying, Brother?" replied the Man of God. "Beware of talking like that. You must understand that I took those words, as though uttered by the Spirit of God." It was thus, in fine, that he was in the habit of acting whenever he had to endure anything from creatures. He regarded them as so many instruments of the Divine Justice, intended to punish him on account of his demerits and his monstrous ingratitude. In the same spirit of humility, he used to strive to hide whatever might redound to his own advantage.

The Friars of the Province, in spite of his desperate resistance, placed him, on one occasion, over one of their Convents as President, although he was not a priest. This

Ch. XIV: The Safeguard of Divine Treasures

Superiorship put him on the rack and was a real martyrdom to him. To be the first and to command others, when everything led him to seek the lowest place and to obey the youngest of the Friars—he could never grow used to such an idea! He contrived, therefore, to conceal his dignity in everything. If there had not been grave reasons to the contrary, he would have gladly dispensed his subjects from receiving the blessing, which it is customary for the Superior to impart to those who are leaving or returning to the Convent. He had an objection to it, because it seemed to make him too conspicuous, but as it could not be altogether omitted, he compromised matters by hiding behind the door, when giving the blessing. As a counterpoise to his Superiorship, he decided to retain his office of Porter.

The holy man once happened to meet, when on a journey, a certain Friar who was, at one and the same time, an eminent artist and a Religious most proficient in virtue. This was Ven. Nicholas Factor. Although they had never before met, they at once recognized each other, and fell into each other's arms. It was a meeting to remind one of that of Dominic and Francis, and of what is related in the *Fioretti* about the conversation of Brother Giles with St. Louis, King of France. They discoursed for a long time of the subjects, which filled their hearts to overflowing; namely, of God, of the salvation of souls, and of eternal happiness. The conversation was interrupted by Ven. Nicholas Factor, who, as though suddenly recalling some fact in the past, said abruptly to Paschal: "Brother, do you remember the Night of the Star? What great and delightful favours you then received from God." The blessed man became agitated, well knowing what his companion alluded to. He would never have breathed a word about this incident, and like so many other events worthy of being recorded, it would have passed into oblivion, had not a providential occurrence obliged him, with all his humility, to reveal it, and bring it to the light of day.

Father Nicholas Factor had gone to Heaven. His death, precious in the eyes of the Lord, had been signalized by so many brilliant miracles, that the Superiors, without delay, ordered that all the known facts of his life should be collected, from the various Convents of the Province, with a view to introducing the Process of Beatification. For this purpose, a precept of obedience was imposed upon each Religious, binding him to declare on oath all that he knew, directly or indirectly, bearing upon the life and heroic virtues of the deceased Friar. Paschal was consequently obliged to appear, in his turn, like the rest. His testimony was of the greatest moment; for it was that of a friend and of a Saint. One can imagine the eagerness, with which the holy man would have acquitted himself of this pious obligation, if only there had been some way to avoid introducing himself upon the scene; but that appeared to be impossible.

In the memorable occurrences of the Night of the Star, he had his own clearly marked place; and since it was now a case of relating all he knew, without curtailing anything, it seemed to be necessary, for that purpose, to claim for himself the halo of sanctity. There was one solid fact, however, and that was the precept of obedience, which urged and constrained him to tell everything. So, with his soul a prey to anguish, and his brow suffused with blushes, the humble Friar related how, on that memorable night, Brother Nicholas Factor had received revelations from God, whilst gazing upon a marvellously bright and beautiful star; and how Our Lord had also shown him a certain Brother called Paschal, in another Convent of the same Order, who was enjoying the same vision and was

Ch. XIV: The Safeguard of Divine Treasures

receiving, from on high, the most signal favours. Of what nature these favours were, Paschal did not say, and the Superiors, seeing how greatly he was distressed, respected his secret, and did not push their inquiries any further. These extraordinary graces, therefore, remain a secret between God and His servant.

In one of his attacks of illness, the holy man besought the Guardian to commit to the flames, after his death, all that he had written, under the impulse of the Holy Spirit, upon the Incarnation, the Angels, the Divine Attributes, and other theological matters. He thus wished to destroy the last vestige of his own science, which he perceived might be turned to his honour. Upon his restoration to health, nevertheless, he continued, as heretofore, to note down, every day, what struck him most, either in his meditations, or in his spiritual reading.

"On this subject," relates Father John Ximenes, "I was harassed by a curious doubt. I said to myself: if Brother Paschal had really and efficaciously desired that his writings should be unknown to posterity, he had only to destroy them in good time; because the day and hour of his death were revealed to him by God. This disturbing thought pursued me everywhere, and I did not know how to get rid of it, until I felt myself inspired to read what Paschal had written on the front page, only recently added to the book. It was like a ray of light. To my great joy, I found there the solution of my painful doubt. This is what the blessed man, with trembling fingers, had traced a few days before his death: 'In the name of the most Holy Trinity, Father, Son, and Holy Spirit—of the three Divine Persons in one only true God, Creator of things visible and invisible, to Whom be glory and power world without end. Amen. I, Brother Paschal, born at Torre Hermosa, of St. Mary of Horta, have written for my spiritual consolation this compilation, taken faithfully from several excellent works.' From these few lines I learned two things worth remembering. The first was that the holy man wished to tread under foot every sentiment of vain glory, by protesting that he was only a transcriber, and that these beautiful reflections were not his own production. The second was that the Holy Spirit, Who had inspired him to write these precious lines, some few days before his death, had likewise and in the same impulse forbidden him to deliver to the flames, writings so replete with pure and sound Catholic doctrine, calculated to produce the greatest good. One of these works was presented to Father John of the Angels, then visiting the Province in quality of Commissary; the second remains in my possession, and I regard it as a priceless treasure. It is never without consolation that I behold again the handwriting of the holy Brother, and that I reflect how everything in this work so exactly expresses the truth, that it would be impossible to rake away or to add to a single line without detriment. The manuscript itself, and everything about it, preaches humility, and in a touching manner reveals the holy Brother's devotion to seraphic Poverty. To economize space he has placed the lines very close together, so that they nearly touch one another, and he has cramped his handwriting for the same purpose. A simple cross separates the paragraphs. There is no margin whatever, the lines running from one extremity of the page to the other. Each leaf is a patch-work of scraps of paper fastened together. The cover is in keeping with the contents, and is a mosaic of minute pieces of cloth of every colour. Everything about it spells that holy Poverty, which is the pearl of the Seraphic Order."

It was humility, too, as much as mortification, which he had in view in going barefoot, or only semi-shod. One of the Friars, seeing him one day walking about with only one sandal, asked him the reason of this singularity. "Well, now," replied the holy man, with a smile, "don't you see only one foot is ailing. Now I ask you, is it fair that these two feet, which are in quite different conditions, should be treated in the same way, and that the one which is in a good state should enjoy the comforts conferred upon its suffering companion?" He had a ready answer for everyone, and hid his acts of mortification under a pleasantry.

Paschal's purity was angelic. Of him, as of St. Bonaventure, it might have been said, that he seemed not to have sinned in Adam. Nevertheless, no one ever employed stronger measures, or took more precautions, to preserve from every taint the frail lily of chastity. Not satisfied with surrounding himself with a hedge of blood-stained thorns, he committed the guardianship of this virtue to its heavenly ally, Humility. From Humility he learned to be distrustful of self, to fly even the semblance of danger, and never to rest upon his laurels. Even in the Saints the fire of concupiscence is never wholly extinguished. One spark, one fiery dart of the Evil One, is sufficient to rekindle the cold embers, and to cause the flames to blaze forth anew. Paschal, when he had arrived at the highest degree of perfection, had painful experience of this truth, and it made him even more cautious than heretofore. It does us good to learn that these terrestrial Angels are made of flesh and blood like ourselves, and that for them, as for us, there are temptations and conflicts.

One day when the Man of God was at prayer, the Demon, envious of such angelic purity, conjured up in his imagination such lively and seductive images that, greatly distressed and thinking himself possessed by the Devil, he arose and wandered about, unable to shake off the nightmare. It was at this perilous juncture that an emissary of Satan presented himself at the door, charged with the express mission of causing the valiant soldier to fall. "For the instruction of all of us," says Father John Ximenes, in his Life of the Saint, "Our Lord permitted Paschal, usually so reserved about everything which directly concerned himself, to recount to me the assault and the victory. It happened at the Convent of St. John de la Ribera of Valencia. Prayer and a glorious flight baffled the snares of the enemy and conducted the Man of God to one of his most signal triumphs."

We cannot better conclude this chapter, devoted to humility and to the other virtues of which it is the safeguard, than by adducing the testimony of a Religious who lived many years with our Saint and made several journeys in his company. "Under every circumstance I found him filled with humility, sweetness, modesty, obedience, and charity, persevering in prayer, faithful to all his exercises; in a word, so proficient in every virtue that I feel a difficulty in saying in which he most excelled. In fact, if I consider his poverty, I find myself obliged to employ superlatives; whilst his charity appears like a shining sun illuminating everything with its beams. When I contemplate his humility, I find myself in presence of a profound abyss. What can be said about his mortification? It was pushed to the very furthest limits, and one might almost accuse this rigid penitent of having exceeded the bounds of the lawful."

This ample and explicit testimony is confirmed by two Religious, who died in the odour of sanctity—Blessed Andrew Hibernon and Bernardine of Corvera. Andrew Hibernon, having striven with Paschal in the race for perfection, completes the picture of his virtues by saying that in the least of his actions, there shone such perfection,

Ch. XIV: The Safeguard of Divine Treasures

that all who had the happiness of knowing him regarded him as a Saint. As to Ven. Bernardine of Corvera, he affirmed one day, in the presence of his Brethren of the Province of Seville, that in the whole Order of St. Francis there was not, at that time, a Religious more proficient in prayer and contemplation than Paschal. He had never set eyes on him, but the eminent holiness of his Brother in Religion had been revealed to him by God.

CHAPTER XV
HEAVENWARD

THE holy Brother had entered upon his fifty-third year when it pleased Our Lord to call him to Himself. Endowed by nature with robust health, and a constitution of iron, he could, by husbanding his strength, have looked forward to a long and green old age; but he had undermined his constitution by his austerities. It was a subject of astonishment that, worn to a shadow, and literally consumed by penance as he was, he was still able to keep about and to discharge his various employments.

The Divine Master, Who had so wonderfully illuminated the eyes of His servant concerning the mysteries of faith and the secrets of the future, did not leave him in the dark, regarding the termination of his own earthly course. For some time previously he had known for a certainty that he was to breathe his last at the Convent of the Holy Rosary. Hence it was that he had hastened with such eagerness to Villareal. He also knew that the time of his deliverance was near at hand; and it was only the exact date which remained hidden in obscurity. When at length the day itself was revealed to him, his whole being was in a state of tremor, and he experienced a portion of the superabundant joy of his Seraphic Father, St. Francis, when it was announced to him that he was about to enter into the House of the Lord.

The holy man could not hide his secret long. The overflowing gladness of his heart showed itself in his exterior, and aroused the attention of those who saw him close at hand. They concluded from it that the holy man had received some intimation from God, concerning his approaching end. The first to perceive this joyousness was Frances Sebastiana, a pious Tertiary who, one Holy Thursday, had remained five hours watching before the Blessed Sacrament, so as to miss nothing of Paschal's silent adoration. Two days before he took to his bed, she saw that he was shedding copious tears during Mass. These tears could not be tears of sadness, for the Holy Brother's countenance was expressive of the liveliest joy. Mystified by this occurrence, Frances returned the next day, and observing the holy man more attentively, she noticed that whilst serving Mass, he was smiling with a mysterious little smile. As he was carrying the Missal across to the Gospel side, after the Epistle, his gaiety increased so that he began to laugh. "What can God have made known to him, of such an agreeable nature?" said the devout female to herself. "Ah, it can only be the news of his approaching departure for Heaven!"

The Religious of the Convent, on their side, had remarked certain things, which gave them food for reflection. On this same day, to the astonishment of all, the sick man, who at other times would never allow anyone to perform for him any kind of menial service, requested Brother Alonso Comacho to wash his feet in warm water. Whilst the infirmarian was bathing and drying his poor fleshless feet, Paschal said to him, as though merely by the way: "You see, Brother, we never know what may happen. It is not impossible that after a few days I might fall seriously ill, and Extreme Unction might have to be administered to me. It is well to take precautions in good time, and to have one's feet perfectly clean, out of respect for the Sacrament." It was a covert way of saying that the day of his departure was drawing near. The infirmarian understood it in this sense, and the Community shared his view.

On the following day one of the Religious, going down very early to Matins, noticed that the outside door was still closed, though the hour for opening it had long since passed. It was an unheard-of event; because so faithful was the Porter to his charge, that he always arrived to the minute, and rather before, than after the time. Only one thing could have prevented him from fulfilling this duty, and that was illness. To make sure, the Religious, feeling rather anxious, went straight to the Porter's cell, and found him stretched out upon his mean pallet, pale and exhausted. "Brother Paschal," he said to him, "it is past the time for opening the Chapel." "I know, my son, I know; but I am not able to do it. Here are the keys. Go and open the door." Thus did the faithful Janitor surrender the humble insignia of his office—those precious keys, which his nerveless fingers were unable any longer to grasp. Doctor Benet was summoned in hot haste.

In accordance with the prescriptions of Spanish physicians of that epoch, he ordered him to be bled. It only enfeebled the patient still more. The illness was, indeed, beyond human remedy, and only a miracle would have restored the sick man to health. The doctor was convinced of this himself, when he had made a closer examination of the symptoms, and as he was a profoundly Christian man, he considered it his duty to warn the Guardian and one of the Definitors then residing at Villareal. "I went further," he says in his deposition, "and summoning all my courage, I disclosed to my holy friend the gravity of his state. 'This is your last illness, good Brother; how does it seem to yourself?' 'It is quite my own opinion, too,' he said calmly. Fearing that I might have caused him pain, or given him a shock by this sudden announcement of death, I begged him to forgive me, in case I should have grieved or alarmed

Ch. XV: Heavenward

him. 'It is quite the contrary,' he said, with a smile. 'You could not give me more welcome news. For years I have yearned for this day, and have besought Our Lord to take me from this land of exile. Believe me, this is my sincere desire. Which day will it be, doctor?' 'According to all appearances, you will not get through Friday.' 'You are mistaken there, doctor. I have asked Our Lord to permit me to live until Saturday, at least.'" Doubtless it was in order to have for the last time on earth the consolation of doing homage to his heavenly Queen, on the day consecrated to her. Paschal then counted upon his fingers the days of his illness up to six. "It will be useless to watch by me, before the seventh day," he said; "spare the Brothers the fatigue."

He gave the same assurance to Father Didacus Castellon, his former Guardian and most faithful friend. The latter was much perplexed, not knowing what to do. His presence was required in Valencia, but on the other hand, he knew that the holy man was sick unto death, and he was most anxious to be near him at the moment of his departure for a better world. In all simplicity, he went and confided his embarrassment to the person, who was its involuntary cause. "Brother Paschal," he said, "if you are really going to die of this illness, please don't conceal it from me, because in that case I will remain at Villareal until your death. Otherwise, I will immediately set out for Valencia, where certain pressing matters require my presence." "Yes, Father Definitor, I am certainly going to die of this illness, but it will not be before Saturday."

He avoided saying anything about what would happen afterwards; but the infirmarian laid a trap for him, and found a means of ascertaining, what was keeping the minds of all in suspense. "Now, Brother Paschal, don't fail to give me warning of the day and hour of your death," said he, "so that I may have time to clothe you in the holy habit, for I am sure you would not like to die without it." It must be understood that, by the doctor's orders, they had taken off his dear Religious habit, which he cherished more dearly than his own skin. Submissive and obedient even unto death, after the example of his Divine Master, he had allowed this to be done without a murmur, and had accepted with docility a softer bed, and other comforts, prescribed by the doctor. Greatly rejoiced to think that he would have the grace of dying, clad in the sacred garb of Religion, he promised the infirmarian to give him timely warning.

In the meantime his suffering became more acute, and a burning fever consumed the dregs of life still remaining in his wasted frame. The friends and benefactors of the Convent, when they learned the situation, were not slow in arriving on the spot. The Friars could not well refuse them the consolation of coming to see the poor Brother, of conversing with him for a few moments, and of receiving his blessing, on which they set a high value. They invaded his cell, therefore, and the dying man's humble couch became a pulpit, from which he delivered to his friends the most touching discourses. Never had his words been so full of unction. Forgetting himself and his grievous torments, he made himself all to all, giving to each one appropriate counsel, and encouraging all who drew near to persevere in the Divine service, to generously practise virtue, and to love the poor of Jesus Christ. Even to the end he belonged not to himself, but to others.

After the Seculars, came the Friars, who in their turn claimed what remained of this precious life. They quitted him no more, and seeing that their treasure was about to be taken away from them, they eagerly received the dying counsels and admonitions of the holy Brother. "Brother Paschal," said one of them, "before you die, tell me some infallible means of attaining my eternal salvation." "I cannot speak long, my son, for I am very weak. Avoid all dangerous familiarity, keep the Rule of our holy Father, St. Francis, to the letter, and you will be saved."

Bartholomew Sart, the apothecary of Villareal, was one of the most assiduous in visiting the holy man, whom he greatly loved. Some medicine had been obtained from him, and Paschal was anxious about the payment of this small debt. "Brother Apothecary," he said to the visitor, "give me an account of the things you have provided for me. I have found a benefactor, who is willing to pay for them all." "What are you talking about, Brother?" replied Bartholomew, quite grieved. "It is the merest trifle, not worth mentioning" (it was a mustard plaster and a bottle of physic). "I shall be only too happy to provide gratis, and for the love of God, all the medicine you may still stand in need of during your illness." "Medicine, Brother Apothecary? There will be no need to give me any more. I do not require medicine any longer." By this last expression, the holy man clearly gave it to be understood that his end was near at hand. "I was then upon my knees," continues Bartholomew Sart, "and I thereupon asked the holy man to bless me. As his weakness was so great that he could scarcely move, I took hold of his right hand, and, having respectfully kissed it, I placed it upon my head. Oh, how wonderful are the ways of Providence! Scarcely had the holy man touched my head, than I felt, as it were, a revolution in my brain, and I was instantly cured of the chronic headache, from which I had been suffering upwards of nineteen years." It was thus Paschal settled the account of the apothecary of the Convent.

Friday and Saturday passed by without the holy Brother reclaiming his habit. At daybreak on Whit-Sunday he urgently requested it. The Friars, seeing his excessive weakness, and fearing to hasten his death by raising him up, pretended not to understand what he wanted, and went out of the room one after the other, so as not to give him a chance of renewing his entreaties. But the Saints are not so easily foiled. Finding himself alone, Paschal summoned up his remaining strength, and with a superhuman effort rose up, took hold of the habit, and tried to put it on. The effort was too great for him; his limbs gave away under him, and he sank unconscious to the ground. The infirmarian, who entered at that moment, raised him up, and after putting his habit on him, carried him back to his bed.

The hour for departure had arrived. By a coincidence apparently fortuitous, but in reality decreed from all Eternity, in the loving counsels of the Deity, the hour of the holy man's departure from the world exactly corresponded to that of his entrance into it. He was fifty-two years old at dawn on Whit-Sunday, to the day and the hour. The biographers have recorded with religious care this providential and touching harmony; they show its fitness, and vie with one another in adducing reasons which called for, and in a certain sense necessitated, it. "It was fitting," it is stated in the Orihuela Process, "that he, whose mortal life had begun on the day when the Church celebrates the descent of the Holy Spirit, in the form of tongues of fire, should on that same day enter into Life Eternal, carried, like Elias in his fiery chariot, by that Divine Spirit, to Whom he belonged by so many titles. It was the Holy Spirit Who watched over his birth, and it was from Him he derived his name, and the marvellous gifts, with which his life was adorned, came from the same source. Paschal was indeed a master-piece of the Holy Spirit. How, then, could his glorious departure to Heaven have taken place under other auspices, or occurred with

Ch. XV: Heavenward

the same fitness on any other day?"[1]

"Brothers, lay me on the bare ground," said the holy man. "I would like to die in the same position as our Seraphic Father." Compassionating his extreme weakness, the Guardian did not think fit to allow him this consolation. Paschal bowed his head resignedly, offering to his Divine Master this last sacrifice, not the least painful of all he had made. And now, all of a sudden, his countenance assumes an expression of alarm. "Jesus! Jesus!" he cries, trembling and like a man in presence of some appalling spectacle. "Brothers, the holy water. Sprinkle me, and sprinkle the cell." And he makes the Sign of the Cross over himself, several times in succession. It was a vision of the Pit which was passing before his eyes. Satan was making his final assault upon the Servant of God. With hands convulsively clasped, the soldier of Christ holds his rosary beads, whilst his gaze is riveted on the crucifix. Presently the temptation vanishes, and a look of heavenly peace overspreads the features of the dying man.

At his urgent entreaty, the Last Sacraments had already been administered to him; and we may easily divine the sentiments of fervour with which he received the Holy Viaticum. So, then, nothing now remained but for him to depart. "Have they rung for High Mass yet?" he asked. When they told him that the bell had been rung and that Mass had commenced, he was filled with joy. He knew by revelation that he was to give up his soul to God on the day of Pentecost, during the sacrifice of Mass and at the moment of the Elevation. What a marvellous and touching recompense for his incomparable devotion to the Sacrament of the Altar! So, as the Convent-bell was tolling for the Elevation of the Host, the dying Saint pronounced

---

[1] MSS. of Process of Orihuela.

twice the Holy Name of Jesus; and then, grasping the hand of his confessor and turning towards him, as the one who held the place of God in his eyes, he gently breathed his last.

In that same moment, at the two extremities of the Kingdom of Valencia, two persons of well-known sanctity saw the soul of the Servant of God, shining with glory, borne heavenwards in a fiery chariot. These two visions, submitted to the strict judgment of ecclesiastical authority, and compared one with the other, are found to be entirely identical in their nature, and invested with all the marks of authenticity. In each of them his external appearance and the lineaments of his countenance are portrayed with such fidelity, that no one could fail to recognize him from the description. And yet these privileged souls had never either seen or known him; they were strangers to each other, and neither of them knew that the other had been favoured with the identical vision.

Before describing the emotion caused in Villareal and its vicinity by this death, so precious in the eyes of God, let us linger for one brief moment, to gather the singularly pathetic testimony of the filial grief of Father John Ximenes, that child of benediction whom Paschal had given to the Seraphic Order, and his Provincial at the time of his death. "At the time our saintly Brother died, I was, in quality of Provincial, engaged in making the visitation of the Convent of Jumilla, situated at the extremity of the Province. It was there that a messenger came to bring the sad news. How harrowing it was to me, only God and I myself could tell. My first thought was to set out at once for Valencia. Accordingly, I started off, and the journey was made by forced marches. It was more than sufficient, to break down my health, already seriously impaired. I was overcome by the excessive heat, and fell so ill at Villena,

Ch. XV: Heavenward

that I was given up by the doctors. Since I was no longer able to go to my holy friend, it was he himself who took the first step, and who came to me. At the very crisis of my illness I was clothed in a habit, which Paschal had worn and which was kept at Almanja. At the contact of this sacred relic, I was miraculously rescued from death. The convalescence took a long while, and it was only after eight months that I was able to walk, and to proceed to Villareal, in order to venerate there the body of the Servant of God."[2] Father John Ximenes could never be consoled on account of not having been present at his holy friend's departure for Paradise.

Death, who habitually respects nothing, suspended his ravages, being held back, and, as it were, chained down, by some unseen force. He did not dare imprint his dreadful tokens upon a body, which had been the living shrine of one of the most beautiful souls on earth. He had to be satisfied with just touching it—with merely breathing on it—but so lightly that the holy man seemed like one buried in a deep slumber. Beneath that icy breath, which calls forth the ghastly pallor of death, his flesh had suddenly taken on the roseate hue of health, and his features, settled in eternal repose, were stamped with a sculptured majesty and grace. His limbs remained supple and flexible, and it seemed as though the blood were still coursing through the veins. Never had the holy man looked so fair, or so instinct with life. The visitors could not convince themselves that he was really dead, and they stood there waiting for him to come out of the trance.

The first panegyrist of the Man of God was the infirmarian, who took off the habit Paschal was clothed in at the moment of his death, to replace it by another less

---

[2] MSS. of the Process. Deposition of Father John Ximenes.

worn. In performing this task, he saw such marvellous tokens of the holy man's heroic penances, that he fell upon his knees, and, seizing the hand of the Saint to kiss it, he exclaimed amidst tears: "O beloved friend of God, all that I observed myself, and all that I could learn from the lips of others, gave me a presentiment, and, as it were, the assurance of what I actually see to-day with my own eyes. I beseech you, do not forget me before the throne of God."

It did not take long for the report of Paschal's death to go from his cell to the Church of the Rosary, then thronged with the faithful, assembled for the festival of Pentecost. When they left the church after the Mass, the sad news flew from mouth to mouth, and soon spread itself with the rapidity of lightning over the whole town and its environs. It produced in all directions a kind of panic. If a plague had suddenly invaded the land the consternation could scarcely have been greater. One would have said that the good Genius of the country and its protector before God had vanished, and that every one was reeling under some terrible blow. Then began a commotion, which was to go on increasing until it assumed gigantic proportions. It was like a general rising. All were afoot and were marching towards the Convent of Our Lady of the Rosary. In the meantime, those who had succeeded in getting inside, plundered the cell where the holy man still lay. True, there was not much to take away, for the little nook was the chosen abode of most high Poverty. But, in the eyes of faith, that wretched, threadbare habit, those worn-out sandals, were simply priceless. Everything became precious, even down to the plaster, whose payment had occasioned the holy man's anxiety a few moments before his death, and the bandages that had been placed upon his arm, after the bleeding performed by Doctor Benet. And these plunderers went off, better satisfied than if they had

Ch. XV: Heavenward

ransacked a King's treasure-chest. The cell soon became too small to contain the crowds, who came to see and touch the body of the Servant of God. The Friary was invaded, and the Religious began to be no longer masters in their own dwelling-place. In these extraordinary circumstances, the Guardian thought that the best course was to have the body taken into the Church, and placed in the Choir of the Religious, until he should receive further orders on the subject.

A group of picked men were placed around the bier, as a guard of honour, and also with a view of defending the holy remains, against the indiscreet devotion of the populace. The faithful entered the Choir by the door to the right, and, having walked around the catafalque, and touched the body in passing, they went out by the door on the left. The very best order was maintained during this procession, and everything seemed to be proceeding satisfactorily. But in the meantime, a storm was brewing outside. The Choir formed a portion of the Enclosure, so that women were not allowed to enter it. Now, who does not know that, when pious demonstrations are in question, far from being behindhand, the weaker sex is ever in the van? It is to the credit of the women, as well as one of their recognized privileges, and now it seemed to them as though they were going to be cheated out of it. Those who had defiled before the Saint were all talking about the heavenly radiance of his countenance, the flexibility of his limbs, and the wonderful moisture which distilled upon his brow. All this was not calculated to allay their pious curiosity, but rather, like oil cast upon the flames, greatly increased the blaze. "We want to see these wonderful things, too, like our husbands, our brothers and our sons," they said with determination; "we have just as much right as they have. When there is question of honouring God's

Saints, the Enclosure does not exist any longer. If necessary, we mean to enter by force and take the Convent by storm." And they would have done it, too, had not the Guardian, in order to avert this pious revolution, adopted measures calculated to give satisfaction to all parties. Yielding to the ultimatum of the devout sex, he caused the body to be carried into one of the chapels in the Church, where it could be venerated by everyone. The events which occurred on Monday and Tuesday of Whit-week are of such peculiar interest, and reveal in such a striking manner the glory of God's Servant, that we are obliged to devote a special chapter to their recital.

CHAPTER XVI
LOVE STRONGER THAN DEATH

ON the morning of Whit-Monday, at a very early hour, all the approaches to the Convent were invaded by a crowd, eager to make their way into the Church. In order not to be forestalled, many had passed the night on the terrace outside the Convent. In view of possible disorder and tumult, the guard had been doubled, and the holy remains had been placed in a chapel, protected by a strong grating. Further, to obviate, as far as possible, all confusion and obstruction, the various battalions of the large army, encamped upon the terrace, like the five thousand fed by the multiplication of loaves in the desert, had been marshalled into companies of forty or fifty. It was thus, group after group, that they went into the chapel. There for a few moments they venerated the Saint together, touching his sacred remains with a chaplet or a medal, and then, much to their regret, they had to retire and make room for others, who were impatiently awaiting their turn, and a like consolation.

The Gospel does not inform us whether, amongst the throng of hungry folk, miraculously fed in the desert, there were to be found some who, after having received their share, glided in amongst the other groups, in order to return a second or even a third time, thus to receive a double or a triple portion. The biographers of our Saint, more explicit on this point, relate that, during the never-to-be-forgotten days, when the holy body was exposed for public veneration, ruses of this description were practised on a vast scale. Some went even further, and, once having

St. Paschal Baylon

established themselves in a good position in the chapel, they tried to stay there at all costs. Why need we be surprised, or impute it to them as a fault? The spectacle they had before their eyes was so marvellously beautiful that it was hard to tear oneself away, after having once had a glimpse of it. There upon his bed of state lay the Man of God, like one plunged in deep slumber. Upon his forehead there distilled a clear liquid, pervading the air with its fragrance, and penetrating even into the soul like a breath from Paradise. When the eyelids were raised, the eyes showed bright and limpid, as those of a living person, whilst over the lips there hovered an angelic smile. Had it not been for the presence of an armed force, the people, in their unthinking enthusiasm, would have cast themselves headlong upon the holy body, and, in order to obtain possession of a fragment of it, would have literally torn it to pieces. The miraculous sweat which distilled from the members of the Saint flowed copiously and continuously during the three days of the exposition, as we are informed by one of those, who, on that occasion, mounted guard in the chapel. It was thus easy to give satisfaction to everyone, each one taking away a piece of linen steeped in this heavenly liquid. We shall relate presently its wonderful properties, and the miracles it was instrumental in performing.

In addition to this standing prodigy, which the people had thus under their eyes, Almighty God, in order to excite confidence in the holy man, and augment veneration for him, was pleased to work other miracles which carried enthusiasm to its highest pitch. On the morning of the second day they broke forth with a suddenness and profusion, for which few parallels can be found in the

Ch. XVI: Love Stronger than Death

annals of heroic sanctity. They would be simply incredible, were they not all attested by witnesses, who relate simply and loyally what they saw with their eyes, heard with their ears, and touched with their hands.

With the help of their testimony, let us endeavour to recall to life those days of wonder, or at least to trace their outline. It is a poor paralytic of Castellon de la Llana, called John Baptist Cebollin, who heads the procession of the recipients of miraculous favours, which is about to defile before our eyes. Elizabeth Xea, that benefactress who was so sorely displeased on account of the changes amongst Superiors, saw this miracle with her own eyes, and it is from her legal deposition that we gather the following narrative: "When I saw the paralyzed man entering the Church, leaning heavily on his crutch, I said under my breath, 'Ah, if good Brother Paschal would only straighten this man's legs for him, what a grand miracle it would be!' Haunted by this thought, I never lost sight of the paralytic. I saw him making his way, with much difficulty, through the serried ranks of the crowd. When he had at length made his way, as best he could, to the catafalque, he bent down, with the assistance of two men who supported him, and taking the hand of the Saint, kissed it fervently. And then what happened? I really don't know how to describe it, but all at once I saw him rise up and begin to wave his crutch in the air, and I heard a cry which seemed to vibrate through the throng of bystanders: 'A miracle! A miracle! I'm cured!' To this shout of victory the crowd responded with prolonged applause. The ranks opened out, to let the victor pass through. Throwing away his crutch, he began to run, to dance, and to leap like a kid. So intoxicated was he with joy that he no longer knew where he was, or what he was saying or doing. In triumph he returned to Castellon de la Llana, followed by a large cortège."

The miracle soon became generally known, and the little town and surrounding country were thrown into a state of commotion. The impulse had been given—it was enough. Excited at the sight of the paralytic, carried away by his narrative, the inhabitants rose as a man and marched upon Villareal. Business was at a standstill; there was now only one concern, and that was to get as quickly as possible to Our Lady of the Rosary to see the wonderful things that were happening there.

Like those sent by the Divine Master through the towns and villages, the highways and the byways, to gather in the halt and the blind, the deaf and dumb, and compel them to come to the feast, the people of Castellon beat up the whole countryside, and brought with them to Villareal all the cripples and invalids of the district. They went to the banquet weeping and moaning, "going they went and wept"; they returned from it with joy and exultation in their heart, carrying their crutches on their shoulders, like so many trophies captured from the enemy, "but coming they shall come with joyfulness, carrying their sheaves."

Greatly impressed by the instantaneous cure of John Baptist Cebollin, John Simon Ferrer and his wife felt themselves impelled to demand from Brother Paschal a miracle in favour of their little Kathleen. But let her mother speak; she will relate in her simple, artless language, better than we could ourselves, the thrilling sensations of that memorable day: "After a long illness she had at seven years of age, this poor child was covered with tumours; the worst of these were on her face, and on her left foot and arm, whilst there were smaller ones nearly all over her body. At times the swellings used to fester and run. Although we were far from rich, we spared no expense to obtain her cure. The most skilful surgeons of

Ch. XVI: Love Stronger than Death

Valencia operated upon the poor little creature, and for two years she was never out of their hands. They slashed and they cauterized to their hearts' content; sometimes they would cut off large pieces of flesh with their scissors. It is impossible to describe what this poor child suffered. During these operations she used to give vent to heartrending cries. Having treated her successively with soap, quicklime, and red-hot iron, the surgeons confessed their impotence, assuring us that it would be useless to try any more experiments and to expose the child to fresh torments. They added that the only remedy was resignation to the Divine Will, because the disease arose from impurity of the blood, and for such a malady there was no human cure. We resigned ourselves, therefore, and the little girl bore her trial patiently for the love of God. Meantime, Brother Paschal died. He was an old acquaintance of ours. How many times had he not visited our house? At news of his glorious departure, all the people of Castellon hastened to his bier, and we saw with our own eyes our fellow-townsman, John Baptist Cebollin, return perfectly cured. 'Why should we not do like the rest?' said my husband to me. 'Let us take Kathleen to see our blessed friend.' It was no sooner said than done. This was Whit-Monday. The people, fearing that the Religious would bury the Man of God, came *en masse*, and it was only with the greatest difficulty that one could get inside the Church. When we managed to enter, after a long and painful delay, the Friars were just going to sing High Mass. When the people saw us carrying the little girl, who was so pale and wasted that she seemed like a corpse, they took pity on us, and the crowd made way to let us pass. On reaching the chapel we all three of us fell on our knees; and my husband made the little girl get as close as possible to the body of our friend and protector. I moistened a handkerchief with some drops of the liquid which distilled from his forehead, and with this precious balsam I rubbed in succession the wounds of the face, the arm, and the foot. Kathleen had succeeded in grasping Brother Paschal's right hand; she clasped it tightly and would not let it go. Oh! the beautiful and touching invocations she addressed to the Saint with the fervour of an Angel—the wee mite! We joined in the prayer—my husband and I. Never had we prayed so hard. The looks of those around were fixed upon us; everyone seemed on the tiptoe of expectation. Suddenly my husband turned toward me. 'Courage, wife,' he said. 'The Saint is going to work a fine miracle for the little one. Look, now, he is opening his eyes!' I gazed in amazement, and, like the child and all those round us, I distinctly saw Brother Paschal's eyes open and afterwards shut."

The servers' bell had just at that moment been rung for the first Elevation. Brother Paschal's eyes were fixed wide open upon the Sacred Host, and regarded It lovingly. They closed again softly as the priest lowered the Host and placed It upon the Altar. Wonderful to relate, scarcely had the Chalice of Christ's Precious Blood been elevated for the adoration of the faithful, than the eyes of the Saint once more opened, and with rapture contemplated the Chalice, and then, as on the previous occasion, they closed when the Elevation was completed. Who could describe the thrill which at that moment passed through the throng? One of the witnesses has attempted the task, and it is her testimony, even yet vibrating with emotion, that we will embody in this narrative. "I always had a great horror of corpses," says Eleanor a Jorda y Miedes, "so in spite of urgent entreaties, I could not make up my mind to go and see the body of Brother Paschal, exposed to public veneration at Our Lady of the Rosary. However, on the second day, seeing that everyone was hastening there, I said to myself: 'Well, after all, why should I be a greater coward than anyone else? Why not go like the rest?' So I went to Our Lady of the Rosary. To my surprise, the sight of this dead body did not give me the least shock. I went up to Brother Paschal, as though he had been alive, kissed his hands and feet, and saw the miraculous dew upon his forehead. In short, I felt so much at my ease, at the side of the holy man, that in order to remain longer under his blessed influence, I resolved not to quit the chapel before the end of High Mass. I must confess, to my own shame, that I was more attentive in watching what was going on round the holy man, than in following the Holy Sacrifice. When I saw him open his eyes at the Elevation, I was so astounded that I gave a loud scream. 'Mamma, mamma!' I exclaimed to my mother, who had come with me, 'look, look! Brother Paschal has opened his eyes.' She looked, and she, too, saw the eyes of the Saint open and then shut at the second Elevation. All who were witnesses of this miracle, like ourselves, had one and the same idea about it, namely, that Our Lord wished in this way to reward Paschal's extraordinary devotion to the Sacrament of the Altar, and that He gave him a new life, so that, even on the other side of the tomb, he might still have the consolation of adoring Him in the Holy Eucharist."[1]

But let us return once more to the pathetic group we left praying at the feet of our Saint. "The sight of the prodigy which had just occurred under our eyes," continued Mary Ferrer, "increased our confidence tenfold, and it seemed that nothing could resist our supplications any longer, so ardent were they. I had not desisted all the time from rubbing the little girl's wounds with the moisture from the Saint's forehead. In proportion to my

---

[1] MSS. of the Process. Deposition of Eleanora Jorda y Miedes

rubbing, the inflammation subsided, until at length the swellings disappeared altogether under the influence of this heaven-sent medicine, leaving only the scars to attest the reality of the miracle. So our little Kathleen was healed. Like John Baptist Cebollin, we left the Church in triumph. The people respectfully made room for us to pass. The crowd cheered us on the way, and joined their thanksgivings to ours. Next day we took the little one to see the surgeon, who had given her such a merciless slashing. He, too, with all his heart, shared in our gratitude and our joy. 'My God, what fine prayers you must have said to obtain such a grace,' said he."[2]

Not to weary the reader, we forbear to describe the long series of prodigies which followed those we have just related. It is fitting, however, to make one exception in favour of the following miracle, in which the Saint shows himself under his double aspect of healer and prophet. After Jeronima Vergues, one of the habitual worshippers in the Convent Church, had met with the misfortune of breaking her leg, Brother Paschal used to come to ask after her, and to console her husband. One day, when he found the poor man more than usually downcast, he had said: "Don't make yourself miserable. Your wife won't die from this accident; in fact, by and by she will be so completely cured, that there will remain no trace of the injury."

When Jeronima heard of the holy Brother's death, she said to herself that the time had come to remind him of his promise. She was helped to the chapel by two charitable neighbours, who supported her on either side. They installed her close to the Saint, so that she could obtain, without trouble, the miraculous liquid which bedewed the face of Paschal, and apply it to the afflicted member.

---

[2] MSS. of the Process. Deposition of Mary Simone Ferrer.

Ch. XVI: Love Stronger than Death

Whilst engaged in this operation, and accompanying it with fervent prayers, Jeronima felt that something extraordinary was happening to her. The nerves and muscles, contracted by the injury, seemed to expand, and everything that had been broken or dislocated seemed to fit itself back in its place. As though propelled by a spring, Jeronima rose from the ground and found herself standing upright on her feet. Paschal had kept his word, and no longer feeling any ill results from her injury, Jeronima walked back home, accompanied by her son and a crowd of people.

And now we have arrived at the third day of Whitsuntide. It marks the climax of popular excitement which had been stirred up, increased, and, as we may say, carried to boiling-point by this long series of miracles, and by the not less wonderful aspect of the body, which continued to defy the power of Death. By this time the Religious of Our Lady of the Rosary, on their feet day and night, were completely spent and were sinking with fatigue. Their Friary, usually so serene and tranquil, resembled an inn, or rather it was like a place taken by storm by the people, who were determined to assert their sovereign rights. Silence, prayer, regularity were no more, and it was impossible to see when and how it would all end. The situation seemed rather to be going from bad to worse; for outside the ranks of the pilgrims were constantly swelling. Thus began the third day, not without serious forebodings. The crowd grew boisterous and almost threatening, especially after a rumour had been set afloat that the Friars wanted to take away the body and put it out of sight.

As on the two preceding days, there were numerous and conspicuous miracles, which seemed to increase, if such were possible, the enthusiasm of the faithful. Perhaps the most famous of these is the following, preserved in the minutest details in the testimony of her who was its subject. Once again it was a fellow-townswoman of John Baptist Cebollin. Decidedly Paschal had a partiality for the good folk of Castellon de la Llana. It was enough to make people of the neighbouring villages jealous. The person favoured this time was called Juana Dominga Sagara, the wife of an honest ploughman of Castellon. At the time of this event she was nearly three score and ten. "I slipped badly one day and broke a bone," she relates. "It could be neither set nor put in its place by the most skilful surgeons. After many fruitless attempts, they declared me incurable, and for more than five years I remained in this painful condition, buoyed up by a vague hope that God would take pity on me and cure me. Now, on the morning of the third festival in the Pasch of the Holy Spirit, in the year 1592, my husband entered my room in high spirits. 'Be quick and get up, old lady,' he said. 'We'll start off at once for Villareal, where a Brother of the Franciscan Friary has just died in the odour of sanctity. He's working ever so many miracles, they say. You must, by all means, go and venerate his body. Who knows? God may do us the favour of curing you through his intercession.'

"His words inspired me with such confidence that I got up with the utmost expedition. As soon as I was ready, they hoisted me on to a donkey. My husband held me up on one side, and my son led the way, holding the animal by the bridle. It was in this style we arrived at Our Lady of the Rosary. As ill luck would have it, the Church was packed with pilgrims, and we had no means of getting inside, even if we waited hours upon hours. Seeing this, I began to cry, and I entreated them, with tears, not to refuse a poor sick woman the favour of being allowed to approach the holy remains, and ask for a cure. My affliction, and the pitiable

Ch. XVI: Love Stronger than Death

state I was in, touched the bystanders, and they did their best to open a way for me. Slowly, slowly, at the risk of being knocked down and suffocated, I gained the entrance of a chapel where the body was exposed behind a strong grating. But the question remained, how was I to get inside? Only the armed force which maintained order and kept back the crowd could open a passage for me. I entreated one of the officers to order his men to assist me. He yielded to my wishes with a good grace, and the policeman escorted me to the catafalque. Then I took Blessed Paschal's hand and kissed it with great reverence and a profound sense of my own unworthiness. 'What's the meaning of this?' exclaimed a person close by, apparently scandalized at seeing me standing in such a place, just before the Elevation. 'Kneel down! On your knees!' Mechanically, I obeyed him and fell upon my knees, without so much as reflecting that for years past my legs had been stiff and lifeless. Then I began to cry like a child, and in a prayer, broken by sobs, I besought the Saint to cure me. When I wanted to get up again with the aid of my crutch, I felt an acute pain in the place where the bone had been broken, followed by a curious cracking sensation. It was as though someone had taken hold of the bones, in order to bring them together forcibly and put them in their right position. I was near fainting, rather from emotion than from pain, and to save myself from falling I clung with both hands to the rail of the grating. At this moment the Elevation bell sounded, and as before, without adverting to it, I knelt down quite easily. Some charitable people carried me out upon the terrace half dead. They bathed my temples to revive me, and gave me a little nourishment. When I came to myself, I felt as though I were no longer the same individual, and that there had been some great change within me. All of a tremble, I ventured to set my foot on the ground, and to stand on the limb which had been crippled. As this timorous attempt succeeded admirably, I ventured by myself, and without any assistance, to mount the donkey. You may fancy the joy with which my husband, my son, and myself, set out on our return journey to Castellon. Before reaching Castellon, we were met by a crowd of relations and friends, who were anxious to know if our prayers had been answered. 'How are you, Juana Dominga?' they cried out with one accord. 'Splendid! I am cured; the holy Brother has worked one of his grandest miracles for me. You are going to see it with your own eyes.' So saying, I got off the donkey's back and threw my crutches away. Then I started off to run towards the doctor's house, situated on the other side of the city walls. Relatives and friends joined in the improvised race, loudly voicing their astonishment. As for myself, I mounted the stairs of the doctor's house with a light step, and entered unannounced into the room where his wife was lying ill. She opened her eyes wide when she saw me, and without waiting to be questioned, I related to her all that had happened. Then I returned to the crowd of people who were waiting at the threshold to give me an ovation. They were nearly carrying me home in triumph. For several days there was a regular procession to our house. The story of the miracle had to be retold, in all its minutest details, to Peter and John, to Catherine and Jane, and to all who presented themselves to hear it. They never tired of hearing it, and I never wearied of telling the story, for the greater glory of God and the honour of His faithful Servant Paschal.

"Eight days after my cure I returned barefoot to Our Lady of the Rosary to hear a Mass of Thanksgiving and to express my gratitude to my heavenly benefactor. Since then, in spite of my great age, I have been well all the time.

I can get up, sit down, walk about without a stick, and I can make the Sign of the Cross. Would you like to have a proof of this, illustrious judges?" added the good old soul, and without waiting a reply, she suited the action to the word, and began to walk to and fro, to sit down and get up again, and finally made a big Sign of the Cross over herself, in presence of the judges of the Process, who were both surprised and delighted by her simplicity.[3] Thus, amidst subdued mirth, ended this deposition, one of the most important of the Process.

On the evening of the third day, the body of armed men, under the pretext of giving breathing-time to the Religious, emptied the Church and bolted the doors. Without losing a moment, the Friars took advantage of this respite and began to prepare a place of sepulture.

Under the Altar of the Immaculate Conception, so particularly dear to the holy man, there was a deep and spacious niche. It seems as though Providence had specially designed it to be the receptacle for his body. It was there they laid him, having previously clothed him in a new habit to replace the former one, which had been torn to pieces by the faithful. The Guardian of the house then caused a thick layer of quicklime to be spread over the body, in order that the flesh might be consumed more quickly. He gave as a reason for this singular proceeding that this would prevent any bad odour arising, as that would be calculated to shock the common people, and thus cause the holy man to lose the high reputation, in which he was held by them. Almighty God made this act of folly redound to the glory of Blessed Paschal, as will be seen in due time.

A striking miracle was worked at the very moment the

---

[3] MSS. of the Process. June 8, 1592.

quicklime was being thrown over the holy remains. Paschal's Confessor, Father James Morales, was present, and thought that he, too, had a claim to derive some benefit from the holiness of his former penitent. "Was I not his ghostly father?" said he to himself. "Why should he not cure me of my sore throat, and the asthma I have suffered from so long?" And, approaching the body, as it was disappearing under the lime, he seized the end of Paschal's cord and applied it to his throat. Nothing further was required. At the contact of the cord the Father was instantly cured.

After the obsequies, conducted from first to last in absolute silence, a little brick wall was expeditiously erected to close the niche, and a curtain was hung in front of it.

On Wednesday morning the Church doors were reopened at a very early hour. The people who had passed the night upon the terrace, poured into the Chapel in a torrent, and not finding what they wanted—the body of the Saint—became infuriated. Soon a rush was made toward the Altar of the Immaculate Conception, with the intention of breaking open the niche and taking out the body of the Saint; but the guard, seeing the object of the manœuvre, forcibly restrained the rabble. However, what was more effectual than even the swords and halberds of the soldiery, in checking this blind rush, and causing the tumult to subside, were the miracles which at that moment commenced anew. When the assailants perceived that, whether present to their eyes or concealed behind yonder wall, the Saint was still their friend and their protector, they calmed down, and the crowd dispersed. Such were the three days of Whitsuntide, which put the seal upon the glory of Blessed Paschal.

CHAPTER XVII
A GLORIOUS SEPULCHER

BEFORE setting about the task of describing the wonders he witnessed at the opening of the Saint's shrine, Father John Ximenes allows an expression of regret to escape from him, in which our readers will readily share. "Ah! why, instead of being so anxious about preserving Paschal's bones, did not that unlucky Guardian rather think of calling in an artist, to preserve for posterity the glorious lineaments of that transfigured countenance?" Our regret is still further increased, when we remember that that epoch was the golden age of Spanish art, and that amongst the schools none was more famous than that of Valencia, only a few miles distant.

If only Blessed Nicholas Factor had still been in this world, we should not have had to deplore this irreparable omission; for he would surely never have left to another, the honour of consigning to canvas the familiar lineaments of his holy friend. But he had already quitted this poor earth of ours for a better world; and so, instead of the masterpiece that would have been produced by his brush, we have only the faint outline of verbal portraiture. When a person is before our eyes, we may indeed identify him from a description. But if we have never had so much as a glimpse of him, how can we recall him to life, and conjure up his image, with such insufficient materials? There are thousands of people in the world who answer to such or such a description—who have a broad or narrow forehead, light or dark eyes, tall or short, and yet who only distantly resemble one another; so that two or three strokes of a pencil would have been more to the purpose than a description like the following.

Saint Paschal was of medium height, and very strongly built. His countenance, without being exactly handsome, was pleasing, on account of its pervading air of goodness. Under his arched and bushy eyebrows, there shone two small blue eyes, full of life and intelligence. Long eyelashes imparted to them a singular depth. Upon his under lip there was a slight scar, which, however, instead of in any way disfiguring his face, seemed to add a certain grace to its expression. In his later years his locks, originally plentiful, had grown thin, and his brow was furrowed by numerous deep wrinkles. At length, too, sinking under the weight of austerities rather than that of age, he walked with a stoop. His feet, worn out by constant travel, were distorted, whilst his hands were so hardened and seared by incessant toil, as to appear as though they were made of the roots of trees. Even to his dying day the holy man preserved a warm, fresh colour, which gave life and animation to his countenance. Such was Paschal as regards his physical traits, during the days of his mortal pilgrimage. And such also are we going to find him in his tomb.

As stated in the preceding chapter, it was not until eight months after the decease of his glorious son, that it was possible for Father John Ximenes, as yet scarcely recovered from his illness, and long hindered by the affairs of his Province, to betake himself to Villareal in order to visit his subjects there, and to venerate the precious pledge they held in safe-keeping. The Friars of Our Lady of the Rosary, and the faithful, had built great hopes upon this visit of the Provincial. They had, in fact, been waiting nearly a year for his coming, with a certain amount of impatience. This impatience arose in great measure from the joyful anticipation of again seeing the Father, whom they dearly loved, and had so nearly lost; but, to speak the truth, there was a still more potent reason. It was said that the Provincial would take occasion from this visit to Villareal to identify the holy body, and that the Religious and the people would have the consolation of once more seeing Brother Paschal.

So general was the conviction upon the point, that a kind of treaty had been entered into, between the people of the surrounding districts and those of Villareal, whereby the latter undertook to despatch a courier, to carry the intelligence of the day and the hour of the ceremony. Father John Ximenes was warned in good time of all these plans, and after seriously debating upon the best course to adopt, he perceived that great inconveniences were likely to arise from doing what was expected of him; and he resolved to find some plan of avoiding the difficulty. For this purpose, he caused a report to be circulated, about a month before his arrival at Villareal, that he did not propose to have any solemn opening of the shrine. His intention, in fact, was to proceed to the recognition of the body, but with the greatest secrecy, and in presence of the witnesses absolutely required for the purpose and bound to silence. Consequently it was necessary not to arouse any suspicion, even amongst the Religious of Villareal. Only one of them was notified of the exact day of the Provincial's arrival. He received orders to knock down the little wall, in front of the niche, and to open the shrine, so that everything would be ready when the Visitator and the witnesses were to go down into the chapel. These instructions were executed to the letter, and with such secrecy that no one had the slightest inkling of the preparations that were being made. For greater security the Father Provincial did not arrive at the Convent until nightfall, thus avoiding a concourse of people and wearisome entreaties.

But let Father Ximenes speak for himself: "When, upon arriving at Our Lady of the Rosary, we had made a visit to the Blessed Sacrament, I went upstairs to my cell, and the Friars came to see me there. We were very pleased to see one another again, and the interview was of a most cordial description. We conversed first upon one subject and then on another, and thus the interview was purposely prolonged, until the signal agreed upon apprized me that everything was in readiness for the visit to the shrine. Under pretence of taking the repose I really needed, after my long day's journey, I dismissed the Friars, asking them to retire to their cells, which they did without delay. When we were certain that all the Friars were asleep, I noiselessly descended into the Church, together with the Father Guardian, my companion on the Visitation, and two other witnesses. The identification of the mortal remains of one of God's children is always impressive; but how much greater is the impressiveness and solemnity of finding oneself before a coffin, which holds the body of a Saint. What were we going to discover under the white shroud of quicklime? In what condition should I find my holy friend, after a sojourn of about nine months in the tomb? The lid was raised, and we all approached the shrine and attested the presence of the crust of lime which concealed the Saint from sight. I would not allow anyone else to have the honour of removing this crust; but detached it bit by bit, beginning with the portion which covered the face. O heavenly joy! In proportion as I lifted the veil, the features of our blessed Brother were disclosed, full of life and animation. It was indeed he himself, and none other, miraculously preserved in the flesh, intact from head to foot, even down to the tip of the nose, ordinarily the first

Ch. XVII: A Glorious Sepulcher

part to show signs of decomposition. When we raised the eyelids, the eyes seemed to gaze at us and smile. The limbs were so supple and flexible, that they lent themselves to every movement we imparted to them. Nothing recalled the presence of death; on the contrary, everything breathed life and brought consolation and joy to the soul. Human language is inadequate to portray such a spectacle!

"On our knees before the shrine we shed the sweetest tears of our life. I took the Saint's hand in mine, and, drawing it towards me and raising it to my lips, I kissed it lovingly. A crystalline liquid, like balm, distilled from the face and hands. When each of the Religious had satisfied his devotion, a fresh layer of quicklime was spread over the body, and then I addressed the Saint in the following words: 'He, Who for eight months hath so miraculously preserved thee beneath the lime, is powerful enough to preserve thee still, for many years to come, and thus give greater lustre to this miracle, until the fitting time shall arrive for translating thy glorious remains to a sepulcher less unworthy of thee.' Having replaced the shrine in the niche, and reconstructed the little wall of bricks, we retired in silence to prepare a report of this first recognition of the body."[1]

Two years later a Commissary-General made the visitation of the Province of St. John Baptist. As he had ample powers, the Religious, frustrated in their previous attempt, thought the time had come to make another effort, with greater chance of success. Consequently they addressed to the Commissary a humble but urgent request, and he, equally desirous of according them this consolation and of ascertaining the condition the body was in, gave full permission to reopen the tomb. This second opening took

---

[1] Deposition of Father John Ximenes.

place on July 22, 1594. It was performed secretly and in the presence of the Religious of the Community only. Not everything was found in identically the same state as at the time of the visit made two years previously by the Provincial. Nevertheless, what is recorded in writing by the witnesses is of a miraculous character. Of the habit and the linen enveloping the body, there remained only a few shreds. The body itself, with the exception of the extremity of the nostrils and some fragments of skin, continued to defy corruption. When placed upright it remained in that position without support. A piece of one of the ears and a finger had been abstracted since the first identification by some indiscreet person.

Under almost similar circumstances, the tomb was opened for a third time, and a visitation made of it, though we are not informed of the precise epoch by our Saint's biographers. An incident which happened on this occasion should not be passed over in silence. Actuated by an ill-regulated devotion, and with no authorization save his own, one of the Religious of the Holy Rosary anticipated his Brethren by some hours at the Saint's tomb, by making a visitation on his own account. By means of a saw, he removed both the feet, and then carried them off to his cell, exulting over this master-stroke of ill-regulated piety. How great was the distress of all, when they found that the two feet were missing, and perceived the recent traces of the saw! In solemn conclave the Superior, delegated to visit the holy body, ordered, under pain of excommunication to be incurred *ipso facto*, that what had been taken away should be replaced forthwith. Some hours later the two feet were replaced in the coffin. Constrained by the precept of obedience, and the threat of excommunication, the culprit had glided back unseen to the tomb, and had made restitution of the sacred relics. On this point, it is remarked by the biographers that, as in the case of the quicklime, so here also Almighty God made an indiscreet action turn to the glory of Blessed Paschal. It was, in fact, from the two feet, separated from the body, that an immense quantity of relics were taken. These relics, being distributed amongst different Convents, and presented to the highest personages, both civil and ecclesiastical, became the means of working many miracles, which spread far and wide the cultus of the Man of God and helped forward his canonization.

The three recognitions of which we have been speaking were visits of private devotion. Something more was required for the glory of the Saint—an official visit made by order of ecclesiastical authority, which had just commenced the Process of Beatification. On July 23, 1611, the Bishop of Segorbe (Castellon de la Llana), Apostolic Commissary, called together the members of the Commission of Enquiry, at Our Lady of the Rosary. The doors of the Church were closed, by order of the Prelate, and the people, who had got wind of the Commission, had, much to their regret, to remain outside. The Commission, presided over by the Bishop, comprised certain ecclesiastics selected for that purpose, the Provincial, the Postulator of the cause, certain eminent personages of the country, doctors and surgeons, and a notary. When the shrine had been placed upon the altar of the Immaculate Conception, the Bishop took a key from the hand of Father Ximenes and opened the first lock; a second and third lock were opened, with their respective keys, by the Guardian of the Convent and by one of the Discreets. Before raising the lid of the shrine, the Apostolic Commissary read the Brief, authorizing him to proceed to the visitation of the body, and promulgated the prohibition upon the witnesses, under pain of excommunication, reserved to the Supreme

Pontiff, against taking away anything whatsoever, and also an injunction to replace the holy remains in the same condition in which they had been found. As some of those present were unacquainted with Latin, a translation in Spanish was read, and a short explanation given.

As soon as the lid was raised, an agreeable fragrance, resembling the perfume of flowers, or scent, arose from the sepulcher. Armed with a pair of scissors, the Bishop proceeded to cut open the habit of the Saint down to the girdle, in order to give the medical facility every opportunity of making an examination of the body, which had now been nineteen years lying in the tomb. The doctors and surgeons acquitted themselves of the delicate task with the carefulness and reverence to be expected from sincere Christians. As soon as they had declared that they had completed their investigations to their own satisfaction, the lid was replaced. On the following day the Commission reassembled to hear the reading of the medical report. The conclusion arrived at, which was based upon the principles of medical science, was in the affirmative, as to the miraculous state of the body. "We, the undersigned doctors and surgeons, affirm on oath, before God and according to our conscience, that the body of the said Brother Paschal Baylon is incorrupt, and that the manner of its preservation is supernatural and miraculous." So ends the report.

The faithful, ever beforehand in the matter, had not awaited the official testimony of science to arrive at the same conclusion. With its mighty voice, oftentimes the voice of God Himself, "*Vox populi, vox Dei,*" the people had from the first, and without hesitation, declared this sepulcher glorious, and had gathered round it, as a new focus of graces and blessings. The inhabitants of the neighbouring villages and hamlets were the first to start the movement, and to come in pilgrimage to the tomb of the Servant of God at Villareal. Soon their place was taken by others, who came from the furthest parts of the Province, attracted by the reports of the virtues and miracles of the holy Brother. The visitors became so numerous that new means of receiving them had to be devised. The few inns of Villareal were inadequate to accommodate these crowds, and new ones had to be built. But on days when there was a great concourse, the whole town was transformed into one large hostelry, and the inhabitants took upon themselves to lodge the pilgrims.

The Religious of the Holy Rosary, too, were unable to cope with a task which had become simply overwhelming. From morning till night they had to hold themselves at the disposition of strangers, to hear their confessions, to take them to the shrine, and often to give them hospitality as well, because there was no shelter for them elsewhere. Such a state of things could not endure, without ultimately destroying that spirit of recollection which is the soul of the Religious life. The Superiors of the Province understood this, and they had another Chapel built adjoining the one where the Servant of God rested, and communicating with it by an iron lattice. The gate of the second Chapel always remained open, and the pilgrims could venerate the body without the Religious being obliged, as they had hitherto been, to act as their guides. This building, though of fine proportions, became in its turn insufficient, and other arrangements had to be devised to cope with the ever-growing throng of pilgrims, who now came, not only from Spain, but also from other European countries and across the ocean.

In a few brief years the *cultus* of the Blessed had spread far and wide over the whole earth, and the hitherto unknown name of Paschal was upon every lip. This worldwide popularity proceeded from a variety of causes. Let us begin by pointing out such as belonged to the purely natural order. The Friars Minor were then in every part both of the Old and the New World, and they had the glory of their Order as deeply at heart, as any of their predecessors. Paschal therefore found in each of his Religious Brethren, a zealous propagator of his glorious name, eager to point out to the world the presence of a new star, shining with marvellous brilliancy in the zenith. Besides being a Friar, the Blessed was a Spaniard also, and this did not tend to obscure his glory. Spain at this time still justified the boast of Charles V., "The sun never sets upon my empire." Exceedingly powerful in both hemispheres, it held beneath its sway the fairest portions of Europe and America. Now, with a Spaniard, patriotism was made to enter into his devotion to the Saints. According to him, from St. James of Compostella down to the latest addition to the shining ranks of the Blessed, there were none, or scarcely any, either in Heaven above or on the earth beneath, to vie with the Saints of his own country. The latest addition was Blessed Paschal, and hence it was that in both hemispheres and in every latitude the soldiers and colonists, who went forth from the old country, carried far and wide the fame of their illustrious compatriot, as a portion of the national glories.

To these two sources of our Saint's popularity we must add a third, more efficacious than either of the preceding, and this time, one of a miraculous character—namely, the share taken by the Blessed himself. By dint of countless miracles, he worked his way everywhere, and became the most active propagator of his glory, or rather of the glory of God in His Servant. It is wonderful to see how well he knew how to make his way in the world, and raise up zealous and powerful promoters of his cause. Here again it was in his native land of Spain that he commenced operations, his first conquest being King Philip II.

In November, 1592, only a few months after the death of the Saint, the notables of Villareal, in view of the vast number of miracles, and the ever-increasing throng of pilgrims at the shrine, sent a deputation to the Bishop, entreating him to take judicial cognizance of the life and miracles of Brother Paschal. The Prelate was only waiting for this move, in order to act, and he immediately appointed a tribunal. "It was then," relates Father John Ximenes, "that I was commissioned by the Prelate to go to Madrid, in order to inform the King about the affair, and to pray him to give it his support. I had an opportunity on this occasion of seeing and admiring the lively faith of this truly Catholic Sovereign, and his profound piety towards God and His Saints. When I arrived at the Escurial, where the Court then was, the King had suspended all audiences, both public and private, on account of his severe and protracted illness. But scarcely had the Grand Master announced my arrival, and the purpose of my visit, than he gave orders that I should be admitted instantly. This was on the Vigil of St. John Baptist, 1593. When I entered the King's private apartments, he came forward to meet me, accompanied by Don Philip, his heir, and the Infanta Isabella-Claire-Eugenie, his beloved daughter. He had arranged that his children should be present at the interview, to strengthen and quicken their faith, and to bind them by yet another tie to the Holy Catholic Church. I had to relate in the minutest detail all that I knew, either of myself or from others, of the holy life, glorious death, and countless miracles of Blessed Paschal. The monarch and his two children listened attentively with silent interest and joy. Then they heaped a number of questions upon me, which I did my best to answer.

"When their pious curiosity had been satisfied, the King bade me to prepare a complete report, promising me his royal favour and support at the Court of Rome. To emphasize still more his sentiments of devotion, he added that it would afford him great consolation if he were to obtain the iron chain with which the holy man girded himself, and the hood belonging to the habit he wore on the day of his death. I promised to do my best to procure these precious relics for him. No one knew better than the Spanish Sovereign how much the Saints can do for the honour and happiness of a people, by the example of their heroic virtues, and by the credit which they enjoy at the court of the King of Heaven. Hence it was that, conjoining on this point political sagacity and Christian prudence, he attached to the subject of canonizing a poor Friar Minor the importance of an affair of State. At the close of the audience, the Archbishop of Toledo, tutor of the Infanta, and the Marquis Denia, who had introduced me to the King, insisted upon my accepting their hospitality at the Escurial. They asked me for relics of the holy Brother, and soon all the great señors, adopting the fashion of the Court, were making the same request. Having learned the value set upon them by his Majesty, they, in the style of courtiers, received them with the utmost veneration."

When Philip III. succeeded his father, he did not forget the audience at the Escurial and Father John Ximenes' narrative. On several occasions, and on his own initiative, he solicited from the Court of Rome, in letters written with his own hand, the Beatification, and later on the Canonization, of the Servant of God. He likewise urged the Superiors of the Order to pursue the affair, with as much earnestness, as though it had been something personal to himself.

Wishing to give his people a public and solemn proof

Ch. XVII: A Glorious Sepulcher

of his veneration for Blessed Paschal, he paid a special visit to Our Lady of the Rosary. Never had Villareal seen such a brilliant pilgrimage. A multitude of retainers formed the vanguard of the cortège. The royal party itself comprised the King and his Queen, Margaret of Austria, followed by the Archduke Albert, Governor of the Low Countries, and his wife, the Infanta Isabella-Claire-Eugenie. Descending from his coach, Philip III. expressed his desire to enter the Chapel, with his suite, to visit the body of the Saint.

In his respect for the ordinances of the Church, and fearing to do anything contrary to the Sacred Canons, relatively to giving honour to a person deceased in the odour of sanctity, he inquired of the Guardian, through his chief Almoner, what marks of reverence he might lawfully give to the holy Brother. "Your Majesty may follow the inspirations of your own devotion, and all will be in order," was the Guardian's reply. The Court heard Mass, and then the noble pilgrims drew near the altar, upon which the shrine had been placed. Standing erect, with head uncovered, the King long contemplated the Man of God in silence; after him followed in succession the Queen and the Princes and the Infantas, and then the whole royal suite. Afterwards the monarch and his Court knelt down, and with touching fervour rendered their homage to Blessed Paschal.

The visit of the Court to Villareal brought other illustrious visitors there. All the viceroys of Valencia considered it a duty, after the example of his Majesty, to come as pilgrims to the sepulcher of the holy Friar. The Grandees of Spain did not show themselves less eager, and one day there came the Duke of Lermes and thirty of the most powerful nobles of the realm. In this brilliant procession of Princes and high dignitaries, the Dukes of Gandia, heirs of Francis Borgia, the sainted General of the

Society of Jesus, held the first place.

Amongst the ecclesiastical personages to visit the tomb of the Saint we may mention the two Papal legates, their Eminences Cardinal Frederick Borromeo and Camillus Massimo. The first had the honour of introducing the Cause, the latter of bringing it to a conclusion. To these is to be joined Cardinal Don Paschal of Arregona, one of the Dukes of Cordona. He owed his birth to the intercession of Blessed Paschal, and hence bore his name. As to the Ven. Archbishop of Valencia, John de Ribera, he continued, in another way, to entertain himself with his saintly friend, and adopted the custom of making a commemoration of him every day in his Office.

In Flanders, it was the daughter of Philip II., the Infanta Isabella-Claire-Eugenie, who, as Governess of the Low Countries, charged herself with the task of making our Saint known and loved, and of propagating his *cultus*. Like her brother, King Philip III., she had preserved an undying recollection of the call of Father John Ximenes at the Escurial, and this memorable interview now bore fruit.

In France, a Queen, who believed herself indebted to the Saint for a special grace, powerfully contributed to make known the name and virtues of her heavenly benefactor. Our Saint made a startling entry into Austria. Having delivered the Archduke Leopold, the Governor of the Tyrol, from a malignant fever, which was dragging him to death, he obtained for him an heir, by his intercession, who came into the world on the very feast-day of his saintly protector. The Archduke, profoundly grateful, caused an altar to be erected without delay in the Chapel of his palace at Innsbruck, and from the intensely Catholic Province of the Tyrol, the devotion to the holy man spread to other Provinces of the Monarchy.

In Sardinia, then a Spanish possession, a gentleman

Ch. XVII: A Glorious Sepulcher

made himself the propagator of the devotion. It was received with such favour, and miracles multiplied to such an extent, that, abstracting from all other prodigies, they alone would have sufficed for the canonization. One fact sums up this universal popularity.

When, in 1625, the Franciscan Friars had assembled from all parts of the world at Toledo, to hold the General Chapter, they testified that, in their respective Provinces, there was scarcely a single Church of the Order which had not got an altar to St. Paschal, enriched with innumerable *ex votos*, each of which recorded some grace obtained through his intercession.

CHAPTER XVIII
THE KNOCKS OF ST. PASCHAL

WHEN Christopher of Arta, the continuator of Father John Ximenes, comes, in his Life of the Saint, to that collection of unheard-of prodigies, known amongst Christian people under the name of the "Knocks of St. Paschal," he pauses, as though appalled by the subject, and doubtful of the effect his narrative may produce. In order to encourage himself in the difficult task, and at the same time to reassure his readers, he recounts a series of similar facts, taken from the lives of the Saints, and accepted by the best critics, and then, before plunging into his subject, he undertakes to show that the prodigies he is about to speak of are attested by thousands of trustworthy witnesses and invested with all the marks of unimpeachable authority. Having thus securely laid his foundation, Christopher of Arta proceeds to trace back the phenomenon to its origin, in order more effectively to study its magnificent developments.

It was in the year when the Cause had just been introduced at Rome that the first sounds made themselves heard in the shrine. In manifesting signs of life at this particular time, the Man of God seemed to wish to intervene personally in his own Cause. He could not have shown in a more striking manner the interest he took in the affair, or have stimulated more energetically the promoters of his glory. The Religious, who first heard these strange sounds, were both surprised and startled. For prudence' sake they kept the matter quiet, and before allowing reports of it to get abroad, they thought it better to refer to the Provincial and ask his advice. The latter, equally prudent, forbade them to speak about it, and enjoined a strict enquiry. This enquiry demonstrated beyond the shadow of doubt the reality of the knockings, their origin in the shrine, and the impossibility of explaining them otherwise than by the intervention of the Saint; for the shrine, being securely fastened by a triple lock, could not have been opened, and the wall, which blocked the entrance of the niche, effectually prevented anyone from entering it.

At the close of the enquiry a very natural anxiety was felt to understand the meaning of this singular phenomenon, and to know what Blessed Paschal wished to convey by these external and sensible signs. The Ven. Anthony Sobrino, then Provincial, considered the matter so important that he ordered special prayers to be offered up in all the Convents of the Province of St. John Baptist, for that intention. Although the desire of fathoming the mystery increased the fervour of the Religious, and although not a few of them were Saints, still it did not please Almighty God to lift the veil entirely. He deigned, however, to throw some light upon the subject in the following vision, and with this they had to be contented. This vision was granted to Brother John of Pavia, one of the most fervent Religious of the Reform. He related it to his Provincial under obedience and upon oath. "Being Infirmarian at the Convent of Villareal, I went into the chapel, after dinner, on the way to the Infirmary. As I was genuflecting before the Blessed Sacrament, I felt myself interiorly prompted to ask Blessed Paschal the meaning of the sounds that were heard in his shrine. At the same moment my soul seemed to be filled with a most vivid light, and in the midst of this light, I distinctly saw formed and spelled out, in characters of fire, these words of the

Prophet Jeremias: *'Quid tu vides, Hieremia?'*[1] (What seest thou, Jeremias?) The reply quickly followed the question and took its place alongside it: *'Virgam vigilantem ego video'* (I see a rod watching). And after these there came other words seemingly pronounced by the Blessed himself. *'Bene tu vides; quia ego vigilabo super Israel'* (Thou seest well, for I will watch over Israel). This internal colloquy impressed itself deeply on my mind. I then perceived with perfect clearness, that this symbolical rod was no other than Blessed Paschal, since Our Lord had entrusted him with the mission of watching over the Province and the faithful, like a sentinel always on guard. The perception of this mystery filled me with such consolation that I turned, all in tears, towards the Saint, and cried out thrice: *'O Vigilans!'* (O Watcher!) What shows still more the supernatural character of this vision is, that at that time, I was not acquainted with the text of Holy Scripture, and that my studies embraced only the rudiments of grammar."

All that we shall have to relate on this point is nothing else but the confirmation and the development of this beautiful vision. In themselves considered, these knocks are an interesting and fascinating subject of study. Those who heard them almost every day noticed that they did not always occur in the same mode, but that they were infinitely varied, and so clearly distinguishable one from another, that they might be arranged in different classes and their significance determined. Sometimes they seemed barely to graze the shrine, so light and discreet were they; on other occasions they broke out violently, and one would have thought the shrine was about to be broken; sometimes they were slow, at others quick; regular, or spasmodic; continuous, or occurring at intervals. On

---

[1] Jer. 1:2.

certain days they sounded like a sweet harmony, on others one seemed to be listening to peals of thunder, or to a furious cannonade.

The Religious of Villareal discovered, moreover, that these miraculous sounds were very often the announcement of events, either fortunate or unfortunate, public or private, the auguries of great calamity or of signal deliverance. Nearly all the events which affected the welfare of Spain, at this epoch, were announced and presaged in this manner. It was remarked that, on the eve of public calamities, the knocks were of a sort to strike fear into the mind, but that they were of a reassuring character when they heralded some triumph. During the period the French were besieging Fuenterrabia, which was of great strategic importance to Spain, gentle rappings of great frequency were heard in the shrine. On September 7 they became more rapid, but still gentler. The people were filled with wonder, and expected some great victory. Nor were they deceived. A few days later a courier brought the news of an unhoped-for success, resulting in the raising of the siege of Fuenterrabia.

In the same year that this siege took place, the troops of the French King encamped under the walls of Tortosa. The night, which preceded their arrival, was one of anguish for the Religious of the Holy Rosary. They were startled out of their sleep by the sound of terrible blows, coming from the shrine, and on going down to the chapel, they counted one hundred and twenty-six knocks, given without intermission, and with increasing force. Not long after they learned of the capture of Tortosa and the retreat of the Spanish army.

But never did the phenomena present itself under so terrifying an aspect as in October, 1640. For fourteen consecutive days blows, resembling a discharge of artillery, resounded from the shrine. They became stronger and more rapid on the Feast of St. Andrew. The Religious and the people, who had long held the clue to these mysterious knockings, recognized in them the announcement of some national calamity; and their presentiments were fully justified. The fourteen days corresponded to the general rising of the Portuguese, and on St. Andrew's Day, the Duke of Braganza was crowned King of Portugal. Omitting other instances of a like nature, we will give one final example which marked the close of hostilities between England and Spain. At the request of Philip IV., the Archbishop of Valencia had ordered public prayers to implore from God the blessings of peace, and, in consequence, there took place at Villareal, as in other towns, a solemn procession and the chanting of the Litany of the Saints. The procession started from the parish church, and after traversing part of the city, finished up at Our Lady of the Rosary. Now, at the moment the Religious were entering the Church, the cantors intoned that beautiful invocation, framed, as it would seem, specially to meet such circumstances: *"Ut Regibus et Principibus Christianis, pacem et veram concordiam donare digneris. Te rogamus audi nos"* (That Thou wouldst give peace and true concord to Christian Kings and Princes. We beseech Thee, hear us). From the depths of his shrine the Saint responded to the invocation with a rap, which sent a thrill through all who heard it, and gave them the assurance that peace was in sight. As a matter of fact, it was concluded soon afterwards, to the satisfaction of the belligerent parties.

From these events, wherein Paschal appears as the watchful guardian and protector of his native land, let us descend to facts of more modest proportions—namely, those affecting the well-being of the Religious Family, whose devoted son the holy man remained, even on the other side of the tomb. On the approach of one of the Provincial Chapters, Father Francis Emper was spoken of amongst the Fathers, as one likely to be elected Provincial. This good Friar got wind of it, and as he had an extreme dread of dignities, he went in his anguish to entreat Blessed Paschal to prevent his election. He seemed to hear the holy Brother saying to him interiorly: "You are going to be Provincial. You are going to be Provincial." "Oh, no, no, holy Man of God! Please not. Preserve me from this misfortune!" he cried. A light tap came to reassure and console the humble Religious. As a matter of fact, contrary to general expectations, and in consequence of an unforeseen incident which occurred at the Chapter, the suffrages were given to another, and he escaped the dignity he so much dreaded.

This same Father, when Guardian of Villareal, noticed that the wax candles were disappearing with unaccountable rapidity. Suspecting that certain of the Brothers were turning to their own personal use, what should be employed only for the altar, he strictly forbade his subjects to help themselves in this way. One of the Brothers, being none too particular, made light of this prohibition, and when he found his stock run out, he went into the chapel to take what he needed. Scarcely, however, had he touched the candlestick, when a knock, proceeding from the shrine, struck such terror into him that he let fall both candle and candlestick, and took to his heels with as much precipitation as if the Saint were in pursuit of him. Next day he humbly acknowledged his fault and the lesson he had received, in the Chapter of Faults.

The Lay Brothers, whose monitor he had been in life, received his admonitions more frequently than the other Religious. The Brother charged with calling the Community slept as soundly as a dormouse, and as he was most zealous for regular observance, he used always to be in dread of being overcome by drowsiness, and so missing the hour for giving the summons. On a certain night, in order to make quite sure, he stationed himself underneath the clock in the choir. This, however, did not prevent him from sleeping the sleep of the just. Awakening with a start, and perceiving some of the Friars praying in the stalls, he asked them whether the hour had struck. As they could not tell him, he addressed himself to Brother Paschal: "O holy man, how am I to know whether the hour has gone by? I beg you, in your charity, not to allow me to call the Community late." At the same instant twelve distinct but gentle taps in the shrine struck the midnight hour, and the Brother hastened away all jubilant to rouse the Community.

In saying that the Convents of the Province of St. John Baptist were so many terrestrial Paradises inhabited by Angels, we might add, as an amendment, that these Angels did not belong to Heaven, and hence we ought not to be surprised to find amongst them some of the failings and foibles of poor human nature. The Sacristan of the Convent of Villareal was a certain Father Joseph Casteñada, a Religious of tried virtue. When, on one occasion, he was ill, the Father Guardian gave him an assistant. Now, the latter took a fancy to the office, and began saying to himself that he was as well able to fulfil it as anyone else. So his disappointment was great when the Sacristan, being once more in a condition to resume his duties, came to ask him for the keys. "There they are; there are your keys!" he said, throwing them down rudely in front of him. "I wonder how it is, that the Superiors can entrust such an important occupation to such a helpless creature as you are?" And he went away growling. Father Joseph was somewhat taken aback at this outburst, which he had not in the least expected, but like the good Religious that he was, he soon regained his composure. Without a word he picked up the keys and went down into the garden, where he gathered a little bouquet of jasmine, to offer to Our Lord in His tabernacle. "Divine Master," he prayed, "I offer Thee this bunch of sweet-smelling flowers, in thanksgiving for the words which have just been addressed to me by that good Brother. What he says of me is only too true. I am indeed of very little use, but with the help of God I will try to improve, and do better for the future." Whilst he was uttering this humble and magnanimous prayer from the bottom of his heart, our Sacristan distinctly heard the body of the Saint turn around in the shrine and knock. The novelty of the thing at first caused him some alarm, but this was quickly changed into consolation. As the Saint continued to rap gently to mark his approbation of this act of virtue, Father Joseph felt emboldened to unbosom himself entirely to him. "Good Saint," he said, "to avoid for the future all disagreeable encounters with this Brother, I propose to keep out of his way as much as possible for the future, and only to come in contact with him, when it is absolutely necessary. Thus there will be peace, and all occasion of conflict will be removed. What do you think about it?" He had scarcely finished when a strange noise was heard. It was as though the shrine had been overturned and was being rolled on the ground. Thus did Blessed Paschal show his disapproval and signify, in his expressive language, what he thought about a resolution which was so far from being heroic. The lesson was understood, and, prostrate with his face on the ground, the Sacristan promised to go straight and be reconciled with the offending Brother.

On returning from the reconciliation, the Father came and knelt down before the shrine, to thank the Saint for having given him this warning and thus recalled him to a sense of his duty. Once again the recompense quickly followed on the sacrifice. For three hours gentle and melodious raps sounded, as it were, a paean of victory, and filled the soul of the good Religious with heavenly joy.

The faithful were by no means forgotten in the favours, of which these knocks were the sign and the instrument. They had, on the contrary, a very considerable share in them. The Brother Porter of Our Lady of the Rosary, for many years a witness of this continuous miracle, used to say on occasions when the Saint rewarded the fervour of pious souls with raps full of sonorous sweetness: "Ah, tomorrow there will be plenty of wax tapers!" He had remarked that these raps were sure announcements of extraordinary graces. Oftentimes, too, they contained a prophecy, and gave to those who came seeking the cure of their maladies the assurance that they would be healed. Sometimes the remedy was in the knocks themselves, which, by affecting the disease in some mysterious way, caused it to disappear. The Acts of the Process relate a host of cures of this sort, not forgetting others a thousand times harder to work—namely, the healing of the maladies of the soul and the misery of sin. The miracles assumed every variety of form and corresponded to every kind of spiritual want; awakening in one the hope of pardon, and piercing another with the stings of remorse, and urging all to break the chains of vice and to practise virtue.

We have already seen the deep reverence the Saint bore in lifetime towards the Word of God, the joy he felt in listening to it, and the paternal interest with which he followed the efforts of the young preachers. He retained the same attractions on the further side of the tomb. The preachers who mounted the pulpit at Villareal had no more attentive auditor than the holy man in his shrine. He did not miss a word of the discourse, and when needful, intervened to mark his favour or his disapproval. On two different occasions Father Ferrer had the joy and the honour of receiving his approval. We will relate the first of these, which occurred on a Thursday in Lent. The preacher had selected for his theme the story of Dives and Lazarus. Having shown that the rich miser's wealth had reduced him to penury, whilst the beggar had acquired true riches by means of evangelical poverty, the preacher, turning towards the tomb of the Blessed, continued:

"But why seek elsewhere for arguments to support this doctrine? Have we not in our midst the saintly Brother Paschal? Not only has he entered into the Kingdom of Heaven, where all riches are contained, but he has even purchased Paradise and has become its owner and its Master. Is not one who holds the keys of a dwelling and can go in and out at pleasure its owner and its master? Now, by those knocks which resound daily in his shrine, Blessed Paschal tells us clearly that his soul comes down from Heaven and gives to his body, hidden in the tomb, power to produce these mysterious sounds that strike upon our ears. What is this but to have the keys of Heaven and to be its owner and master? Whence is this marvellous power, whence are these infinite riches derived, if not from evangelical poverty, which in him was rigid in the extreme?"

At the conclusion of this passage, visibly appreciated by the auditors, a loud knock was heard, which greatly increased their emotion, and gave an assurance to the preacher that he had spoken the truth, and in nowise exaggerated the excellence of evangelical poverty.

Other preachers were less favoured than Father Ferrer. Their mishaps naturally lead us to speak, in this chapter, of the reluctance with which some excellent souls accepted this assemblage of marvels, and of the strong opposition sometimes offered by them to what they considered as old women's tales, better suited to amuse the credulity of the people than to promote solid devotion.

Contradiction proves works of piety, and discloses their real worth, just as a man's virtue is tried and manifested by temptation. What is based merely on popular excitement and credulity, melts away under the first breath of adverse criticism, whilst, on the contrary, that which survives such attacks and emerges triumphant from the ordeal, is shown by that very fact to rest upon a solid basis of truth. Now, the knocks of St. Paschal hold their ground, in spite of all the attempts that have been made, for one reason or another, to discredit them.

Many rejected them *a priori* as undeserving of serious consideration. Others thought such occurrences unlikely. So they were, but does not the proverb remind us that "Truth is stranger than fiction"? Amongst the opponents, we must not forget that class of men who, entering unbidden into the Divine counsels, wish to dictate to Almighty God what sort of miracles He ought, or ought not, to work. Many good souls there were, who held their judgment in suspense and said, "Let us wait." Finally, the wisest came, saw, and dispelled their doubts, convinced by the evidence of the facts they had under their very eyes. In the last category were two Fathers of the Society of Jesus, who had come on pilgrimage to the tomb of Blessed Paschal.

After paying their devotions to him with much fervour, they remained in the chapel to discourse about the sounds which were said to proceed from the shrine. Both were able theologians. They weighed the *pros* and *cons,* and raised various objections which occurred to the mind of each. This argumentation, though reasonable and lawful in itself, occasioned sore vexation to Josephine Mas, a pious woman, who, at that moment, was reciting her prayers in a corner of the chapel. Burning for the glory and privileges of her Saint, she could not bear that what was to her clear as noonday, and beyond dispute, should become a subject of debate. Discontinuing her prayers, therefore, she lent an attentive ear to what the two Fathers were saying, and when, at a certain point, it seemed that they were inclining to the negative, she could bear it no longer, and felt that it was high time to intervene and to cause light to spring forth and so clear up these doubts. Consequently, she addressed to Blessed Paschal this whispered prayer: "My good Saint, the moment has come for striking a decisive blow, in order to prove the truth clearly to these two Religious. Don't let them remain in the dark any longer. If you hear me, I promise, on my part, to explain to them what is meant by the knocks you give, and thus they will be doubly convinced of the reality of the miracle." The good Saint was not deaf to the prayer of his faithful client, and a loud report, which shook the Church, startled the two Religious. Their amazement increased when Josephine Mas came up to tell them about the prayer she had just said for their enlightenment. Fully convinced, by this time, they cast themselves down before the tomb, thanking Our Lord with tears of joy, for having made them witnesses of such a prodigy.

Father Diego Candel, a Discalced Carmelite, did not give in so easily; it required no less than three admonitions to bring full conviction to his mind. Nevertheless, he was very devout to Blessed Paschal, and joyfully agreed to preach his panegyric. It was just this panegyric which was tormenting him. As he did not feel convinced in his own mind about the reality of the miraculous sounds, it seemed to him that it would be better not to mention them, whilst, on the other hand, how could he pass them over in silence, without impairing the belief of the people? So, in order to free himself from this anxiety, he went to the Saint himself, and asked light of him whilst kneeling before his tomb. "O glorious Servant of God, I firmly believe that you are most powerful with God, but as regards those knocks, that are so much talked about, I must confess to you that my conviction is far from being so strong. If they are real, I beg you, for my spiritual consolation, not to refuse to allow me to hear them." Three knocks immediately resounded in his ears; but, thinking he was a prey to some delusion, he asked that a second proof might be given him at once. "Ah, it seems that faith is coming to me," he then said. "Great Saint, confirm me with a third proof, so that I may be able to speak of this prodigy in the pulpit." And the third proof was given. It is said that never did preacher speak with greater conviction and fire of the miraculous knocks, than this new Thomas.

Our Saint brought conviction to another orator, who preached his panegyric, but was doubtful on this same point. This panegyrist was Don Frederic of Villaraja, Canon of Valencia, and uncle of Father Michael, then Guardian of Villareal. When he reached the portion of his discourse upon the Saint's life, in which the subject of the knocks would most appropriately be introduced, he thought to skilfully evade the difficulty by saying: "This great Saint is dead, and yet he still, in a sense, lives, if we are to credit the testimony of those who maintain that they have heard signs of life in the tomb. Far from me be the thought of denying such a fact; but I must confess I have my doubts concerning it."

No one in the audience was more grieved or shocked by these words than the preacher's nephew, Father Michael. How he repented having invited him! But the principal question was, how to efface the unhappy effect produced on the minds of the people. Only the Saint could repair the scandal, so it was to him the poor Guardian had recourse without delay. "Blessed Paschal," he said to him, "the Guardian of Villareal cannot presume, like his predecessors, to give you a precept of obedience; nevertheless, as Superior of a Convent, where you were living for many years as a subject, I think that I have some right to require you to cure my uncle of a more than distressing doubt." The Saint obeyed, without a precept of obedience, and a vigorous knock proceeding from the shrine interrupted the Canon's discourse. Utterly confounded by this solemn reproof, he burst into tears, and thus, as the Chronicle says, his eyes disavowed publicly what his lips had affirmed.

It is interesting to learn that Father Michael had at one period himself been amongst the number of doubters, and that, in taking such a lively interest in the Saint's glory on the above occasion, he was but making atonement for his former scepticism. The fact we allude to is all the more interesting, inasmuch as it enters into the history of a person with whom it behoves us to become acquainted. This person is a nephew of the Saint—his brother's son. Paschal had obtained for this child of singular purity and wonderful simplicity, the grace of vocation to the Seraphic Order. He received the name of Brother Diego, and was assigned as his residence the Convent of the Holy Rosary, where lay the body of his holy uncle. Scarcely was he clothed in the habit than he adopted the custom, when leaving or returning to the Convent, of going to ask the *Benedicite* of his sainted relative, after receiving the blessing of the Superior. Kneeling before the shrine, and acting as though his uncle were still living, this good nephew related to him, with the simplicity of a child, all his actions and intentions; asked his advice and submitted everything to his approval; and then he mentioned, one after another, the benefactors from whom he had received anything when on quest, and warmly recommended to him their affairs, both spiritual and temporal. At the conclusion of the prayer, certain gentle tappings were generally heard, and a sound in the shrine like that of a body turning round. The Religious, who sometimes observed the young Friar, unbeknown to him, very soon perceived that the uncle had a certain partiality for this nephew, and indulged in a kind of nepotism, in his regard, by favouring him particularly. They took advantage of this fact, and frequently had recourse to his meditation, in order to hear the miraculous knocks.

Now, it so happened that on one occasion Father Michael paid a visit to Villareal, and he eagerly embraced this favourable opportunity of testing the reality of the alleged miraculous knockings. For this purpose he had recourse to Brother Diego, and the latter, whilst promising to be his advocate, advised him to have patience until after Whitsuntide, which coincided that year with the Feast of Blessed Paschal. "My holy uncle," he said, "never gives signs of life during days when there is a large concourse of people, on account of the excitement and disorder that might ensue from it. After the Feast, we shall see." When everything had returned to its wonted calm, Father Michael, who occupied a cell remote from the Church, very distinctly heard a knock, which interrupted him in his labours, and was so violent as nearly to upset the inkpot. He had not yet recovered from his astonishment, when Brother Diego entered his cell and said to him: "My uncle has just been knocking; that was the noise you heard." An hour after a second bang resounded in the cell, and the Brother hastened to bring the information that his uncle had knocked again. "I am only half convinced. Brother Diego," said the Father to him; "all that may be only a freak of the imagination. If you wish me to retract what I have preached, on the subject of these miraculous blows, you must get the Saint to make me hear one which it is impossible to doubt about." He heard what he wanted that same day at the second *Memento* of his Mass, which Brother Diego was serving. "Are you convinced this time?" said the Brother, when he entered the sacristy after Mass. "What else could you expect my uncle to do, in order to convince you?"

What has already been recorded concerning the miraculous knockings is sufficiently astonishing; but our astonishment will increase on learning that all that has hitherto been related is only the prelude to still greater prodigies. These latter give to the prerogative reserved to our Saint a kind of world-wide extension. "In order that the whole of Christendom might enjoy this privilege, and in order that this grace should no longer be confined within the narrow limits of a sanctuary, inaccessible to the majority of the faithful," says Father Pañes in his "Life of St. Paschal," "it has pleased Our Lord to enlarge the sphere of His mercy, and to endow the relics and images of His servant with the power of causing the miraculous sounds to be heard. In this way those who live afar off, or whom sickness or other good reasons prevent from coming on pilgrimage to Villareal, can hear the sounds and receive this grace at home, or wherever else they may be." Thus the entire world becomes the field of this miracle; because everywhere the relics and images of the Saint answer like an echo to the mysterious blows which resound in the shrine at Villareal.

Those who in the name of Divine wisdom sought to put an end to the miracle, when it had as its theatre only the Chapel of the Rosary, were even more sorely tried when they learnt that the knocks of St. Paschal, overleaping every obstacle, were heard in all parts of the earth. God could only work a miracle for reasons of the greatest weight, they had said, and here He was, as it were, sporting with prodigies, and sowing them broadcast, for reasons apparently of no great moment. So true it is, that the Wisdom of God is not as the wisdom of men, and that the exigencies of His mercy are other than those of human science and prudence.

The first manifestation of this new series of miracles, and perhaps the most astounding of all, is related, in the minutest detail, by witnesses at the canonical Process of Valencia. In reading the account, we seem to be dreaming, and one would scarcely venture to speak of such occurrences, had they not been attested by the Archbishop and his Suffragans, the Court Dignitaries, and in fact by the entire city.

Don Antonio Saavedra, Secretary of the Viceroy, had in his service a little black Mohammedan boy, six years of age. Don Antonio placed him under the patronage of Blessed Paschal, asking the Saint to incline the heart of this child to the true faith, and to be as a Guardian Angel to him. The effect of this patronage was soon evident, for, of his own accord, the little boy came, at the end of five months, to solicit the grace of Baptism. He learned the rudiments of the Christian faith with such extraordinary readiness, and appeared to have such a clear insight into the mysteries of our holy religion, that the catechists were in a state of astonishment. As Don Antonio was fully persuaded that the gift of faith had been accorded to this young Mussulman, through the intercession of Blessed Paschal, he desired that the name of Anthony Paschal should be given to him at the sacred font. On the day of his

Ch. XVIII: The Knocks of St. Paschal 241

Baptism, this truly Christian master led the neophyte, still clad in his small white robe, to the tomb of the Saint, and there, holding his protégé by the hand, he presented him to the Saint, again beseeching him to be a father to him, and to continue what had been commenced under such happy auspices. To betoken, in a more sensible manner, that this new Christian was the spiritual son of Blessed Paschal, he hung round his neck a reliquary, containing a picture of the Saint, and a fragment of the bone of his foot.

Two months after this great day, when he had become a child of God, Anthony Paschal felt some light taps on his breast. It was the reliquary, which seemed as though alive, and was giving the child a living proof of the interest taken in him by his heavenly protector. These taps were frequently repeated, and became, as it were, of continued recurrence. When the people of the house wanted to hear them, they had only to say: "Anthony Paschal, is the Saint knocking just now?" And the child would reply "Yes" or "No," as the case might be. "Let us see your reliquary," pursued the curious. "Very well." And then, with great simplicity, he used to take off the reliquary and show it to them, saying very devoutly: "Blessed be the most Holy Sacrament of the Altar." And the miraculous knocks made themselves heard at once. After uttering the salutation of the Eucharist, the child, all absorbed in devotion and under the influence of a plainly-marked interior emotion, remained silent and was unable to utter another word. At first the rumour of this singular manifestation did not get outside the walls of the viceregal palace, and precautions were taken not to divulge it without proper investigation. Although the child's innocence and candour precluded the suspicion of trickery, he was closely watched, and in order to assure conviction of the reality of the facts, the experiment was repeated so often, that even the most incredulous had to give in. It was only then, that they ventured to entrust the secret to certain intimate friends. The latter kept the secret very badly, it would seem, since it soon became public property. Henceforward every distinguished visitor at the palace requested the favour of seeing little Anthony Paschal, and of hearing his salutation of the Blessed Sacrament, and listening to the miraculous knocks. As the spectacle was edifying, the Viceroy and his wife did not make any difficulty about yielding to the wishes of their visitors, and the child was called in each time he was asked for.

A providential occurrence placed the miracle in a new light, and obtained for it the sanction of ecclesiastical authority. The Canonical Process had just commenced at Valencia, and the Tribunal was sitting at the Archbishop's residence. At the conclusion of one of the sessions, the Archbishop, Don Luis Alphonsus de Cameros, accompanied by his Suffragans, the Bishops of Segorbe and Marona, and other Ecclesiastics, came to pay their respects to the Viceroy. The conversation turned naturally on the Process of Beatification, and they discussed everything connected with it. To the great surprise of the Viceroy, the Archbishop made no allusion to the facts, that were happening every day at the viceregal palace. It was requisite to make him break through this prudent reserve and to get him to declare himself categorically. This task the Viceroy set himself to accomplish. He therefore related with much animation all he knew about the child and his wonderful reliquary. As the Archbishop continued to preserve silence, and seemed embarrassed and perplexed, the Prince said to him: "Does your Grace call in question the reality of the facts?" "No, not exactly, but—" And he commenced to raise a number of learned objections. "Well, then," replied the Viceroy, "there is a simple way of

Ch. XVIII: The Knocks of St. Paschal

settling the matter. We will call in the child, and your Grace can see for yourself what is to be thought about it." As the Archbishop did not see his way to demur on this point, the servants went in search of Anthony Paschal, who soon appeared on the scene. When he had knelt down in front of the Archbishop, the Viceroy said to him: "Anthony Paschal, show your reliquary and recite the praises." "Blessed be the most Holy Sacrament of the Altar! Blessed be Mary, conceived without stain!" And the miraculous knockings succeeded the praises, without a moment's delay. The Archbishop counted fifteen of them, divided into groups of five. His emotion was so intense that he shed tears, and, kissing the reliquary, said: "Verily, God is wonderful in His Saints." Then the Suffragan Bishops and the Ecclesiastics present venerated the reliquary in turn. Blessed Paschal had pleaded his cause for himself and had convinced his judges.

The Archbishop had to endure a little unpleasantness in consequence of this incident. The Procurator of the Cause came to see him the following day, and the Prelate, thinking to please him, related what had occurred the preceding evening, and how he could now pronounce upon the miracle not merely as a judge, but also as a witness. The Procurator appeared very much vexed, inasmuch as this upset the regular order of procedure. So, leaving the Archbishop's house, he went straight to the Residence, to reproach the Viceroy with having challenged an experiment, which had transformed judges into witnesses. The Prince, who regarded only the glory of the Saint, took the reproof anything but well. "To listen to you," he said sharply to the Procurator, "one would think you were the adversary of the Cause, instead of its promoter." And he turned on his heel.

Let us not forget to add what puts the climax upon this

signal favour, and shows to what a degree little Anthony Paschal had entered into the graces of his glorious Patron. All the pictures and relics of the Saint which were presented to the child had scarcely been touched by his hands than the miraculous knocks commenced to proceed from them. This assumed such proportions, that the Procurator of the Cause and the Friars of the Convent of St. John of Ribera were disturbed by it. They feared that, on account of its very frequency, the miracle would lose its prestige, and would in a certain sense be discredited. Nothing of the kind happened, however, thanks be to God. The prodigy, by its multiplication, served to increase the friends of the Saint and the promoters of his *cultus*. As it is impossible to relate anything more than a tithe of the marvellous facts, which fill whole volumes in the Acts of the Process, we shall confine ourselves to recalling a few of the most salient, particularly those having reference to the Holy Eucharist.

The Ven. Father Diego Danon, renowned in the Province of St. John Baptist, for his heroic virtues and holy death, was one of the first to place himself under the protection of his glorious confrère. Having procured a fragment of bone, he encased it in a reliquary which he wore hung round his neck. He never parted with it till his death. This relic became a standing miracle. Day and night it ticked in the manner of a clock. It was, indeed, the spiritual clock of this saintly Father. It was in vain he sought to distract people's attention from the sound, by loudly rattling the beads, which he always carried in his hands. No one was deceived by this manœuvre; all who approached him distinctly heard the taps given by the reliquary. During the first quarter of an hour of the meditation, which followed the midnight office, the blows became accentuated. "I could speak without end upon this subject," adds one of the witnesses, "because I lived six years with Father Danon in the Convent at Granada, and had much intercourse with him. I will add only one detail, and that is that, a little before his death, Father Danon revealed to his confessor that Blessed Paschal had bestowed many favours upon him, by means of this relic, and that the happy effects produced in his soul would only be known on the Day of Judgment."

Father Alphonsus of St. Thomas, Discalced Trinitarian and a celebrated preacher, relates in his deposition that having often heard the miraculous knocks of St. Paschal spoken of, he conceived a strong desire of procuring a relic of the Saint. Once he had obtained possession of this treasure, so ardently coveted, he was favoured, like Father Danon, in an exceptional manner, and the relic became a source of copious graces and blessings to him. During one of his meditations in choir he counted sixty raps. They flooded his soul with such delight, that it seemed as though the Church itself were not large enough to contain the ocean of joy in which he was plunged. On one occasion, when he had administered the Last Sacraments to one of the Benefactors of the Community, he presented the relic to him to venerate. "Remember me to-morrow at Holy Mass, in case I should pass away during the night," said the dying man to him. The Confessor promised not to forget him in the memento for the dead, but, distracted by other cares, he did not remember his promise. When he reached the second memento, the redoubled pulsations of the reliquary put him on the alert. Fearing that he had committed some fault against the rubrics, he carefully reflected as to how he had failed, and what the Saint of the Eucharist could have to reproach him with, on this head. He was unable to discover anything, and so proceeded with his Mass. Before he had finished, the recollection of the promise made on the preceding evening occurred to his mind. Confounded at this forgetfulness, he hastened to make amends for it by reciting a *De Profundis* for the repose of the soul of his penitent, who had died during the night. The relic responded to this prayer with an approving rap.

Amongst these miraculous knocks some had a direct relation to the Holy Eucharist. They form a class apart, and cannot be forgotten or left out in the life of the Patron of Eucharistic Associations. They contributed, in a large measure, to revive faith in the Blessed Sacrament, and to popularize that salutation which little Anthony Paschal had always on his lips: "Blessed be the most Holy-Sacrament of the Altar." Some of them took place in the Church of the Holy Rosary, and were the direct work of the Saint, lying in his shrine. Others, infinitely more numerous, were produced in almost all parts by his relics and images.

How could the watchful Sentinel, in his ceaseless vigil, by day and by night, be unmindful of the Blessed Sacrament, the adoration due to it, the reverence that should encompass the tabernacle, and the purity of heart demanded in the celebration of the holy Mysteries? In his shrine, and through his relics and images, Paschal was still the intrepid champion of the rights of the God hidden under the sacramental species, and an avenger of the outrages committed against this most August Sacrament.

On one occasion a Spanish Grandee, the Duke of Alcala, entered the Church of Our Lady of the Rosary, with his suite, at the time when the Father Guardian was celebrating his Mass at the altar of St. Paschal. Accustomed to making himself at home everywhere, and unused to putting any restraint upon himself, this high and mighty señor made his entry into the House of God as though it had been a theatre, talking in a loud voice to his retainers, who were not slow to copy their master. This noisy entrance and the hum of conversation so upset the celebrant, that he could no longer remember what part of the Mass he had arrived at. In order to recover himself, and, still more, to vindicate the honour of Almighty God, he commanded Blessed Paschal, in his quality of Guardian, to quell this scandalous tumult, and to recall these fine gentry to a sense of their duty. A blow struck with force upon the shrine followed this command. The Duke and his people had not to inquire as to whom this warning was addressed. Bewildered and terrified, they became silent, as though by magic, and by their respectful deportment and the veneration they paid the Saint, they repaired the unseemliness and scandal of their tumultuous entry.

The following incident is still more characteristic: On a certain great feast-day, at the moment the last Mass was just finishing, the Religious and the faithful saw some strange parishioners arrive at the Church of the Holy Rosary. It was a gang of brigands, armed to the teeth, having as their captain an unfrocked and fallen priest. "Is there another Mass?" demanded this wretch, of the Guardian. "No," replied he. "All right, then; in order that my people may fulfil the precept, I will say Mass myself." And without other preparation than that of unbuckling from his girdle the holsters for holding his pistols, he quickly donned the priestly vestments and mounted to the altar with an assured step, carrying his head high and with as much coolness as if he had been a saint. Great was the distress of the Religious and the faithful on beholding this desecration, which no one was able to hinder.

The Mass proceeded quietly until the Consecration. At this point the sacrilegious priest faltered. In vain he strove to pronounce the sacramental formula; his tongue was paralyzed, and the greater efforts he made, the less was he able to succeed. The faithful, whose eyes never left him, saw him stop, without being able to divine the reason. The hour of grace had struck, and a ray of divine light had just entered into this darksome soul. For the first time, in long years, the renegade raised his heart to God, and taking Blessed Paschal as mediator, he besought him to obtain for him the grace of being able to continue and to finish the Mass. In return, he promised, if heard, to be converted and to repair by means of penance the scandals of his unhappy life. "A blow from the shrine knocked at his heart, harder than flint, and he burst into tears," says one of the biographers. At the Elevation of the Host a second knock was heard, and a third at the Elevation of the Chalice. With what emotion the faithful now followed this stirring Mass! They divined the mystery of grace, when they saw the unhappy wretch leaving the altar, with his head bowed down, and his face bathed in tears.

The brigands looked at one another, and asked themselves anxiously what was going to be the upshot of this adventure. They were not left long in suspense. Their former chief, coming to them, related what had happened, and declared his unshakable resolve to amend his life. As they had themselves witnessed the prodigy, they departed without recrimination or violence, and the converted sinner, his chain being now broken, re-entered the Convent alone. "Send me one of your Religious, full of learning and prudence," said he to the Guardian, "so that I may be able to treat with him upon a matter which is of great importance and extremely involved." This affair, so difficult of settlement, was, as may be guessed, that of his conscience. The Guardian offered him Father Nuniesa, Commissary-General of the Order, a man of great learning and consummate prudence, who had just come to Our

Lady of the Rosary to make a Novena to Blessed Paschal. The penitent accepted him with gratitude; he was the very man he wanted. When, after numerous and protracted sessions, this interminable general confession was finished, the convert, faithfully keeping his word, retired from the world, and repaired his past scandals by an exemplary life.

It is impossible to admire sufficiently the constant and active solicitude of the Saint in his shrine for all that affected the integrity and the glory of the Sacrifice of the Mass. His attention extended to the smallest details. If the sanctuary lamp was going out for want of oil, the Sacristan was soon reminded of it by a knock, discreetly given. At a push, the Saint, resuming the functions of server at Mass, which used to be so dear to him, came forward to supply what was wanting. Here is one beautiful example: When Father Augustin was one day celebrating at the Altar of St. Paschal, the server was called away suddenly, and left him at the first Memento. When the Elevation drew near, and he had not returned, the good Father, who had a tender, not to say rather scrupulous, conscience, began to debate anxiously in his own mind whether it was right for him to go on, and to consecrate in the absence of the one who should ring the bell at the Elevation. The Saint reassured him, and advantageously replaced the usual tinkling of the bell by his miraculous raps at each of the Elevations, and they sounded with such harmoniousness from the depths of the shrine, as to throw Father Augustin into a sort of ecstasy.

The reverence which the holy man had borne towards priests in his lifetime, because he "beheld in them the Son of God," he still continued to testify to them by urging them to become more and more worthy of their vocation. We meet again here with the good Carmelite Father, whom he had hithertofore delivered from a formidable doubt. What he now asked his heavenly Patron to obtain for him was the grace of being a true and holy Religious. To show how deeply the prayer of his client had touched the heart of Our Divine Lord, the Saint struck a blow of such penetrating sweetness at the moment of the Elevation, that the soul of the celebrant seemed to be melting away. Here, too, we meet once more with Father Casteñada, the Sacristan with the little bunch of jasmine. He was agitated with the desire of knowing whether the Saint would be pleased, if petitions were addressed to him, in the name of the devotion and the love he bore towards the most Blessed Sacrament. This was to touch the Saint in a tender spot; so that the reply was not long in coming, and knocks full of sweetness marked his assent, and the gratification such a mode of address would cause him.

It remains to mention one other feature of these miraculous sounds, and one which seems especially designed to put the finishing stroke to all this assemblage of marvels. This time it is no longer for the advantage of others, or to bring them help and consolation, that the Saint makes himself heard in his shrine; but it is for his own consolation that he produces his knocks, to satisfy his insatiable devotion to the Eucharist, and to continue his role of perpetual adorer of the Blessed Sacrament. One day the blows coming from the shrine seemed to be striking on the tabernacle. It was the faithful disciple who craved an audience and wished to speak with his Lord. Oh, ineffable marvel! The Host replied to this appeal, and knocked in Its turn. Then between Master and servant there ensued a mystic dialogue, a sort of duet of unspeakable charm. Only the Angels were worthy to hear it and were able to appreciate its divine harmony.

Father Diego Mazon received from God a revelation, which seemed to give him a foretaste of the delights of

Paradise. The life of this holy Religious, who died in the odour of sanctity, sufficiently authenticates this miracle. On account of the ecstasies, which frequently surprised him whilst saying Mass, the Superior had assigned him a private oratory where there was nothing to hinder his communications with God. His Mass, which was frequently interrupted by tears, usually lasted two hours. Conversing one day with his Provincial about the knocks of St. Paschal and his many miracles, Father Diego confided to him the following precious anecdote: "Whilst I was saying Mass at the Altar, near the picture of St. Paschal, I heard the sound of a knock coming from the picture, after the first consecration. It struck the Host I held in my hand, and the Host replied to this loving invitation. The knocks succeeded one another, each echoing each, and this lasted so long that it seemed as though I should never be able to finish my Mass. I was also afraid lest I should allow the transport of emotion, which stirred my soul, to appear externally." This incident admirably corroborates other facts of the same nature, which figure in the Process. It renders easier of acceptance the testimony of those who affirmed that they had heard divine responses in the tabernacle to the mysterious sounds in the shrine.

To such of our readers who may be disposed to take alarm at this invasion of the supernatural, we will reply with Christopher of Arta, one of the best biographers of our Saint: "It is sufficient for us to know that such prodigies, without being absolutely necessary, always correspond with certain needs in those on whose behalf they are worked. They serve, indeed, to confound infidels, heretics, and the impious, and to convert sinners. They fortify the just in their faith, console the faithful, provide much food for devotion, not to mention other effects not less salutary, in the witnesses of these marvels, and also upon those who hear them related."

This suffices, and more than suffices, to explain and to justify their wondrous profusion. Everything lends itself to the supposition that these prodigies, multiplied without end in a Catholic land, were God's answer to the impious negations and the innumerable sacrileges of heretics. It was the period when the new Iconoclasts burned the images of the Saints, and scattered their ashes to the winds.

By glorifying, through the agency of miracles, the relics and the images of one of His most illustrious servants, Almighty God solemnly affirmed the lawfulness of the religious veneration given to them by the Holy Catholic Church. By sowing miracles in such profusion, He protested against the outrages offered to Him in His Saints, and repaired the injury in His own Divine way.

> "Con tus golpas admirables
> Celas de Dios los honores.
> De Hereges y peccadores
> Conviertas innumerables."[2]

Even in our own days this miracle has not ceased, of which it is said by the author of the Spanish Martyrology: "It is the most wonderful thing in the world, and nothing similar to it is found in the Acts of the Saints."[3]

In Spain and in the southern provinces of Italy, where

---

[2] O Paschal! By thy wondrous blows
Thy burning zeal for God is shown.
A host in sin and error steeped
By them to truth and grace are won.

[3] "Quod est valde mirabile et nullibi in Sanctorum Actibus scriptum reperitur."—Tayanno: "Martyrologium Hisp."

Ch. XVIII: The Knocks of St. Paschal

the most lively devotion to our Saint prevails, his knocks are heard, as of yore, in their various forms. The best known of all is the mysterious warning given by the Saint to his faithful clients, three days before their death. Religious worthy of all credence have asserted in the most formal manner that they have frequently witnessed this phenomenon during their ministry to the sick. In those countries it occurs so often that no one is astonished by it. By this salutary premonition the Adorer of the Blessed Sacrament prepares his clients for their last Communion, for the Viaticum, which hallows the passage from time to Eternity, and assures the beatitude of Heaven. It is the last grace and the most precious of all. Nothing, we may well believe, is better calculated to promote devotion to the Patron of Eucharistic Associations, and to increase tenfold the number of his clients, than this last-mentioned miracle. It will be sufficient to make it known to our readers, in order to awaken in them the desire of practising devotion to St. Paschal, which produces such abundant fruits.

CHAPTER XIX
A GALAXY OF MIRACLES

"WITH death, all perishes."

This assertion, though nothing but a blasphemous gibe, in the mouth of the infidel, who wishes to drive from his mind the disturbing thought of the soul's immortality, is nevertheless almost literally true, when applied to our earthly existence. As regards this present world, it is allowable to assert, without suspicion of impiety, that everything perishes with death. Power, honour, riches, talent, beauty—all must equally succumb to the universal destroyer. Of the orator, whose words held the crowd spellbound, of the conqueror under whose footsteps the earth trembled and shook, what remains? The Holy Scripture answers: *A tomb.* "Only the grave remaineth for me."[1] Doubtless the names of the great ones of this world are writ large on the pages of history; doubtless their statues are raised in public places, and even the semblance of immortality accrues to them, from the influence their thoughts and actions exercise upon posterity; but this is the sole kind of immortality these favoured scions of the human stock can pretend to, and in reality it is so small a matter, that we can say truly that the tomb has swallowed them up, and that, as regards the world, they have ceased to exist.

It is not to them, but to the living, that aspirants after favour and preferment betake themselves. One who should kneel before their sepulcher to solicit their patronage with the high and mighty of the hour would be rightly regarded

---

[1] Job 17:1.

as a lunatic; for their ashes are forever cold, and no living response can issue from them. Visitors at our museums, perhaps, may halt respectfully before historic relics, exposed in the glass cases, and contemplate with transient emotion all that is left of the great men, whose names once resounded through the world; but no one would dream of seeking relief in his pains, or help in his needs, through the agency of these lifeless remains. Thus does the fashion of this world pass away, and together with it, all who have been the greatest and most commanding characters, upon the stage of life. Their memory passes away with the pompous clatter of their obsequies. "Their memory hath perished with a noise" (Ps. 9:7).

It is entirely different with those great Servants of God, whom we call the Saints. If the assertion were not too much like a paradox, one might say that they only really begin to live on the day of their death, and that from that moment, which proves so fatal to human glory, dates the unparalleled influence they exercise upon the world. Thus their after-life is itself a living reality, more fruitful, and more replete with splendid achievements, than that portion of their existence which elapsed from the cradle to the grave. Their sphere of action, hitherto circumscribed, is then wonderfully enlarged, and knows neither hindrances nor limitations. After the likeness of their Divine Master, raised up upon the cross, they now commence to exert a mysterious and all-pervading attraction. Their history beyond the tomb then begins, never more to end—a history crowded with life and interest. People approach these chosen friends of God, marvelling at their wondrous power, to entreat them to obtain for them spiritual and temporal favours, and, wonderful to relate, the Saints reigning in glory answer all these petitions, and liberally scatter the blessings of

Heaven, thus continuing to play their part of perpetual benefactors of humanity. Wherever a thread of their clothing, or morsel of their bones, is to be found, miracles take place and wonders abound. These favourites of God are nearer to us, and more truly amongst us, when they have left us, than in the days of their earthly pilgrimage; and it is possible to derive the greatest benefits from intercourse with them; for now, at least, we can take them in all security as our advocates, and rely upon their patronage, without any fear of finding them wearied by the multitude of our requests.

Perhaps no life of a Saint is illuminated with such a blaze of posthumous glory, as the life of Blessed Paschal. What still remains to be told, after all that has been related concerning the miraculous knocks, gives evidence of a prodigiously active life, displaying itself simultaneously in a thousand different places. It is, indeed, now that he has at length become all things to all men, and that, without any distinction of country, race, or clime, he appears wherever faith and piety summon him, or demand his aid.

At the first Process, after the judges had discarded everything, that was not of primary importance, they had still one hundred and seventy-five conspicuous miracles, any one of which, alone, would have been sufficient to determine the Beatification. At the second Process they had become so numerous, that the bare list of them filled several volumes. Only three were submitted to examination, but so brilliant were they, that they carried the votes at the very outset.

We shall follow the example of the Postulator, and, in order not to be overwhelmed by our subject, we shall merely recall two or three of these miracles. They will serve to give the reader a notion of the credit enjoyed by our Saint at the Court of the Heavenly King.

Ch. XIX: A Galaxy of Miracles

The witnesses, cited in the different Processes of Beatification and Canonization, form a veritable army, comprising entire populations of certain localities, who came forward to relate to the ecclesiastical judges, what they had seen and heard, and the innumerable graces bestowed upon them, through the intercession of the holy Brother. Those witnesses who had enjoyed the privilege of conversing with him during his lifetime did not fail to recall the fact. "I had," they would say, "the good fortune of being personally acquainted with Brother Paschal. He used to come to our house, and we went to see him at the Convent. Oh, what a holy man! When shall we see his like again?" Without exception, they all showed a legitimate pride in the fact of being numbered amongst the friends of a Saint. These witnesses are, indeed, charming and attractive personalities. From the eight volumes in folio of nearly 1,000 pages each, containing their testimony, may be gathered, as perhaps from no other document, what the Spanish people really were, at this troublous period of history—constant in their faith, which they knew so well how to preserve in its integrity, and not less solicitous for purity of morals, and the virtues, which are the honour and glory of a Christian people.

On the resumption of each of the Processes, the judges took cognizance of the non-appearance of several of the earlier witnesses, who had died in the interval. After reading this obituary notice, the Notary Apostolic questioned the priests and the faithful present, and adjured them to tell what they knew about the missing witnesses, so that the value of their testimony might be determined. Nothing could be more beautiful or touching than the answers returned to these interrogations. It will not be out of place to quote a few of them. "What do you know about Clementia Sagasta?" asked the Notary Apostolic.

"Clementia Sagasta? Ah, the worthy woman! God rest her soul! She was always ready to oblige her neighbours. You should have seen how she kept her household, and how well her children were raised!" "Witness, what do you know about Salvador Balaguer?" "Salvador Balaguer? He was a thorough Christian, frequented the Sacraments, and gave good example to everyone. His word was as good as gold, and he was straightforward and honest in his dealings." And so these eulogiums continued, and the humble and solid virtues of these honest folk received their due meed of praise.

All the witnesses were perfectly instructed, in regard to what kind of honour is permitted, or forbidden, by Catholic doctrine to give to the Saints, and none amongst them attributed to these friends of God the omnipotence which belongs exclusively to the Almighty. "Glory be to God, Who works these wonders through His Saints," they would say. "It was He Himself Who cured us through the intercession of Blessed Paschal." In thus affirming the genuine Catholic belief regarding the *cultus* of the Saints, they thereby triumphantly refuted the calumnies of heresy, and denied the errors which sectaries are pleased to attribute to the Church, upon this point.

On several different occasions the ecclesiastical judges questioned the witnesses, as to whether the Religious, the custodians of the shrine, did not derive some advantage or profit from the eagerness of the multitude, and whether they did not reap a golden harvest from their beatified Brother. The numerous replies to these interrogations are all to the honour of the Religious of Villareal. They constitute the highest eulogy that could be given to a Community of Friars Minor. There is not a discordant note; all are emulous in exalting the disinterestedness of these true sons of St. Francis. "There is no way," says one of the witnesses, "of getting the Friars to accept money, under any pretext whatever, so fearful are they of losing their treasure, which is most high Poverty. They continue to-day, as in the past, to live by questing for alms in kind, though it would be so easy for them to draw from other resources."

Interrogated in his turn, Doctor Benet gave to his reply an original turn, which for the moment held the minds of his hearers in suspense. "Ah, well!" he said, "since the oath which I have just taken obliges me to tell the whole truth, without reserve, I must acknowledge that the Religious of Villareal have, in fact, derived certain benefits from the devotion of the people to Blessed Paschal, and that these benefits are very appreciable, I have been able to convince myself from my own observations. I will enumerate some of them to you. What they have gained, in the first place, is the servitude into which they have fallen, since their beatified Brother was raised to the altar. At every hour of the day and night they are compelled to be at the beck and call of the first person who comes to the door, to carry the relic to the sick and dying, and to read the Gospel over them. Their second acquisition is the loss of peace in their own home, thanks to the perpetual commotion going on round the Friary, heretofore so tranquil. Finally, yet another gain that has accrued to them is the great difficulty they now experience in giving themselves to that recollection and silence, which is the principal charm of their life; and other benefits of a similar nature have come to them in the same way. Such, learned judges, is what they have gained."

And the judges smiled and gave tokens of approbation. The good Doctor, adhering strictly to the truth, could have made allusion to a certain very real benefit and true gain—that of the increased respect, veneration, and confidence felt by the Christian people towards the Brethren of Blessed Paschal, detached, like him, from the things of earth, and aspiring towards those of Heaven.

From Doctor Benet and other practitioners already mentioned, it can be seen that Doctors and Surgeons occupied a prominent place in this interesting gallery of witnesses. Our Saint counted amongst them some of his best friends and most fervent admirers. There was perhaps some merit herein, for the Man of God made more than one incursion into their territory, carrying away each time, and under their very eyes, the flower of their patients. Thus he became a formidable rival, with whom it was difficult to compete. Be it said to their honour, that they never even thought of protesting against the encroachments of this confrère, without a diploma, or of denouncing him before the tribunals, as an unlicensed practitioner. The miraculous cures effected by the Saint were the cause of more than one sharp mortification to these excellent physicians. When an invalid was cured contrary to all the rules of medicine, the relatives and friends were not slow in declaring before them that their prescriptions had nothing at all to do with the recovery. On one occasion things went even further, and a revolution occurred—happily, a bloodless one. "I was nothing but skin and bone, a perfect living skeleton," relates the poor woman on whose account the rising took place. "My purse was as lean as myself. All my little savings had vanished, like those of the woman of the Gospel story, in physic and drugs. But when I asked the help of the Saint, my dried-up flesh was suddenly restored to health, and I regained all my strength in one brief moment. The people, who beheld this marvel, gave vent to hurrahs, and also to cries of death. 'Hurrah for Blessed Paschal! Death to ointments and elixirs! Throw all those phials and plasters, and all that chemist's shop in your cupboard, out of the window.' Then bottles and phials went whizzing through the window, and smashed into fragments amidst the enthusiastic cheering of the crowd. Fortunately the proceedings ended here, and no one proposed to send the doctors and druggists after the physic."

These Spanish physicians appear before us with grave and solemn deportment, and freely do they quote Galen and Hippocrates in their depositions. "According to the axioms laid down by these two fathers of medicine," they declare sententiously, "the patient should, in such case, be given up."

But to return to our subject—the miracles of our Saint—he has at various times disputed with his illustrious confrère, St. Anthony of Padua, the privilege of causing lost things to be found again. Those who had been objects of some favour did not think they could better testify their gratitude to the Saint, than by furnishing him with fresh occasions of exercising his power and goodness. Clients were never difficult to find, because on this earth of ours there is never a lack of miseries of every description.

There was, for instance, Catherine Seratta, who made a speciality of recruiting the sick and afflicted; like a broker or a commercial traveller, she was always going about in search of samples of fine complaints and diseases to present to the Saint. "As I was myself miraculously cured of all my maladies," she says, "I made it my duty to procure the same benefit for others, and I strongly urged the sick and stricken to do like myself, and ask deliverance from the Saint."

Amongst the clients we find some who, a little bit treacherously, led the Saint to work a second miracle, to give them, as they said, the conviction that the first was really his doing. "O holy Brother Paschal!" said a poor woman to him, "if you cure my poor little girl, I will firmly believe that it was you who worked the other miracle that happened in our house." And the good Saint, in order to dispel this doubt, which, to put it mildly, looks rather suspicious, came back and worked a second miracle in the place.

As our book takes us into Spain, it would be deficient in local colouring, did it not provide a distant glimpse of a bull-fight. "It is nearly five years ago," relates Seraphine Mirralles, "when Cecile Alberich de Benincarlon came to our house, accompanied by one of our friends from the same locality. The poor woman's right arm and hand were paralyzed, and it was only with difficulty that she could put her foot to the ground. As the travellers arrived after dinner I said to them: 'Wait a little time, whilst I am preparing a good meal for you. The best thing you can do is to go to the *corrida*.[2] All the people are excited over the fight which takes place to-day. They say it will be a really interesting one.' 'Thank you,' said the poor woman, 'but I assure you I am not inclined to eat anything, and much less am I dreaming of attending a bull-fight. It was not for that I came all the way to Villareal, but to visit the tomb of the holy Brother, and to see if Almighty God would restore to me the use of my arm and hand, through his intercession.' So I let her go, as she wished, to Our Lady of the Rosary, and continued making my preparations. About an hour later somebody rushed into the house, calling out: 'A miracle! a miracle! Cecile is cured!' I was so delighted that, leaving the dinner and the saucepans to look after themselves, I sat down and cried for very joy. In the meantime the woman's husband arrived, and the general

---

[2] Course.

happiness was complete. There was no more thought about the *corrida*. Cecile's arm had regained all its suppleness, and the hand that was healed looked an even fresher colour than the other."

Sometimes the Saint set about his miraculous cures, through the medium of a vision. We have many beautiful examples of this. There are two which, besides being interesting in themselves considered, are of interest on another score. They providentially supplement the information we have regarding the attitude of the holy man in prayer, and certain traits of his physiognomy, so that they have every right to our preference. The first is accompanied by really touching circumstances:

In a cottage at Huesca, in the Kingdom of Granada, a little girl, three years old, named Catherine Ledesma, was dying. In consequence of a fright, she had been seized by nervous tremblings, complicated by fever. She had been given up by the doctors, and for four days had been unable to swallow anything, and was hovering between life and death. Her mother, like Agar in the wilderness, had left the room so as not to see her child die, and was hiding her grief in some obscure corner of the house. With greater courage, the father remained standing near the little one's cot, awaiting in anguish her last fleeting breath. When all seemed to be over, he closed the eyes of his little Kitty, and wrapped a shroud around her. Then, turning to Blessed Paschal, his Saint of predilection, he said to him, weeping: "O my dear Saint, what are you doing? I have recommended this child so often to you. I have made such big promises to you, if you would cure her, and now she is dead! Ah, my sins must indeed be enormous, to have prevented you from asking this miracle of God." Scarcely had he ended this gentle remonstrance, when Kitty began to stir beneath the sheet he had wrapped around her.

Awakening as from a deep sleep, and looking at her father, she said to him: "Papa, where is he—the Saint I was with? Let me see him." The poor father thought the child's mind was wandering. "What Saint are you talking about, little one?" he said, trembling. "Why, papa, St. Paschal, who is at St. Francis'; he was the one who was with me, and came to cure me." These words, uttered in a strong voice, reached the mother, and she ran into the room, all bewildered. Kitty then asked for the picture of the Saint, and received it with transports of joy. She went on kissing it, as she exclaimed: "It's you that saved me, dear good St. Paschal; I shall have to put myself under your protection now, and you will have to teach me to become very good, and to love God with all my heart." These expressions, and others, too, quite beyond one of her age, increased the joy and the astonishment of her parents. The little one was clothed in the Franciscan robe, to fulfil a vow her father had made, and she wore it three years. This apparition of the Saint to the child had left in the father's mind a doubt, or rather an apprehension, that perhaps it might only have been imagination or the effect of delirium. Wishing to clear the matter up in his own mind, he one day took Kitty to Our Lady of the Rosary and, pointing to the picture over the altar, said to her: "There, there is your St. Paschal." "No," said Kitty, "that is not he. The one I saw, and who was with me, is in the chapel where you brought my shroud as an *ex voto*." And to convince her father that it was so, the little creature went down on her knees, joined her hands, and raised them to the level of her face. "Look now. That's how I saw him, papa!" It was exactly the posture the Saint used to adopt in prayer. After that proof, there was no doubting the reality of the apparition.

    The second apparition we have to relate, resulted in the restoration to health of a young Religious of the Convent

Ch. XIX: A Galaxy of Miracles

of St. John Baptist, Father Jerome Cirujada. It is from him we learn all the details. "For more than a month I was racked by a fever, and reduced to such a state of weakness, that my recovery was despaired of. Father Ximenes, who took a great interest in me, came to see me, on this occasion in the Convent of St. John of Ribera. 'Father Provincial,' I said to him, 'I beg you to have the habit of St. Paschal sent to me.'

"When it was placed on my bed I grasped it with both hands and kissed it with faith, mingling tears with my prayers. The Novice-Master then read over me the Gospel and the Prayers for the sick, after which he took the relic back to the Novitiate. Not only were my drooping spirits raised by this visit, but I also received the assurance that I should get well. About midnight, whilst I was rather impatiently awaiting the Infirmarian, who used to bring me regularly a little nourishment at that hour, I suddenly perceived, as I turned my head round, a Religious of our Order at the foot of the bed, and raised above the ground. From the form of his hood, I knew that he was a Lay Brother. 'Why, it's Brother Paschal,' I exclaimed, weeping. 'O great Servant of God, obtain for me my health back again, and I promise that I will serve the Lord in the future with all the strength of my soul!' It was, indeed, the Saint himself. 'My son,' he said, smiling and blessing me, 'do not be disturbed. You will recover, and on the Eve of Our Lady's Feast in September, you will leave the Infirmary, to hear Mass.' Having blessed me a second time, he vanished, taking my fever away with him. To hasten my convalescence, the Superiors gave me a change of air, and I was taken to the Convent of Torrento, one league from Valencia. Scarcely had I taken up my quarters there, when the Religious informed me of the arrival of Brother Alonso Rubio, who they said resembled Blessed Paschal in an astonishing degree. Here, said I to myself, is a first-rate opportunity of telling whether the Brother who appeared to me and healed me was really Blessed Paschal. And, without giving a hint to anybody, I scanned the new-comer with an interest that may be divined. My wonderment and joy were unbounded, when I discovered that Brother Alonso resembled, feature for feature, the Brother who appeared to me. Perhaps I ought to have rested satisfied with this proof, which was already more than sufficient; but there still remained one point I wished to be cleared up. The opportunity of settling it was not long in coming. On returning the following day to Valencia, in company with Father Didacus Castellon, who had been Blessed Paschal's Superior for a considerable time, I asked him with an air of unconcern if it were true that Brother Alonso Rubio resembled Blessed Paschal. 'Yes,' he replied, 'I knew them both well, as I was their Guardian, and the likeness was so striking, that one was often taken for the other.' 'But was not Blessed Paschal of a lighter complexion than Brother Alonso?' 'Yes, certainly; Brother Alonso is much swarthier.' It was all that I wanted to know. 'If that is the case,' I then said to Father Didacus, 'I shall be able to tell you an important secret, and relate to you a miracle which was worked on me. Let us sit down here—we had just come to the torrent of Rambla—and I will tell you the story.' When I had finished, Father Didacus, who had listened to it with increasing interest, said to me in a tone of reproach: 'Now, why did you never speak of this before? For what reason did you conceal the miracle until to-day?' 'It seemed to me that it was not a matter to talk about. Inasmuch as I was favoured with an apparition of the Saint, people might have taken me for a great Servant of God, whereas in reality I am only a poor miserable sinner. If I have made this disclosure to you, a

Ch. XIX: A Galaxy of Miracles

Definitor of the Province, it is because, in case I should die, I desire that what God has been pleased to do for the least of His children, may be made known for the greater glory of God and the honour of his well-beloved Servant, Paschal.' "[3]

We have already seen the predilection of our Saint for the doctors and surgeons, who with incomparable devotion and for the love of God gave their services to the Friary. One of the most devoted of these, after Doctor Benet, was, without doubt, the surgeon, Salvador Mata. This excellent man could be summoned at any time. He hastened with such joyous alacrity, that one might have thought that he was the person obliged, and that the Friars were doing him a favour by putting his services in requisition. He was continually repeating to them that they must never mind calling him, but to make use of him as they wished. We are now going to see how the Saint, after his death, was able to recompense this devotedness.

"The holy Brother Paschal worked no less than three miracles in our house," says the surgeon, in his deposition. "Here is the first of them. My eldest child, five years old, was on the point of death. Devoured by a burning fever, the only nourishment he had taken for twelve days was a little barley-water. From my own experience about illness, and from what the doctors said, I could not be under any illusion. The child was lost. Weighed down by sorrow, and unable to bear my burden alone, I went, one evening, to seek for sympathy from the good Brothers of St. John of Ribera, and to ask their prayers for the recovery of my little Salvador. Father Anthony Sobrino, touched with compassion, at the sight of my deep distress, promised to get the Novices, who were very fervent, to say the *Salve*

---
[3] MSS. of the Process. Deposition of Father Jerome Cirujada.

Regina, according to my intention, and he bade two of the Religious to come to our house immediately, with the relic of Blessed Paschal's habit. It was not long after the death of the Man of God. 'Be of good heart,' he said. 'This Brother is generally reputed to be a Saint. Recommend yourself to him, and I believe the child will be restored to health.' Comforted by these kind words, I hastened back to the house with the two Religious who carried the relic, and on the way, I made the promise of clothing the child with the habit of the Reform, and of making him wear it, until he had grown up, in the event of his being cured. When we entered the sick-room, I said: 'Look here, Salvador. We have brought from the Convent the habit of a holy Brother. Recommend yourself to his prayers, and you will be cured.' The child smiled, and when he had been raised into a sitting posture, in order to get a better view of the Blessed Paschal's habit, he took it in both hands and kissed it fervently. The Religious then read the Gospel and the Prayers for the sick, and after exhorting us to confidence, they went away, taking the relic with them. An hour later my father-in-law, the child's grandfather, arrived, greatly agitated, and fully expecting to find his grandchild at death's door. 'How are you, Salvador?' he said to him, approaching the bed. 'Oh, much better, grandpapa! Brother Paschal has obtained my cure from God. Put my clothes on. I want to have a walk.' When we had dressed him, he began to run about the room, quite delighted to stretch his legs again. They were still rather weak, and we were afraid he would fall down. After the legs, it was the turn of the stomach to be tested. 'Now that I have had a walk, I would like something to eat. Oh, I am so hungry.' We had to satisfy him, whether we liked or not, and after he had finished a wing of chicken and two eggs, he exclaimed: 'I would like a little more, please.' Although we feared greatly it would give him indigestion, we gave him what he asked for. As he was going to sleep, he cried and said: 'They won't give me enough to eat!' Next morning he was up and around early, and as merry as a lark.

"A year later, little Salvador was again very ill, and I called in my friend, Dr. Leonardo. The latter, through inadvertence, administered to him some terribly strong drug, which in a few hours reduced him to extremities. The doctor hastened back, perceived the imminent danger, and, as a last resource, prescribed a potion, which the little invalid obstinately refused to swallow. Death was approaching rapidly, and not a moment was to be lost. On the advice of my wife and mother-in-law, I sent off posthaste to the Convent, to ask for the habit of the holy man, or any other object that had belonged to him. Without any delay some of the Religious, all of whom took a great interest in us, came with a reliquary, containing a particle of bone. 'Salvador! Salvador!' they called out, in a loud voice, as they approached the dying child who was hidden away under the blankets. 'Who is calling me?' And he put his small head out of the cot. 'It is we, the Friars of St. John de la Ribera, who are bringing you a relic of Brother Paschal. You will be cured by it as you were last year.' 'Let me see it!' When the veil had been removed, he cried out: 'Give it to me!' And Salvador seized upon it eagerly and pressed it to his chest. 'Ah, that is not enough, my child,' said one of the Friars. 'There is still something to be done, if you want to get well, and that is to take your medicine at once. Brother Paschal tells you to do so.' 'As you say that Brother Paschal tells me to do so, I will take it; but I would not have taken it for papa, or mamma, or even for grandpapa.' And he swallowed the draught, at one gulp, without wincing. Next day he was cured, not so much in virtue of the remedy, as by the intercession of the Saint.

"The third miracle worked in our home saved the life of our little Louis, then twenty months of age, and still at the breast. Dr. Leonardo, when leaving, said: 'You will have to part with him.' It was only too true; the child no longer gave any signs of life, and we covered him with a shroud, waiting for the time to carry him to the grave. But this was not to count upon the great faith of my wife. 'The little one is like one dead, but is not Blessed Paschal powerful enough to restore him? Go and get his relic from the Convent, and he will return to life.' As she had foretold, scarcely had the child been touched by the relic than he showed symptoms of life, and he was saved. Some hours later Dr. Leonardo passed by. Seeing the neighbours gathered round the door, he asked them if the baby was dead. 'No,' they replied, with a tinge of satire, 'he is doing remarkably well. Go into the surgeon's house and you will see for yourself.' From this, learned judges, you will readily understand," says the deponent, in conclusion, "why I am so devout to Brother Paschal, and why all of us at home hold him to be a great Saint."[4]

Blessed Paschal was not satisfied with disputing with Death, for those already marked for the grave. Such would have been only a partial victory, and he wished for a complete one. So he entered into Death's own domain, and compelled him to give up his prey. This is the most brilliant of his triumphs, and it has occurred so often, that those who have been recalled to life by the Saint, form quite a lengthy procession. Strange as it may seem, this procession is headed by a horse! And yet, after all, when we come to reflect upon the subject, is it something so very strange? Has not all pain, no matter what its nature may be, a claim on human pity? In the eyes of the Saints there

---

[4] MSS. of the Process. Deposition of Salvador Mata.

Ch. XIX: A Galaxy of Miracles 271

did not appear anything ridiculous in this. And so they treated with the tenderest compassion those lowly creatures of the all-merciful God, which the Seraphic Francis called his brothers and sisters. They did not consider it to be a degrading or vulgarizing miracle, when it was worked in favour of a poor dumb animal, that was in pain or needful to its owner. As anticipating by several centuries our modern societies for the prevention of cruelty to animals, they deserve to be made their patrons.

We will now recount the marvellous history of this steed, which, however, was neither Alexander's Bucephalus, nor Roland's fiery charger; it approximated more closely to Rozinante, the property of the Knight of the Sorrowful Figure. "We are pedlars on a small scale," said Frances Rippolles in her deposition, "and for the purposes of our trade, we for a long time employed a horse, whose services were invaluable to us. He used to draw, from village to village, the wagon containing our stock, and when required, he also served as a mount for my husband. Now, to our great misery, the poor brute was attacked by a very dangerous malady, called in our part of the country the *tochon*. In default of a veterinary surgeon, Sanclemente, the farrier, tried a remedy, which, however, had no effect. The swelling went on increasing. He lay on his side in a corner of the stable, and refused the bran and oats we gave him. It seemed all over with Coco, for that was the name we called him by. 'There is only one thing to be done,' said Sanclemente to us, 'and that is to get a rope, and drag that horse, as best you can, to the ditch!' We had, in fact, to make up our minds to this, but only with the deepest regret. This poor beast was a part of our small belongings, and he was our bread-winner. What should we do without him? If we could have even bought another it would not have been quite so bad, but our means did not allow us to dream of providing any successor to him. Whilst I was ruminating over all this in tears, the thought of Blessed Paschal occurred to my mind. As he works so many miracles, why should he not work one for us, when we are so devoted to him? 'Let us go to his tomb,' said I to my husband, 'and let us beseech him to restore our horse to us.' When we returned from Our Lady of the Rosary, we had not the courage to go and see if the poor animal had expired, so we sent on the little maid-servant to our place. She came running back in no time, breathless with excitement. 'Hurrah! Coco is alive and all right again. Come and look; he is galloping round the field.' We followed her, and, to our immense delight, we saw the horse rolling in the grass, and gambolling, like a foal, in the heyday of youth. His neighs admonished us that he was hungry. When he had been led back in triumph to the stable, he attacked the fodder with avidity, and compensated himself for the privations of his long fast. Since then, he has always been in the pink of condition, and has been of the greatest service to us. No one was so astonished as Sanclemente, the farrier. He rubbed his eyes to make sure it really was our horse. 'What remedy did you employ?' he asked my husband. 'That of invoking Blessed Paschal, and you see it has taken effect.' "[5]

This same remedy proved equally efficacious when applied by Angela Melgar, who related the touching story in which she herself took such a leading part. "On the Feast of St. Michael, my husband went to hear Mass at the Convent of St. John de la Ribera. There was High Mass with sermon. He returned about noon, and so charmed was he with what the preacher had said concerning the virtues and miracles of Blessed Paschal, that he called together the

---

[5] MSS. of the Process. Deposition of Frances Rippolles.

servants, and exhorted them warmly to place themselves under the patronage of the Saint. During the ensuing night he died suddenly from an apoplectic stroke, without having had time to receive the last Sacraments. It was this circumstance which grieved me more than anything else. Then I remembered the advice the dead man had given us, on returning from the sermon; and, without even delaying to kindle a light, I immediately began to search for a little piece of the holy man's habit, which I kept carefully stowed away in a cupboard. Although it was hidden under a pile of cloths, I put my hand upon it at once, and this I took to be a good augury. Then, approaching the corpse of my husband, I invoked the Saint fervently. 'O holy Brother, do not forget that, at this present moment, reports of your miracles are being everywhere disseminated, and that your canonization may be brought about by them. Now, then, is the time to work one, which will greatly promote your Cause. Please remark that if I ask you to raise my husband to life again, it is much more for the salvation of his soul than for the sake of his mortal life. You know as well as I do the disquieting circumstances under which he has entered into Eternity. Then bring him back to life again, so that he may have time to settle his accounts with God. The Process of Canonization will then progress by leaps and bounds.' The prayer ended, I applied the relic, with faith, to the icy brow of the dead man, and, at the contact, a tremor ran through him. Coming back, as it seemed, from another world, he looked around and crossed himself: 'My Jesus! What has happened? Was I not dead? And yet I am alive!' The neighbours hurried in, and soon the room was full. The man, just returned to life, related to them how, after he had finished his night prayers, he fell, struck down, as it were, at the foot of the bed. And it was thus, in fact, that we found him—his eyes bloodshot, his tongue protruding, and presenting altogether a very horrible spectacle. As I still felt anxious about the confession, I went in search of our parish priest, and, on returning, I found my husband so far recovered, that I urged him to get up. Strange to say, he would not consent, and insisted on remaining in bed. The only concern of the poor man was the salvation of his immortal soul. He comprehended that this was the end, for which God had called him back to life, and so he prepared himself with the utmost diligence for the reception of the last Sacraments. When he had received them, he peacefully gave back his soul to God, three days after his restoration to life. I had been answered, as regards the principal thing, which was the salvation of his soul, but I reproached myself ever afterwards with not asking the accessory—namely, the prolongation of his life."[6]

Another widow, who was poor, and burdened with a large family, and afflicted with greater trials than Angela Melgar, fell down on her knees likewise by the side of the dead body of her husband, who had been carried off by a pestilential fever, and boldly asked the Saint to restore him to life. "How can you expect me to remain all alone with these little children?" she said to him. "No, it is really out of the question. You must without fail take pity on us, and restore my husband to me. If you will be so good as to raise him up, the tapers which are ready for his funeral will be for you, and I will come with him and the children on pilgrimage to your tomb." The Saint was not deaf to this naïve and heartrending appeal, and even before it was ended the dead man was restored to life. Then the poor woman, beside herself with joy, rushed through the streets as one demented, announcing to all the happy tidings of her husband's resurrection. The vow was faithfully

---

[6] MSS. of the Process. Deposition of Angela Melgar.

observed in all particulars. The family visited the Saint's tomb together, and the chapel received the bequest of the tapers originally intended for the funeral.[7]

The limited space at our disposal in this small volume, compels us to interrupt the account of the innumerable prodigies wrought by St. Paschal. "These miracles are so numerous," says Father John Sanchez, Guardian of Villareal, "that if I undertook to relate them all, it would take me days and days." We leave it, then, to our readers' imagination to picture to themselves the dimension of the volume which should contain a printed account of all these miracles.

In his anxiety not to pass over any of these wonders, Father Pañez, one of our Saint's biographers, had recourse to the following method. Classifying, as in a medical dictionary, the various ills which poor human flesh is heir to—neuralgia, fevers of all descriptions, gout, palsy, asthma, blindness, fractures, wounds, etc.—he has devoted a separate chapter to a consideration of each of these complaints and accidents, rich in examples of persons cured through the intercession of the Saint. "This voluminous work is only an abridgment," he says at the end of his book. "Each class of maladies could have provided me with matter for several volumes." Has any physician, even the most skilful, ever been able to boast such signal services, or to present a list of such wonderful cures?

The *ex votos*, each of which is a memorial of some grace obtained, soon invaded the walls of the Saint's chapel. They became so numerous that it was necessary to remove them in order to make room for others. The latter soon shared the fate of their predecessors, and were placed

---

[7] MSS. of the Process.

with them in a chapel designed for that express purpose. To give some idea of the great quantity of such souvenirs, it will be sufficient to state, that two years after the death of the Man of God, 400 miracles were already to be counted. With such rich materials to work upon, little doubt could be entertained regarding the happy issue of the Process of Beatification.

Pope Paul V took a keen interest in the success of the Cause. It afforded him great pleasure to listen to Father Francis Suessa, Postulator of the Saint, relating to him the virtues and the miracles of this great Servant of God. Even before the Beatification he was fond of calling him "Blessed." One day someone made him a present of a medallion of silver, with a representation of the holy Brother, his head surrounded by an aureola. This was an infraction of the law, calculated to delay the promotion of the Cause. However, although Paul V was not blind to this fact, he contemplated the figure of the Saint with evident satisfaction, and would never part with the medallion.

In favour of our Saint, he suspended the operation of a recent law, which deferred for a certain period all causes of Beatification, and thus in 1618, only twenty-six years after the death of the Man of God, he had the happiness of placing him in the ranks of the *Beati*. Moreover, he permitted his feast to be celebrated with special ceremony at St. Francis a Ripa, by the Friars Minor of the Reform, and to add to the solemnity he graciously sent a choir from the Sistine Chapel. In the evening he came in person, and pontificated in the Church of the Friary.

His successor, Gregory XV, manifested the same zeal, and he was preparing to issue the Decree of Canonization when he was interrupted by death.

Under Urban VIII, in consequence of certain modifications introduced into the Canon Law upon this

Ch. XIX: A Galaxy of Miracles

point, everything had to be commenced over again. Almighty God permitted this, at the instance, we may conjecture, of Blessed Paschal himself. Humble, even on the other side of the tomb, he could not allow that Peter of Alcantara, Founder and Master of his Province, should follow after him, and so, in order to yield precedence to his Father, he raised a thousand unforeseen obstacles which retarded his canonization for more than half a century. These delays seem inexplicable after the eloquent and conclusive report of St. Robert Cardinal Bellarmine, and the acceptance of fourteen signal miracles, which in full Consistory drew this enthusiastic exclamation from one of the Cardinals: "*A saeculo non est auditum tale*" (From the beginning of the world the like hath not been heard). The final obstacles were removed under the Pontificate of Alexander VIII, and the Decree of Canonization was promulgated in 1690.

It seemed impossible to surpass the festivities, which in Italy and Spain had given a joyous response to the Beatification. They were surpassed, however, and on the day of his Canonization, these two Catholic nations vied with each other in the magnificence and splendour of their celebrations. In a voluminous work, printed at Valencia, on the morrow of the Canonization, we have a description of the festivities observed in Spain, and in a volume not less bulky, printed at Naples, an account of the festivities in Italy. The most beautiful inspirations of faith and piety, aided by eloquence, poetry, and the fine arts, were lavishly employed on that solemn occasion, to publish and exalt the glory of the new Saint.

It was on October 6, 1690, that Pope Alexander VIII. solemnly promulgated at St. Peter's the Decree which placed the name of Paschal in the list of Canonized Saints, and on the same occasion several other canonizations took place. According to traditional usage the banners of the new Saints were carried in procession, and at the conclusion of the ceremony they were hung from the ceiling in front of the side chapels. The God of the Eucharist had prepared a final joy and fitting reward for His faithful adorer. Quite by accident, as it seemed, the standard, representing Paschal on his knees before the Host, was displayed just in front of the Chapel of the Blessed Sacrament. It was only after the festival was over that this was observed, and all were in admiration at this providential coincidence. It seemed as though St. Paschal had come and taken up his station of his own accord before the Tabernacle. And what they admired still more was the way in which Our Divine Lord had arranged everything so that, on the day of His faithful adorer's supreme triumph, he should be found in presence of the Object of his adoration.

From many excellent works on the subject, we learn what a profound and lasting impression these festivities, and the example of St. Paschal, have left upon the consciousness of the Christian people, and in what measure they have served to increase faith and devotion towards the most Holy Sacrament of the Altar; but perhaps there is nowhere to be found a more eloquent tribute to the influence of Paschal's example than a certain touching little custom, which has survived many changes and revolutions. At Villareal and in the surrounding country, when the sound of the bell announces the Elevation, the faithful are wont, in remembrance of the holy Brother, to stop, uncover their heads, and, kneeling down in the middle of the road, to say in a loud voice:

"BLESSED BE OUR LORD JESUS CHRIST IN THE MOST HOLY SACRAMENT OF THE ALTAR."

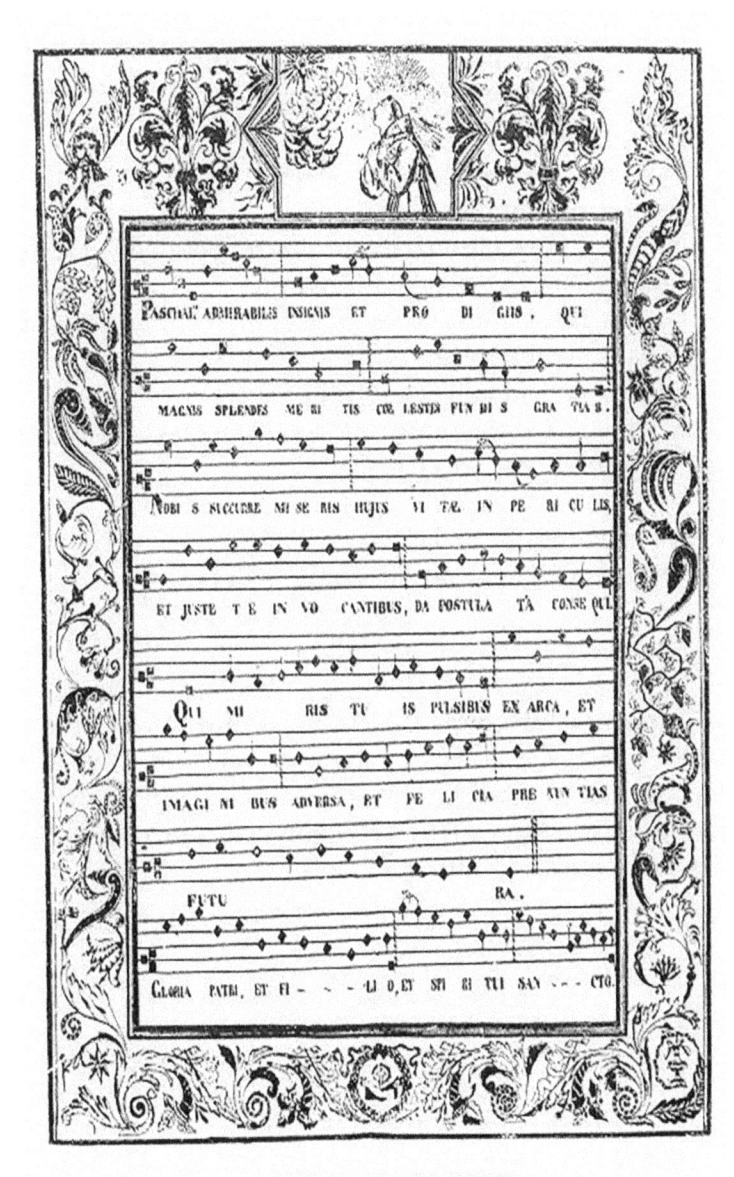

RESPONSORY OF SAINT PASCHAL.

RESPONSORIUM IN HONOREM SANCTI PASCHALIS BAYLON.

Paschalis, admirabilis, qui magnis splendens meritis coelestes fundis gratias.
Nobis succurre miseris hujus vitae in periculis, et juste te invocantibus, da postulata consequi.
Qui miris tuis pulsibus ex arca, et imaginibus adversa, et felicia proenuntias futura.
Gloria Patri, et Filio, et Spiritui Sancto.
Sicut erat in principio, et nunc, et semper, et in saecula sacculorum. Amen.

V. Ora pro nobis Beate Paschalis.
R. Ut digni efficiamur promissionibus Christi.

Oremus.

Deus qui Beatum Paschalem Confessorem tuum mirifica erga Corporis et Sanguinis tui sacra Mysteria dilectione decorasti: concede propitius, ut quam ille ex hoc divino convivio spiritus percepit pinguedinem, eamdem et nos percipere mereamur: Qui vivis.

RESPONSORY IN HONOUR OF ST. PASCHAL BAYLON.

O Paschal blest, whose merits bright
A glorious Saint proclaim:
How manifold the graces wrought
Through power of thy sweet name!
Amidst the storms and toils of life
Thy clients safely shield;
To us each blessing sought through thee
May God in bounty yield.
O thou, who by thy wondrous blows,
From shrine and pictures giv'n,
Dost herald forth calamity,
Or joys sent down from Heav'n.
Amidst the storms, etc.
All glory to the Father be,
And His co-equal Son;
The same unto the Paraclete,
While endless ages run.
Amidst the storms, etc.

V. Pray for us, Blessed Paschal.
R. That we may be made worthy of the promises of Christ.
Let us pray.

O God, Who hast adorned Blessed Paschal, Thy Confessor, with a wonderful and tender devotion towards the sacred Mysteries of Thy Body and Blood; graciously vouchsafe, that we also may become worthy to receive those same rich and abundant graces, which he obtained from this Divine Banquet: Who livest and reignest with God the Father, in the unity of the Holy Spirit, God, world without end. Amen.

Lightning Source UK Ltd.
Milton Keynes UK
UKHW010636021221
394874UK00003B/73/J